John Hancock

John Hancock

*First to Sign, First to Invest
in America's Independence*

WILLARD STERNE
RANDALL

DUTTON

DUTTON

An imprint of Penguin Random House LLC
1745 Broadway, New York, NY 10019
penguinrandomhouse.com

BOOK DESIGN BY KATY RIEGEL

Library of Congress Cataloging-in-Publication Data

Names: Randall, Willard Sterne, author.
Title: John Hancock: first to sign, first to invest in America's
independence / Willard Sterne Randall.
Other titles: First to sign, first to invest in America's independence
Description: [New York, New York] : Dutton, [2025] |
Includes bibliographical references and index.
Identifiers: LCCN 2024057091 (print) | LCCN 2024057092 (ebook) |
ISBN 9780593472149 hardcover | ISBN 9780593472156 ebook
Subjects: LCSH: Hancock, John, 1737–1793. | Statesmen—United
States—Biography. | United States—History—Revolution, 1775–1783. |
United States. Continental Congress—Presidents—Biography. |
Signers—Biography. | Governors—Massachusetts—Biography. |
Businessmen—Massachusetts—Boston—Biography. | Boston
(Mass.)—Biography. | LCGFT: Biographies.
Classification: LCC E302.6.H23 R35 2025 (print) | LCC E302.6.H23 (ebook) |
DDC 973.3092 $a B—dc23/eng/20250312
LC record available at https://lccn.loc.gov/2024057091
LC ebook record available at https://lccn.loc.gov/2024057092

Printed in the United States of America
1st Printing

The authorized representative in the EU for product safety and compliance is
Penguin Random House Ireland, Morrison Chambers, 32 Nassau Street,
Dublin D02 YH68, Ireland, https://eu-contact.penguin.ie.

For Nancy

Contents

John
Hancock

Prologue

In the September 1930 issue of *Harper's Monthly Magazine*, New England historian James Truslow Adams published an unprecedented attack on John Hancock, the Founding Father whose flamboyant autograph on the Declaration of Independence has become synonymous with a signature. Entitling his article "Portrait of an Empty Barrel," Adams excoriated Hancock, the Boston businessman who financed, organized and helped to lead Massachusetts throughout the American Revolutionary era.

Adams, a retired investment banker and onetime diplomat who had turned to writing history, dismissed Hancock's three decades as an unpaid public servant who had risen through the ranks of colonial politics from Boston selectman to three-term president of the Continental Congress, at the time the equivalent to president of the United States. Ridiculing Hancock, Adams wrote: "His chief resources were his money and his gout, the first always used to gain popularity, and the second to prevent his losing it."[1]

Adams was undoubtedly influenced by the 1913 publication of economic historian Charles A. Beard's controversial book *An Economic Interpretation of the Constitution*. Professor Beard contended that economic forces underlay the movement for the formation and adoption of the federal Constitution and determined its most important provisions. The founder of the revisionist progressive school of American history, Beard asserted that all of the merchants, moneylenders, security holders, manufacturers, shippers, capitalists, financiers and their professional associates supported the Constitution.[2] To Adams, Hancock fitted all of these parameters.

Two years after his *Harper's* critique, Adams, as editor of the multivolume *Dictionary of American Biography*, tasked himself with writing Hancock's biographical entry. He denounced Hancock as "shallow and vainglorious" and "easily manipulated."

In his own time, as early as 1809, fellow Founding Father John Adams lamented that Hancock had been virtually "buried in oblivion"—even in Boston where, as head of the House of Hancock, one of colonial America's preeminent mercantile firms, he had been central to commerce and politics. There had been little effort to preserve his legacy. The Hancock family mansion atop Beacon Hill was torn down in 1863 when neither the city nor the state would maintain it.

In 1817, John Adams, once a caustic critic of his fellow Founder, wrote to William Tudor, "I am not writing the life of Mr. Hancock; his biography would fill as many volumes as [John] Marshall's Washington and be quite as instructive and entertaining. . . . But if statues, obelisks, pyramids or divine honors were ever merited, John Hancock deserved these from the town of Boston and the United States."[3]

Not until 1876, the centennial of the signing of the Declaration of Independence, was there even so much as a plaque commemorating Hancock in Boston. And another two decades would pass before—in 1898, more than a century after Hancock died and was buried in what was essentially an unmarked grave—Massachusetts erected a modest memorial column in the Granary Burying Ground, just off Boston Common. Historian Alfred Young explains that Massachusetts's "new elite was not comfortable with a rich man who pledged his fortune in the cause of revolution."

By the time of James Truslow Adams's 1930 critique, only one biography of Hancock had appeared. One possible explanation: While Hancock had authored innumerable state papers, he apparently left no trove of personal papers, in contrast to more prolific Founding Fathers like Thomas Jefferson, James Madison, Alexander Hamilton and fellow Bostonian John Adams. Moreover, Hancock had no descendants who could periodically commemorate his contributions.

James Truslow Adams's disparaging appraisal of Hancock began at once to influence the verdicts of future generations of chroniclers. Immediately after Adams's scathing profile of Hancock in the *Dictionary of American Biography*, Samuel Eliot Morison, Harvard's distinguished official historian, devoted fully six pages of his 1936 classic, *Three Centuries of Harvard*, to Hancock's troubled relations with the college as its treasurer during the Revolution and as ex officio president of its senior governing board.

Following suit, in 1945, Harvard Business School economic historian W. T. Baxter published *The House of Hancock*. After itemizing and praising the accomplishments of John's uncle Thomas, Baxter concluded his profile of Hancock with words closely paraphrasing Adams, calling him "The Empty Barrel." As historian

Donald Proctor points out, of the scant handful of Hancock biographies, all have largely relied on the voluminous writings of the signer's political opponents.[4] But John Hancock was far more than a citizen of Massachusetts. From the Stamp Act crisis of 1765 to the outbreak of the Revolutionary War ten years later, he emerged as a prominent figure in protests against increasing imperial controls. For the next fifteen years, Hancock was a major shaper of American political development. He can be properly appreciated only through an attempt at understanding the political life and times of which he was a part, a task made more difficult by the fact that many of Hancock's activities were shrouded in secrecy by the very nature of his business, others because they verged on treason.

A deeper dive into archives that have been recently digitalized and into the papers of other better-known Founders has now made it possible to reconstruct John Hancock's contributions and his controversies. In the process, much of the mythology created during the century since James Truslow Adams's vituperative appraisal can be peeled away.

For example, John Adams insisted in his 1809 memoir that Hancock had expected to be selected as commander in chief of the Continental Army. Adams described a red-faced Hancock's reaction when, instead, he nominated George Washington. This scene has never been corroborated by any other delegate to the Second Continental Congress. Adams's claim came a quarter century after the supposed event—during which time Hancock and Adams had fallen out over bitter post-Revolutionary party politics. Adams's autobiography was also published after Hancock's death, denying him the opportunity to refute it. This book will show how John Hancock and George Washington worked in tandem through three terms of the incoherent and ultimately unworkable Continental Congress to resolve the numerous political and logistical problems of supporting and supplying the Continental Army, together struggling to keep the Revolution alive. (Incidentally, Hancock named his only short-lived son John George Washington Hancock.) *John Hancock* will explore Hancock's thirty-year relationship with other Founding Fathers as they labored together to give birth to the United States of America.

CHAPTER ONE

"The Known World"

Born in Braintree, Massachusetts, into a family of Puritan clergy, John Hancock seemed destined to be the third of his name to become a parson in a small town. His grandfather, John Hancock I, attended Harvard College on a scholarship. Son of a shoemaker, he had somehow taught himself enough Greek and Latin to pass the written and oral examinations required for admission. Matriculating with the class of 1689, he was accorded a class ranking that indicated his social standing: thirteenth of fourteen. After he graduated with a bachelor's degree, it took Hancock I ten years of guest preaching before he found a congregation—in what became Lexington—that liked what he said enough to offer him a permanent pastorate. He filled the Lexington pulpit and its meetinghouse for fifty-four years, becoming known as "the Bishop" for his imperious manner.

John Hancock I married the daughter of a neighboring clergyman. They had five children, including two daughters—who also married parsons—and three sons, the oldest inheriting his father's name but not his imperious disposition. Asked the proper duties of the church elders, the Bishop answered that there were only two: saddling his horse and holding his bridle.

The Bishop's eldest son, John Hancock II, entered Harvard with the class of 1719. He was a "conspicuously orderly boy" who had little success impressing congregations. After taking a job as the college librarian, he was twice rejected to fill empty pulpits. On his third attempt, he asked a classmate to send the search committee a letter of recommendation. It ended, "He could make a very handsome bow, and if the first didn't suit he'd bow lower a second time."[1]

Seven years after John II's graduation, the town of Braintree suffered the death of its popular pastor. Still without a job in the church, John delivered a conciliatory sermon on the "solemn covenant of Liberty" that could be realized only through hard work performed collectively by the community. Members of the Adams and Quincy families were among the Third Parish Church pewholders listening. The search committee unanimously selected Hancock as the town's next pastor. In November 1726, for John Hancock II's ordination, his father, the self-styled Bishop, came down from Lexington to deliver the sermon.

Young Parson Hancock II proved so popular that he was able to talk the tightfisted parish elders into building him a larger parsonage where he could bring his bride, a widow nine years younger than he. They had three children, naming the second, born on January 12, 1737, John Hancock III. Among other newborn parishioners Parson Hancock baptized was John Adams, the son of a farmer who served as a part-time cobbler and the church's deacon.

Surrounded by farms, Braintree sat on a low hill a few miles south of Boston. The setting had been described lyrically a century earlier by its first English settler, Thomas Morton: "In all the known world, it [cannot] be paralel'd for so many goodly groves of trees, dainty fine round rising hillocks, delicate faire large plaines, sweet cristall fountains, and clear running streams that twine in fine meanders through the meadows, making so sweete a murmuring sound to hear."[2]

By the time John Hancock III was born, farmers had stripped the land of most of its oaks, elms and maples to build their houses and barns.

For the first seven years of his life, the third John Hancock—who would eventually become the signer of the Declaration of Independence—lived in the Spartan manse beside the meetinghouse on the village green. At age five, he began an education—intended to prepare him for the ministry—at a local school run by Mrs. Belcher. At six, he transferred to a school run by Joseph Cleverly, where he began to learn the rudiments of reading, writing and figuring. It was here that Hancock met John Adams, who had a rather dim view of their schoolmaster Cleverly: "He was through his whole life the most indolent man I ever knew. . . . His inattention to his scholars was such as gave me a disgust to schools, to books and to study."[3]

But there was hardly time for John Hancock to form his own opinion. When he was seven, his father died after a brief illness, leaving his now twice-widowed mother, Mary, with three children under the age of nine. The family had little time to grieve; they had to vacate the manse to make way for the next pastor. Fortunately, the seventy-two-year-old Bishop Hancock, presiding over an empty parsonage, invited them to come live with him in Lexington.

There, he planned to mold the next Parson Hancock. He didn't know, at the time, that his second son would fundamentally alter the path of young John Hancock III's life.

~ℓ~

The Bishop's second son, Thomas, decided to forgo a Harvard education and the meager living of a clergyman. At thirteen, Thomas left the Bishop's manse in Lexington after signing papers for a seven-year apprenticeship with Boston bookseller Samuel Gerrish, from whom he was expected to "Learn the Art or Trade of a book binder" and the rudiments of commerce.[4]

In Gerrish's popular shop in Cornhill, young Thomas absorbed the intricacies of currency exchange and letters of credit, of importing and merchandising. He met many of Boston's leading businessmen, whose gossip about the reputations of merchants in London and the other American colonies he overheard and stored away. At the end of his apprenticeship, he traveled to England to cultivate personal contacts with British merchants. Soon after his return, he placed in the *Boston News-Letter* an advertisement announcing that "Thomas Hancock, at the sign of the Bible and Three Crowns," was offering for sale a printed sermon by a noted Boston preacher "and all manner of other improving tracts."[5]

Prospering, he ventured into local politics, at first at its lowest possible level, winning election as the town's hog reeve. In his role, he was in charge of policing hogs that roamed through Boston's unpaved streets, corralling and holding each stray swine until he collected a fine, which he pocketed as side income. With the profits of his combined endeavors, Thomas branched out, forming a partnership to ship general merchandise for sale in New York province.

One of Boston's most eligible bachelors, he married Lydia Henchman at age twenty-seven, forming an alliance with one of Massachusetts's first families: Lydia's grandfather had been a hero of King Philip's War; her mother was bookseller Gerrish's sister.

Thomas Hancock's bookshop on the town dock, stocked with merchandise from both sides of the Atlantic, was to become Boston's most prosperous general store in a dozen years. According to an advertisement in the *Boston News-Letter*, in addition to books and stationery, Thomas sold a wide variety of imported cloth (calico, chintz, muslin, cotton, taffeta, damask and silk) as well as thread, fans, girdles "and sundry other sorts of Haberdashery," including "silk Shoes, Men's and Women's Hose," millinery, compasses, hourglasses, leather, cutlery, tea, sugar and corn. Hancock became the first Boston merchandiser to organize a store into departments. He advertised "Excellent good Bohea Tea, imported in the last ship from London. . . . N.B. If it don't suit the ladies' taste, they may return the tea and receive their money again."[6]

To maximize his profits and trim the cost of importing merchandise from Britain, Thomas formed partnerships with other merchants, including building a paper mill, the first in New England, that benefited his stationer's trade. But as he branched out, stationery and books became less than one percent of his sales; hardware from brass compasses to swords accounted for ten percent. His dress department became the largest. His store was full of customers from Boston and surrounding towns virtually every day. Because he could buy at wholesale, his annual sales hit £10,000 (about $1.5 million today). Adding a warehouse, he supplied other merchants and offered them volume discounts.

Only five years after he opened his stationery store, Hancock launched his first single-masted ship, a sloop; it carried rum, beef, cotton and hemp to whaling towns along the New England coast and Newfoundland and picked up cargoes of whale oil and bone to sell in London. He paid his London factor three percent of the proceeds both to market his cargo and to act as his purchasing agent. Another eight percent went to the captain and crew. That left eighty-nine percent of the proceeds to be used to buy goods to ship back and sell in his store on Clark's Wharf, the second longest in Boston.

Turning to international bartering, Thomas commissioned shipbuilding. He sent lumber to treeless Newfoundland, traded it for salted cod to sell to plantation owners in the French West Indies and exchanged the cod for molasses to send to Holland for distilling into rum. Then he imported the rum to sell in his Boston emporium.

~e~

To befit his newfound stature as a conspicuously prosperous merchant, Thomas Hancock decided to build an opulent house on a two-acre plot on the crest of Beacon Hill overlooking the town and the harbor. In the latest Georgian style, constructed of square-cut blocks of granite joined at the corners by brownstone quoins, the mansion was palatial by Boston standards, ranking among the most imposing in colonial America at the time. Two windows flanked a wide entrance crowned by a large balcony. In all, the mansion had fifty-three windows—including three third-story dormers—which were fitted with the best crown glass imported from England. Thomas Hancock had admonished his London agent to take "particular care about my window glass, that it be the best and every square cut exactly to the size."[7]

Bisecting the mansion, a wide center hallway led family, friends and clients past a ten-foot-tall "chiming clock" adorned with sculpted figures overlaid with "burnished gold" to their left and into a parlor with imported Georgian mahogany furnishings upholstered in damask to match the drapes. To their right, they would be ushered into a long gallery lined with portraits and prints in heavily gilded frames. Green-and-scarlet velvet "Flockwork" wallpaper—"a very Rich and Beautiful fine Cloth" with wool and cotton tufts—covered the walls. Brass candlesticks topped three marble-hearth fireplaces. Across the hallway, English wallpaper, described by Hancock as "better than Paintings done in Oyl," depicted "Birds Peacocks Macoys Squirrels Fruit & Flowers."[8]

A spiral balustraded staircase led to bedrooms with yellow damask drapes matching the coverings of four-poster beds. The master bedroom, its walls and canopied bed draped in crimson, lay opposite the guest room, both offering views of Hancock's two-acre formal gardens. From English nurseries, Hancock ordered trees, shrubs and plants: "Procure for me two or three dozen Yew trees, some Hollys and Jessamine vines . . . Pray send me a Catalogue of that Fruit that you have that are Dwarf Trees and Espaliers."[9] His ship captains had orders to carefully bring home specimens from other lands.

To his London agent, Hancock boasted, "We live Pretty comfortable here on Beacon Hill. . . . My Gardens all Lye on the South Side of a hill, with the most beautiful Ascent to the top; and its Allowed on all hands the Kingdom of England don't afford so fine a Prospect as I have both of Land and Water. Neither do I intend to Spare any cost or pains in making my gardens Beautiful or Profitable."[10]

～℮～

As Thomas Hancock emerged as one of Boston's leading citizens, the town's six hundred freemen elected him to its highest office, selectman. He joined four of the town's wealthiest merchants, all white male Harvard graduates. He was reelected at Boston's annual Town Meeting for the next thirteen years. Acting as both legislators and executives, the selectmen controlled Boston's commerce and finance. The unpaid post carried with it assurance of lucrative government contracts parceled out by Massachusetts's royal governor without negotiation or competitive bidding. But it also carried the shared civic responsibilities of supervising the almshouse, schools, roads, the town granary and the cemeteries.

With the death of his older brother, Thomas became the family patriarch and lent money openhandedly to his relatives or invested it for them. He enlarged his father's parsonage in Lexington after John Hancock II's family took refuge there. And a year later, in 1745, Thomas and Lydia rode out to Lexington in their carriage with a proposition. After fourteen years of marriage, they still had no children. They offered to raise their handsome eight-year-old nephew, John, as their own son. They would give the boy a better life than the Bishop could afford to provide him, pledging to send him to Boston Latin School and on to Harvard College—not to suit him for pulpit and gown, but to introduce him into the new and risky world of international commerce. John's grandfather, while he was disappointed that he could not shape another clergyman, could hardly refuse, and John's mother agreed that the move would be best for her son.

John Hancock's journey from the crowded small-town manse in Lexington to the largest town in America took place over only a few miles and hours but would profoundly alter his way of life. Thomas Hancock's elegant carriage transported John to a mansion atop Beacon Hill and the privileged status of adopted son and putative heir to one of colonial America's wealthiest entrepreneurs.

Aunt Lydia ushered John into a large front room with a panoramic view of the ships crowding the harbor and of the serpentine streets of the town. News had just arrived of the victory of New England's armada of one hundred ships and its thousands of troops in the forty-nine-day siege of the French fortress at Louisbourg in Nova Scotia. From his window, John could enjoy the celebration— the bonfires, the illumination of every window with candles, the pealing of the church bells.

A constant stream of mercantile visitors and officers in the brilliant scarlet of King George II's army and the blue and gold of Royal Navy officers rode up Beacon Hill to confer with Uncle Thomas over contracts for supplies and shipping. The House of Hancock had received lucrative British government contracts to round up the ships and to supply the entire Louisbourg expedition with food, clothing, tents, arms and ammunition. Hancock's countinghouse became the logistical hub of Britain's wars with New France, earning Hancock £100,000 (about $15 million today) and making him the richest man in Boston.

Atop Beacon Hill, Thomas presided over Aunt Lydia's lavish dinners, displaying his fondness for Madeira wine ordered from Portugal "without regard to price, provided the quality answers to it," poured from "6 Quart Decanters" into "2 doz. handsom, new fash'd" rock-crystal wineglasses. Amid the elegance of liveried servants, decanters of imported wines and silver salvers heaped with fish and game, an eight-year-old boy could hardly be expected to understand the lively gossip of trade or of parliamentary and royal court politics, but he could appreciate its importance to his family's stature.

Assigned a private tutor to help him catch up to his wealthy peers, John plunged into the standard eight-year regimen of education for a male member of Boston's literate society. Within a month, his uncle rode down the hill with him to the two-storied, gambrel-roofed edifice of Boston Latin School. There, behind the Anglican chapel, John met the ruler of School Street, Master John Lovell, legendary for drilling and terrifying his pupils. One of twenty applicants, John read aloud briefly from the King James Bible to demonstrate his literacy. Lovell admitted him and, because John was nearly nine years old, advanced him to join the third-year class to be with other boys his age.

For the next four years, before seven each morning, John rode down the hill in his uncle's coach to begin the ten-hour school day. As the schoolhouse bell clanged, John took his place among the one hundred privileged pupils on one of the oak benches that lined the classroom—where, under the unforgiving eye of an usher, he began his Latin studies with *Lily's Grammar* and Eutropius's history of Rome. If John's attention wavered, he could expect a whack across his hands from his teacher's wooden ferule.

With knowledge steeped in the classics, John advanced from bench to table after three years of rote memorizing. There he could began to translate Aesop's fables into Latin verse. By translating Julius Caesar's *Commentaries on the Gallic War*, Cicero's Orations,

Virgil's *Aeneid* and Ovid, he learned to read, write and debate in Latin. In his final year, he translated the Greek of Xenophon and Homer. Absorbing history, poetry, geography and philosophy through these works, John was quickly mastering the lingua franca of an English gentleman.

At the end of each school day, John ran down the street to Abiah Holbrook's writing school for his favorite hour of the day. There, he shaved his quill to a sharp nib in order to shape, in an exquisite calligraphic style, his name. Hancock knew that practicing penmanship was very important for legible correspondence and a merchant's ledgers.

CHAPTER TWO

"No Pleasure Without Pain"

At thirteen, Hancock stood for Harvard College's intimidating entrance examination—part oral and part written. The test was administered by the college president and several tutors and included translating passages of Virgil from Latin and the New Testament from Greek—tasks he was well trained to complete. Once admitted, he was the second youngest in a class of twenty, ranked number five in class order, a recognition of his family's social standing. In only two generations, the Hancock family had moved from near-last rank to one of the top spots. Class order determined a student's room size, his proximity to the front of the chapel when he was praying, his order of service at mealtimes and his place in college processions.

The college's campus consisted of three redbrick Georgian buildings arranged around a quadrangle flanked by an orchard and outhouses. Because there was a shortage of dormitory rooms and because his uncle could afford it, John boarded off campus in comfort with the family of a clergyman eager to augment his meager stipend by taking in three freshmen. In his second year, John moved onto campus and into Massachusetts Hall.

The first of his five roommates was a cousin from Dorchester; the last, Anthony Wibird of Portsmouth, New Hampshire. Slim and handsome, his brown hair always combed, Hancock dressed impeccably in custom-tailored clothes. According to John Adams, who entered Harvard a year after John Hancock and knew both men well, the seven-years-older Anthony could hardly have contrasted more sharply with his fashionable roommate:

> P[arson] W[ibird] is crooked, his head bends forward, his shoulders are round and his Body is writhed and bended, his head and half his body have a list one Way, the other half declines the other Way, and his lower parts from his Middle, incline another Way. His features are as coarse and crooked as his Limbs. His nose is a large roman Nose with a prodigious Bunch Protuberance. . . . His mouth is large and irregular, his teeth black and foul and craggy. . . . His lips are stiff, rigid. . . . His eyes are a little squinted . . . his Visage is long, and lank, his Complexion wan, his Cheeks are fallen.[1]

The unlikely roommates hit it off, though, and after they graduated, Anthony would go off to Braintree, where he would take over the pulpit John's father had once occupied and live in the manse where John had been born. Deacon Adams's acerbic son, John, would have to endure Anthony's sermons from the family pew.

John Hancock's college life began, as had his father's and grandfather's, with compulsory daily attendance at chapel, where he heard a sophomore intone the college rules in Latin. Outfitted in a dark gown, Hancock was tutored for his first classes by Henry Flynt, an old friend of the Hancocks. John's grandfather and father had tried and failed to persuade Master Flynt to marry one of the Bishop's daughters; instead he chose to remain a bachelor.

John's classmate Benjamin Church would limn an uncharitable verse portrait of their aged tutor:

An ugly Monster, he in Sight appears / Form'd so by Nature not deform'd by Years / His matted Wig of piss-burnt horse-hair made / Scarce covers half his greasy shining Head / His Face a mixture of Deformities, like flaming meteors, shine his Gorgon Eyes / A very Scare-crow is his awful Nose / A frightful Grin his hideous Jaws disclose / You, when he yawns, tremendous teeth may see / And hence he's called his Dental Majesty.[2]

John's day began at five a.m. and ended twelve hours later with prayers. Donning his black gown, Hancock ate a breakfast of bread served with half a pint of home-brewed beer. After a study hour, the first class started at eight, with Flynt lecturing in Latin and reading from a long-ago-prepared text. The main meal of the day came at midday, with all students and tutors obliged to assemble in the Commons, the tutors at the front of the hall and the hundred or so students seated at benches and tables in class order.

Scholarship-dependent student waiters brought trays of food from the kitchen. Sometimes these men had been admitted with good social standing but for some reason their families could no longer afford the expense. For example, Samuel Adams's father, a maltster and member of the town's influential Caucus Club, had helped to found a land bank that printed and circulated its own paper currency according to the value of a borrower's land and crops. Parliament declared the currency illegal, its backers criminals. Only the elder Adams's political connections saved him from prison, but he was ordered to replace the illegal currency with Massachusetts pounds. Bankrupt, he had to inform his son that he could no longer afford to pay his tuition. If young Adams, a third-year student, stayed on, he would have to pay his own way by waiting on tables. A lifelong loathing of the British government and aristocracy was born of the boy's humiliation.

Wealthy or impecunious, each student was issued a wooden bowl, washed once a week, and had to provide a spoon, the sole utensil. The menu was monotonous: one pound of baked beef with "sufficient" vegetables and a half pint of beer. After the midday meal, students scattered to their tutors' rooms to spend their afternoon dissecting and disputing the morning's lecture. After more prayers at five, supper was served at seven thirty. The dinner menu was no more varied: the usual slab of meat pie and a tankard of beer. Like college students of any epoch, Harvard undergraduates complained that the food was "rotten" and that there wasn't enough of it. Wealthier students like Hancock cut Commons and ate somewhere else in Cambridge; as a result, only those less well-off followed the school's unenforced rule that all scholars must eat together.[3]

Emphasizing Latin, Greek and Hebrew, Harvard's curriculum afforded Hancock ample ancient history and politics. By studying Euclid, he learned to compose a syllogism; after memorizing passages of Homer, he recited quotes for his tutors. In addition to the classics, Hancock was exposed to Enlightenment thinkers, with his studies merging the ideas of John Calvin with those of John Locke, whose *Essay Concerning Human Understanding*, Hancock's favorite, served as the college's ethics textbook. After mastering the Latin writings of Cicero, Livy and Sallust, he was introduced to Montesquieu and Hume. Recent reforms at the college also introduced him to geography, geometry and astronomy. He liked to peer through the campus telescope and inspect the school's orrery, a model of the solar system.

Since grades didn't seem to matter, students found time to get into skirmishes with the school proctors. At age fifteen, John Hancock's first brush with authorities came when he and three classmates went to a local tavern and drank heavily, at the same time getting a Black servant named Titus, the former slave of the college's president, so drunk that they were charged with "endanger[ing] his life."[4]

Hauled before the college president and tutors, they faced a range of penalties, from a warning to a fine to expulsion. A more lasting sanction was to be degraded, the lowering of a student's class ranking. The faculty tribunal decided that the two ringleaders of the drinking spree would drop seven places in class order. For his part in "very much promoting the Affair," John Hancock dropped four places, from fifth to ninth. Both his father and grandfather had passed through Harvard without a single demerit. There is no trace of the reactions of Uncle Thomas and Aunt Lydia. Twice more, Hancock received penalties but for less serious infractions. Once, he was fined for failing to attend compulsory chapel, once for praying when he should have been studying.

While he had no further serious blemishes on his record, John Hancock did not forswear tippling. He even composed a six-stanza college drinking song, entitling it "A Pot of Good Ale." He devoted one stanza to parsons like his father and grandfather:

Our old Parish Vicar when he's in his liquor / Will merrily at his Parishioners rail / Come pay all your Tythes or I'll kiss all your wives / When once he shakes hands with a Pot of Good Ale.

While John was still an undergraduate, his mother married a third husband, another country parson. John immortalized her with her own quatrain:

The widow who's buried her husband of late / Has scarcely had time to weep or to wail / Thinks every day ten, till she's married again / When once she shakes hands with a Pot of Good Ale.

In July 1754, John Hancock and his class received their bachelor's degrees amid customary pomp: The royal governor and the county sheriff appeared in their robes. In addition to the official guests, hundreds crowded the campus to sell their own wares and buy others, turning the event into a festival. John's mother, brother and sister came up from Braintree, while Uncle Thomas and Aunt Lydia drove down from Beacon Hill to join the celebration.

At age seventeen, John Hancock left behind the world of classical authors and entered the modern orbit of ledger books, the lecture hall replaced by the countinghouse, with its rows of gray-faced clerks on stools keeping track of every order and farthing passing through the House of Hancock. Uncle and nephew could now begin to forge their commercial partnership.

Meanwhile, British warships dropped anchor near Clark's Wharf, the nearest to the sea. Its proximity to the ocean after a ship had made the long crossing gave the Hancocks a considerable commercial advantage.

Only weeks earlier, in the forests of western Pennsylvania, a young Virginia militia colonel named George Washington had inadvertently struck the match that ignited the French and Indian War, with all its lucrative government contracts for the House of Hancock.

Amid early rumors of renewed fighting between Britain and France for control of North America, Thomas Hancock had presciently begun to stock up on ammunition. His December 1753 order from London included six hundred half barrels of pistol powder. By the time John rode home from Harvard to Beacon Hill in his uncle's grand carriage, the Hancock warehouse bulged with war matériel. It became John's daily duty to register each shipment in account books and to track inventories.

When he passed through the front door of the House of Hancock—its new, ivory-inlaid coat of arms admonishing *Nul Plaisir Sans Peine* (No Pleasure Without Pain)—John put his poise and elegant penmanship to work as his uncle's personal assistant and amanuensis. At his desk in the counting room, he learned the intricacies of international transactions as he meticulously transcribed his uncle's scribbled notes into polished letters and orders to London agents, writing out half a dozen copies for different ships to increase the chances that at least one letter would survive privateers and storms at sea to reach its intended destination.

John allocated part of his time to accompanying his uncle to clubs and taverns. Every day from one to four in the afternoon, merchants gathered at the Exchange Coffee House to discount bills of exchange and gossip about politics and trade. In his memoirs, John Adams would later attest that, with lace at his cuffs, young John Hancock worked hard, becoming "an example to all the young men of the town. Wholly devoted to business, he was as regular and punctual at his store as the sun in its course."

Even before the French and Indian War, a secret message arrived at the House of Hancock from Charles Lawrence, royal governor of Nova Scotia. The British were preparing to attack the French fortress at Beauséjour (near present-day Moncton, New Brunswick) on the Bay of Fundy. The House of Hancock could receive the monopoly to provide all of the expedition's supplies in exchange for open-ended credit. After accepting, Thomas Hancock rushed word to his London banker, arranging for £20,000 (about $3 million today) in credit.

Requesting a man-of-war escort, Hancock dispatched his own ships to Britain to rush to his wharf a mountain of arms, powder, blankets, and tents—all the accoutrements of an army in the field. Writing out every order and keeping track of every shipment, John Hancock learned how to equip an army.

In June 1755, thirty-one ships crammed with two thousand New England colonial troops and their supplies set sail from Boston Harbor for Beauséjour, where they overwhelmed the French garrison. Then, with eighteen ships chartered from the House of Hancock, Governor Lawrence set about deporting three thousand Acadians and burning their settlements. As if in atonement, when one group of exiles escaped to Boston and was imprisoned, Thomas Hancock appealed successfully to the Massachusetts Council to release them. In 1759, in the climactic battle of the French and Indian War, oxen and teamsters provided by the House of Hancock dragged cannon up a narrow path from ships on the St. Lawrence to the Plains of Abraham, enabling Sir James Wolfe to win his final, decisive victory.

For its pains, the House of Hancock received a five percent commission for all services rendered throughout the six-year-long French and Indian War. Thomas Hancock also emerged with an appointment to Massachusetts's executive council, the province's highest civilian office. To provide his uncle the time to fulfill his new duties, John assumed more of the burden of lending money, negotiating real estate deals and acquiring merchandise, his distinctive signature on all the orders.

        —◡—

As the euphoria of British victory over the French wore off, Parliament plunged into a thorough review of its revenue from taxes in its American colonies. A glimpse at the national debt revealed a staggering £137 million—roughly $20 trillion U.S. in today's money—carrying annual interest of £5 million. Meanwhile, the cost of administering the empire, including newly conquered territories, consumed £8 million (about $1.2 billion) annually. Faced with this burden, the ministry concluded that the Americans had benefited disproportionately from the war and should begin to pay their fair share of the debts.

Since exactly a century before, when Parliament passed the first Acts of Navigation and Trade, British efforts to regulate their colonies' maritime commerce had collided with colonists' notions of their right to trade freely. Fathered by Oliver Cromwell at a time when England scarcely owned a merchant fleet and its American colonies had none, the Navigation Acts were ratified when Dutch global trade threatened to engulf Britain's overseas commerce.

The Navigation Act of 1756 mandated that a colonist's cargo must touch a port in England and pay customs duties there before being sold, no matter its ultimate destination. The act further stipulated that goods from America, Asia or Africa had to be in English ships crewed by a majority of Englishmen to land in England, Ireland or Britain's American colonies.

American colonists considered the thrust of the act unequivocally unfair.

They henceforth would have to purchase all manufactured goods from or through Britain and they were not free to set up their own manufacturing plants. Moreover, to protect England's growers, the Mother Country would buy only a fraction of American harvests. And to protect the profits of British merchants, Parliament proclaimed that Americans could export to Britain only certain "enumerated" commodities—and then only in English ships to British ports: "English goods in English bottoms." The act remained little more than words on paper for nearly a century, its enforcement haphazard at best and prohibitively expensive. The cost of the combined customs service and Royal Navy crackdown, an estimated £8,000 annually, far exceeded the resultant revenues, up from a meager £259 in 1755 only to £1,189 in 1761. In all, the Navigation Acts would produce only £35,000 in thirty years; the Molasses Act, £21,000 in thirty-five years.

Because the British government had followed an unwritten policy of "benign neglect," a clever and careful status quo had existed since the settling of the first British colonies in North America in the early seventeenth century. Colonists in the West Indies depended on the mainland English colonies for such imports as horses, fish and flour, livestock and lumber, barrel staves and naval stores—and even the ships that brought them. In exchange, the Caribbean islanders provided mainland colonists with unlimited sugar to make rum and molasses. Yet the West Indies were unable to keep pace with the demands of the mainland colonies. British officials turned a blind eye as North America made up the shortfall by trading with the island colonies of the rival Spanish, French and Dutch empires.

In peacetime, goods flowed freely between the mainland ports and the West Indies. The British home government remained content to make ample profits from manufactured goods—furniture, glass, fine clothing, carriages—exported to the colonies by English factors. American colonists preferred English manufactured goods that were cheaper and better made than similar products from Continental Europe. Colonial merchants' profits seldom resided six months in the colonies before being remitted to Britain and exchanged for luxury goods.

This laissez-faire policy lasted until the 1730s, when the British government, pressured by West Indian plantation owners who sat in Parliament, demanded a monopoly on the rich sugar trade. Asserting its right to regulate colonial trade, Parliament forced through the Molasses Act of 1733. At first provisional for five years, it was renewed over and over again. The new duty was steep—six pence to the pound—and proved too much for mainland merchants. They simply began to evade the duty, quickly devising practices to circumvent it. What had been, a day before Parliament passed the act, perfectly acceptable commercial practice became illegal overnight. Once legitimate merchants, if they did not abandon their businesses or face ruinous duties, now became, in the eyes of the British, smugglers.

Mainland merchants quickly learned that they could face considerable losses by having sugar and molasses brought legally from Spanish, French or West Indian ports—or they could make profits by having cynical West Indian merchants clandestinely land the goods along thousands of miles of North American seacoast. Thomas Hancock sent instructions to his ships' captains in the Netherlands with cargoes bound for his Boston wharf to unload in Cape Cod. After evading customs duties, they were to haul the goods overland to Boston.

CHAPTER THREE

"Make a Stir for Us"

As soon as British victory in the French and Indian War had been assured, British customs agents in Massachusetts, determined to crack down on smugglers, sought ships to seize contraband and warrants to enter and search warehouses. Customs officials requested writs of assistance but merchants challenged the legality of these special warrants. The writs were intended only to break up illegal trafficking in French contraband; now that the war was over, merchants were sure no more would be issued. When there were no large seizures, there were no protests.

But customs officials applied to the Massachusetts Superior Court, which complied by granting a number of writs. Armed with the writs, the officials swooped down on the waterfront and began to seize allegedly illicit cargoes. In the autumn of 1760, a Dutch ship arrived carrying an extraordinarily rich cargo from Holland valued at an estimated £10,000 (about $1.5 million today). The ship's presence prompted Charles Paxton, surveyor of customs in Boston, to begin conducting raids in Massachusetts ports, apparently in response to instructions from London. Merchants in Boston, Salem and Plymouth yowled. Why were the warrants being issued for only Massachusetts?

Every Boston merchant knew that customs collectors profited handsomely from the sale of any goods they confiscated: One-third of the proceeds went to the Crown, one-third went to the province's treasury and all the rest went to the customs collector. Paid informants tipping off the customs collectors were so reviled that, to protect their identities, customs didn't even have to identify them, even to the Admiralty court. The collectors had only to clarify the amount arranged for their payment, which came from the Crown's share.

A delegation of merchants, including Thomas Hancock, maintained that search warrants could be issued only by the Court of the Exchequer in England. Did the Massachusetts Superior Court have the same authority, the same powers as the Court of the Exchequer in England? If it did not, the seizures were illegal.

Bostonians grew increasingly indignant that they should be subjected to search warrants, which they felt were contrary to the rights of Englishmen, a throwback to the reign of the despotic Stuarts before the English Civil War. To the Hancocks and fellow Boston merchants, these warrants were beyond illegal: They were unconstitutional, meaning that they violated principles that transcended those of Parliament, of the king and of all the committees and boards of trade made up of men who were totally ignorant of America. None of these courtiers had ever visited the colonies; their only goal was to make the colonies profitable for Britain, to keep the balance of trade favorable to England.

The case came to trial in March 1761. Arguing for the Crown,

Jeremiah Gridley declared that the necessity of the case took away "the common privileges of Englishmen." Even if the merchants were indignant when tax collectors entered their homes, arrested them and seized their property, wasn't the collection of revenue to support fleets and armies more important than the liberty of any individual? There were many precedents for the exercise of writs of assistance in England, he argued. "If it is the law in England, it is the law here, extended to this country by act of Parliament."[1]

It was midafternoon before James Otis rose, bowed and launched into a fiery rebuttal. "This writ is against the fundamental principles of English law," he contended. According to Locke's *Second Treatise on Government*, unrestricted general warrants were unconstitutional. It was an Englishman's right to keep his home secure against search and seizure. It was the right of English subjects not to be taxed without their consent. English colonists were full English subjects; they had the same rights as English subjects on English soil. As such, they could not be taxed without representation in Parliament. "If an act of Parliament should be passed in the very words of this petition for writs of assistance, it would be void."[2]

British American colonists had always believed that they held rights assured by "the laws of God and Nature," but no one had ever before objected to Parliament's authority to make laws regulating trade. These were considered external taxes based on external legislation passed by Parliament and had long been accepted. By asserting colonists' rights as British subjects, Otis was defying the members of Parliament to abridge if not abrogate their natural rights as Englishmen.

After days of attorneys battering each other with citations and legal precedents, Chief Justice Thomas Hutchinson stopped the trial. He would make no immediate decision but would continue the case until the next court term. Meanwhile, he would write to the Board of Trade in London for advice. Customs officials in Boston could continue exercising their writs, searches and seizures until the matter was settled.

It would be fully six years before Britain's attorney general and solicitor general upheld Otis, declaring that writs of assistance were invalid in America. Indeed, such writs could be issued only by the Court of the Exchequer in England. But the searches, seizures and fines had already ruined many merchants.

Britain's triumph in the French and Indian War brought celebrations in London but a depression in America. Suffering from gout and acute nervous disorder, Thomas Hancock decided it was time to begin preparations to turn the business over to John. But first, John would have to acquire more social polish. Lydia and Thomas agreed that their nephew should follow the route of wealthy young English gentlemen and make a grand tour of Europe. To refine his skill at negotiating, he would meet and develop personal ties with the House of Hancock's British agents and bankers.

Thomas paved the way by sending letters of introduction to all his business connections in Europe. To his principal London agent, he wrote, "I have given my nephew Mr. John Hancock, who has been with me many years in business, an opportunity of going to London, to see my friends and to settle my accounts. I am to desire you to be so kind as to provide him with good lodgings where you think it will be most convenient for him to meet with reputable people."

Describing John as a "sober, modest young gentleman" whose "industry, good behavior and ability has recommended him to me," Thomas confided his plan for the future: "On his return from England I propose to make him a partner with me in my business."[3]

To provide protection while crossing an Atlantic aswarm with French privateers, Thomas arranged for his nephew to travel with Massachusetts's homeward-bound royal governor, Thomas Pownall, giving him authority to negotiate a ransom if John were captured. Thomas admonished his nephew to heed Polonius's advice to his son, Laertes, in *Hamlet*: "This above all, to thine own self be true." He also urged John to be "frugal of expenses, do honor to your country and furnish your mind with all wise improvements." As a going-away memento, he gave John his treasured watch with the admonition "Keep the pickpockets from my watch."[4]

Evading French warships and privateers, the merchantman *Benjamin and Samuel* made an otherwise uneventful thirty-seven-day Atlantic crossing that summer. John settled into rooms in fashionable Westminster and began his metamorphosis from provincial clerk to an English gentleman with fittings in the latest London fashion. With Pownall's assistance and his uncle's letters of introduction, he made the rounds of Thomas's overseas agents, going from office to office to introduce himself to the merchants responsible for keeping the goods flowing to the House of Hancock. He usually made a favorable impression, as they reported in letters to Thomas. "He is a worthy, well-disposed young gentleman," one put it.

To bankers, John presented Hancock bills of exchange so that he could draw on his uncle's funds for his expenses. But at least one balked at the presumptuousness of this young American: When

John tried, without written authorization from his uncle, to withdraw £1,000 (about $150,000 today) all at once from his uncle's account to pay off his uncle's debt to Pownall, the banker refused to hand over such a large amount of cash. Furious, John vowed that he would never again have any dealings with this bank. He went to his uncle's other banker, who readily advanced £800 (roughly $120,000 today). When John reported the incident to his uncle, Thomas wrote back, "I shall not forget."[5]

In the Thames between business meetings, John learned to swim, something he had never learned at home. Seeing London's society at play and being seen amid it, he sipped coffee or tea for a fee in the pleasure gardens of Ranelagh and Vauxhall, where he was dazzled by the evening displays of fireworks. Other nights, he took in the latest David Garrick play in Covent Gardens. One possible activity he didn't report in letters to Aunt Lydia and his mother was visits to one of London's fashionable disorderly houses.

During his two-year sojourn, John spent on himself at least £500 ($75,000 today)—five times the yearly earnings of a skilled English cabinetmaker. Away from the disapproving eyes of Boston's Puritans, he pursued an elegant lifestyle, mingling at the royal court in the latest fashions. When his uncle winced at his high expenditures, John admitted, "I am not remarkable for the plainness of my dress. . . . Upon proper occasions I dress as genteel as anyone and can't say I am without lace. . . . I find money some way or other goes very fast, but think I can reflect it has been spent with satisfaction and to my own honor." He added that he thought his conduct necessary: By upholding the prestige of the House of Hancock, he hoped to bring home more contracts.[6]

In an effort to cut expenses, John left London and headed into the countryside. In September, he made an excursion west to

Bristol, port of embarkation for many Boston-bound ships; then he swung north to Manchester. And that was the extent of his grand tour: John never crossed the English Channel.

In October, King George II died. London social life died with him. All the theaters closed, John wrote to his mother, "and no diversions are going forward."[7] At first, John was determined to stay for the coronation of George III, but he became ill. His uncle's business agent Jonathan Barnard insisted John give up his bachelor digs and come live with his family. A young servant girl took care of him: John wrote home to his younger brother, Ebenezer, that she was "remarkably tender and kind," reminding him of his aunt Lydia.[8]

While young George III's ambassadors searched Europe for a suitable queen, the soon-to-be king postponed his coronation. John didn't want to miss it: He never expected to see anything so important again. But from Boston, John heard of Aunt Lydia's deep depression after her father's death: She needed John to come home. Uncle Thomas implored him to cut short his visit. John dutifully paid his bills and headed for Portsmouth to find a fast vessel home.

He stopped off long enough to meet with Matthew Woodford, a government contractor who was in charge of provisioning sizable British garrisons in Nova Scotia and Newfoundland and who needed a reliable American contact. John had learned how to negotiate diplomatically, and he offered to help Woodford. John asked him to sign an agreement granting a lucrative contract for the House of Hancock.

When John landed in Boston in the fall of 1762, he could see that his uncle's health had deteriorated: He was "just creeping about pretty poorly," his gout worsening. Impressed that John had not only enhanced the firm's reputation but had landed important contracts, Thomas changed the name of the firm to Thomas Hancock and Company. He took an advertisement in the January 1, 1763, edition of the *Boston News-Letter*: "I have this day taken my nephew Mr. John Hancock into partnership with me having had long experience of his uprightness and great abilities for business."[9]

Taking over most of the business affairs of the House of Hancock in the midst of a postwar economic slump, John received the blessing of his bedridden uncle to branch out into new endeavors that did not rely on cash-strapped neighbors. In the summer of 1763, John visited Nantucket and arranged a new partnership with the whaling firm of Folger and Gardner. During his London sojourn, he had learned of the lucrative commerce of supplying both whale oil, which fueled England's lamps through its long, dark winters, and whalebone, which could be transformed into corset stays for fashionable women.

Binding together his Nantucket partners with agent Jonathan Barnard in London, John boldly set out to corner the whaling market. He commissioned larger, faster vessels, including the hundred-twenty-ton, two-masted, square-sailed *Boston Packet*—the largest ship in the Hancock fleet—to transport the maximum number of barrels of oil. John also commissioned a fast new twin-masted brigantine specially designed to carry both whale oil and merchandise. He named the ship *Lydia* after his aunt. After buying up all the oil in Nantucket in the spring, John dispatched the two fast ships, packed to the gunwales with barrels of oil and bales of bone, to arrive in London before any other supplier.

His principal competitor, the firm of William Rotch & Sons of Nantucket, already held a virtual monopoly on the spermaceti taken from whales hunted off the Falkland Islands in the South

Atlantic; the spermaceti was prized in Britain for its use in making clean-burning, virtually smokeless candles. The Rotches had once driven Thomas Hancock from the oil market by shipping directly from Nantucket to London—following the Gulf Stream—which was faster than the desultory Nantucket–Boston–London route John's uncle had followed. But because of John's new ship, his London partners were ready to send back each one crammed with autumn orders of general merchandise for the Hancocks' whole-sale and retail markets even before competitors' cargoes arrived in England.

~e~

By the summer of 1764, John was managing most of the Hancock enterprises. In addition to whale oil and government contracts, he personally oversaw construction of the vessels to carry provisions to the British Canadian garrisons, and he corresponded with the English merchants who supplied the ships. He managed the Hancocks' sprawling patchwork of real estate, which included twenty-two thousand acres of undeveloped land in central Massachusetts, its forests a source of potash coveted in England for soapmaking; property in Maine being held for speculation; and developed parcels in and around Boston. These included the dozen stores, offices and warehouses on the Hancocks' wharf, which provided a steady flow of rental income.

Along with John's elevated status came an invitation to join the Masonic Lodge of St. Andrews, whose members included prominent Bostonians such as his old Braintree neighbor Josiah Quincy, the lawyer James Otis Jr. and Dr. Joseph Warren. John was also invited to become a member of the Long Room Club, a secret society recently formed by malt broker Samuel Adams to discuss colonial politics. Warren and Otis were members of this organization, too, along with silversmith Paul Revere, whose shop was a near neighbor of Hancock's Wharf. Thomas had bought out the other shareholders of Clark's Wharf—the second longest in Boston Harbor and the closest to the sea—and renamed it Hancock's Wharf.

For most of every day on the wharf, John talked orders and contracts with merchants, shipbuilders and sailors; now, after he closed his shop in the evening, he had new outlets where he could enjoy talking, drinking and playing cards with lawyers and politicians, craftsmen and journeymen.

One Sunday early in the summer of 1764, John Hancock first saw Dorothy Quincy coming out of church. "Dolly," as everyone called her, was the youngest of Judge Edmund Quincy and Elizabeth Wendell Quincy's ten children. Dorothy had spent most of her early years in Braintree in a lively household, where the Quincy girls' callers included John and Samuel Adams. Hancock began to visit the Quincy mansion frequently. Dolly was seventeen at the time; John, ten years older.

Judging by portraits by John Singleton Copley, both John and Dolly were slim, with high foreheads, dark eyes and slender lips; they almost looked like siblings. Garments Hancock wore to his inauguration as governor, preserved by the commonwealth, suggest that, if we allow for shrinkage in their laundering, John was five six.

Aunt Lydia could now worry less about John: She had no doubt been disturbed by the rumors that John had a mistress, an older woman named Dorcas Griffiths. Dorcas was a tenant shop owner on Hancock's Wharf who dispensed liquor, linen drapery, groceries and, some said, sexual favors from her rooms, where Hancock frequently visited her. Now that John began to see Dolly, he seemed to have lost interest in all other feminine company—and Dorcas left town with a British sailor.

After Dorothy's mother died on November 7, 1769, Aunt Lydia met with Dorothy's father and won his approval to have Dorothy, now twenty-two, spend much more time with her in Beacon Hill. Dolly would stay for days at a time, meeting frequently with John with Lydia chaperoning. Indeed, she became Lydia's companion on her numerous social visits around town. As John and Dorothy spent more time together, it seemed obvious to the town gossips that their engagement was inevitable. Aunt Lydia did not quash the scuttlebutt: She was determined to link the Hancock name with the more distinguished lineage of the Quincys, who claimed descent from Baron de Quincy, the first earl of Winchester, one of the barons who forced King John to sign the Magna Carta.

Dorothy and her siblings had grown up in a genteel world of sudden wealth. When she was only one year old, in the middle of King George's War, her father, Edmund, had commissioned the *Bethel*—a small privateering ship—in partnership with her uncle Josiah and the men's brother-in-law, Edward Jackson. Off the coast of Gibraltar, the *Bethel* overtook a Spanish galleon bound from Havana to Cádiz. At night, *Bethel*'s captain tricked the Spaniards into believing he was heavily armed, when in fact *Bethel* had only wooden cannon and a small crew. After the Spaniards surrendered the *Jesus Maria and Joseph*, the Bostonians discovered the galleon was carrying a treasure of 161 chests filled with gold and silver. After the Spanish vessel was escorted by the *Bethel* to Boston, the treasure was divided among the partners. Dorothy's mother would never again have to operate a small store out of their Braintree house to help feed their family.

Edmund immediately purchased a grand house on Summer Street in Boston and set about turning his Braintree house into a country estate with formal gardens, a waterfall and, from the street to the house, an allée of lime trees. He refurnished the house and added a harpsichord and scores of books to his extensive library. When Dorothy was old enough to go to school—Quincy believed in educating all his children—he brought her into town to attend a girls' academy.

~ℓ~

Thomas Hancock survived the usual eighteenth-century course of medical treatments—emetics, purges and bleedings—for another year and a half after making John his partner, but little could be done to alleviate the pain in his gout-swollen arms and legs. His outings from his Beacon Hill mansion narrowed to occasional carriage rides, his arms and legs cushioned in flannel, to attend meetings of the executive council at Province House. On August 1, 1764, he managed to climb the stairs to the second-floor council chamber. Upon entering, he collapsed. The other councillors carried him to his coach and rushed him back up the hill, where he died two hours later of a stroke.

The death of Thomas Hancock at age sixty-one left his twenty-seven-year-old nephew, John Hancock, one of the wealthiest men in colonial America. Dividing an estate worth an estimated £100,000 (about $15 million today), Thomas left his widow, Lydia, £10,000 ($1.5 million) in cash, the Beacon Hill mansion and all its furnishings and grounds. He divided £8,000 ($1.2 million) among his sisters, nieces, nephews and friends. To his alma mater, Harvard College, he left £1,000 ($150,000) to endow a professorship in Near Eastern languages; to the town of Boston, £600 ($90,000) to build a hospital for the insane. To the Society to Propagate Christianity, he left £700 (about $100,000) to establish a Native American missionary program. To his five slaves, he left each £20 annuities (about $3,000 a year) and their freedom.

Everything else he left to John: the House of Hancock's wharf; his warehouses and shops and their inventories; his ships; and all his land and properties in Massachusetts and Maine. Only three days after Thomas was buried, Lydia signed over the Beacon Hill mansion and all its contents to John—with the condition that she could live there for the rest of her life. At her request, John commissioned Boston's leading portrait painter, John Singleton Copley, to create a full-length portrait of Thomas Hancock to hang in Harvard's library.

John also commissioned Copley to paint a portrait of himself as if interrupted from a day's work. Copley posed John sitting thoughtfully in a simple wooden chair at a worktable, a quill pen poised in one hand, the other turning the page of a ledger. He wears a plain blue broadcloth coat over a simple white shirt; his stockings are white silk. His hair is pulled back and tied with a ribbon. Hancock positioned the portrait prominently in the foyer of his mansion so that every visitor would see it—and he even ordered pen-and-ink copies to distribute.

For Aunt Lydia, Thomas's death left a vacuum on Beacon Hill, which she wished to fill by the marriage of John to Dorothy Quincy. Lydia was intent on grooming Dolly to be a hostess. More and more often, Dolly was invited to Aunt Lydia's dinner parties, where guests were served soups, meats, fish, fruits from her orchards and pastries, with plenty of good wine. When Dolly stayed at her father's home, John wrote long notes to her and sent them by courier at all hours.

Aunt Lydia continued to prod John to spend even more time with Dorothy. Each seemed to bask in the other's company in public, yet no announcement of an engagement seemed forthcoming. John had immersed himself in his taxing new responsibilities as the head of the House of Hancock.

CHAPTER FOUR

"We Are a Gone People"

John Hancock could hardly have inherited his uncle's business at a worse moment. The postwar slump deepened into a full-scale depression. Despite writing to agents, suppliers and customers that, undaunted, he intended to press on, he could not ignore the evidence that several Boston mercantile houses had collapsed within months of the news that the long war was over. Many had placed orders for merchandise before they learned that it would no longer be needed. A crewman on one of Hancock's ships returned from England infected with smallpox. The entire crew was quarantined, the ship ordered to be burned. Twice before in the past fifty years, Boston had been decimated by smallpox, as much as ten percent of its populace dying in each outbreak. By Christmastime, Bostonians were fleeing, leaving few customers for Hancock's mounds of unwanted merchandise.

Hancock nonetheless decided he should advertise a full line of goods for those who stayed. "At Store No. 4 at the east end of

Faneuil Hall Market," he offered "a general assortment of English and India goods; also choice Newcastle coals and Irish butter, cheap for cash." At the same time, he called on "those persons who are still indebted to the estate of the late Hon. Thomas Hancock... to be speedy in paying... to prevent trouble."[1]

While few creditors had the money to pay up, Hancock decided he could not refuse them additional credit and force them to go bankrupt for want of stock to sell. Indeed, Hancock decided it was a propitious moment to expand. Concentrating on the whale oil market, he sent his Nantucket partners orders to speed to London a record £17,000 (about $2.5 million) worth of oil, tripling his usual order. He put unemployed carpenters to work building even more ships to carry the oil, potash and lumber to England.

In an early form of what would later be called "franchising," Hancock set up at least four of his clerks with their own shops to manage in and around Boston, supplying them with building materials, labor and an initial inventory worth £1,500 (about $225,000 today) of goods. While each franchisee could purchase goods from another supplier, the House of Hancock could now undersell anyone. The franchisee was free to sell anything Hancock did not. Once trained by Hancock, the franchisee could advertise under John's sign, Hancock and Company, and would enter a fifty-fifty profit-sharing agreement with him. Effectively, John became the partner of each franchisee.

~ℓ~

But as the year 1765 began, John Hancock wrote to his London agents that he was forced to cancel his spring orders, citing "great uneasiness." The failure "of some persons of note has put us all into great anxiety. . . . Trade has met with a most prodigious shock and the greatest losses to some people ever known in these parts of the world. Times are very bad and precarious here and take my word, good friends, the times will be worse here." Hancock added a warning: "If we are not relieved at home [in England] we must live upon our own produce and manufactures."[2]

In April, John Hancock was appointed to his first public office. At twenty-eight, he became the youngest ever to serve as one of Boston's five selectmen. In effect, he took his seat in the chair vacated by his uncle's death. Yet "no alteration appeared in Mr. Hancock," John Adams attested in his memoirs. "The same steady, ready, punctual, industrious, indefatigable man of business. Not less than a thousand families were every day dependent on Mr. Hancock for their daily bread."[3]

At this singularly inopportune moment, in order to pay for British troops to garrison the colonies' frontiers, Parliament decided to pass the American Revenue Act, the first law ever enacted to extract cash directly from colonists. The list of new tariffs would affect almost every American, at the same time doubling the duties on goods from competing empires' colonies in the Caribbean. And Americans could now export raw materials only within the British Empire.

In Boston, Samuel Adams warned the Town Meeting that this latest infringement of colonial rights would "annihilate our charter rights to govern and tax ourselves. . . . Are we not reduced from the character of free subjects to the miserable status of tributary slaves?" Alarmed, the Massachusetts Assembly launched the first intercolonial protest movement by establishing a committee of correspondence to link with the other provincial assemblies.[4]

In Virginia, tobacco planter George Washington, a member of

the House of Burgesses, publicly criticized the new levy. Punitive levies would only drive Americans to make themselves less dependent on imported English goods by manufacturing goods for their own markets. Washington called the tax an "ill-judged measure":

> What more can they desire? All taxes which lessen our importation of British goods must be hurtful to the manufacturers of them. Our people will perceive that many luxuries which we have hitherto lavished our substance to Great Britain for, can well be disposed with while the necessaries of life are to be procured for the most part within ourselves. . . . Who is to suffer most in this event, the merchant or the planter?[5]

In response to even this timid colonial response to its new taxing policy, Parliament retaliated heavy-handedly by imposing the first excise tax ever levied on Americans, a stamp tax that had to be paid in scarce gold or silver. Stamps of various denominations were to be affixed to legal documents of all types—including liquor licenses and all permits, wills, and bails—as well as to ships' papers, bills of lading, bills of sale, insurance policies, appointments to office, articles of apprenticeship, wine containers, newspapers, almanacs, pamphlets, leaflets, even playing cards and dice. Some stamps were prohibitively costly. A college diploma required a £4 (roughly $600 today) stamp when half of Harvard's students, on scholarships studying for the ministry, had no money.

But the tax would fall heaviest on merchants and shipowners like John Hancock. The paper on which all legal documents were written would have to be purchased from England with the stamp already embossed on it, and stamped paper was outrageously expensive. The contracts of apprentices and clerks required costly stamps roughly equivalent to a five percent wage tax.

At first, Hancock complained only about the time he would have to waste filling out more forms. And in the short term, he actually stood to benefit as weaker mercantile firms dropped out of competition. Indeed, combined with the postwar depression, the new regulations would reduce the number of ships traveling between Boston and Caribbean markets by eighty percent in one year. But Hancock foresaw the long-term threat posed by the new tax. He knew that his London agents had close ties to the Board of Trade. He warned them, "The heavy taxes on the colonies will be a great damp to trade. If such duties are laid and we must be obliged to bear all, we shall have little or no demand for supplies from England."[6]

He urged his agents to lobby Parliament to rescind the "very cruel" act. "We were before much burdened. We shall not now be able much longer to support trade. . . .[I]n the end Great Britain must feel the effects of it. I wonder the merchants and friends of America don't make a stir for us."[7]

Joining America's first trade boycott, Hancock, like other Boston merchants, stopped importing English lace and ruffles. Mechanics followed suit, wearing only leatherwork clothes tanned in Massachusetts. A nonimportation movement spread south to Virginia.

By June 1765, enforcement of the new customs duties had drained what little cash remained in circulation. Not only shopkeepers and artisans were closing their doors—even major importing firms like Hancock's were struggling. Hancock had only £2,000 ($300,000) in his London bank account. While English firms owed him £3,000 ($450,000), he was still carrying £9,000

($1.35 million) in business debts on the books when his London agent began to refuse his orders. (His personal fortune remained unaffected: His uncle had taught him to keep his personal and business accounts separate.)

When his London agent did not respond to his entreaties to intercede with the Board of Trade, Hancock, at first ever so deferentially, began to see himself as a spokesman for Boston's merchants. He wrote to his old friend former governor Pownall, who now filled an influential post on the Board of Trade. "I wish we could be helped out of our present burdens and difficulties. . . . Our trade is prodigiously embarrassed and must shortly be ruined." Hancock had convinced himself that pressure brought to bear by his powerful connections in London could sway Parliament to rescind the odious act. "If the Stamp Act takes place," he wrote again to his agent, "we are a gone people—do help us all you can."[8]

On September 11, when fourteen boxes of stamps arrived in Boston, Hancock, calling the stamps "the most disagreeable commodity that were ever imported," again appealed to his friends in London. If the stamps were "carried into execution" on November 1, the day the act was to take effect, "they will entirely stagnate trade here. . . . It is universally determined here never to submit to it. . . . The consequences will be bad and I believe more fatal to you than to us. . . . For God's sake, use your interest to relieve us."[9]

The name of each colony's stamp commissioner was published in August. At the same time, Samuel Adams gathered members of once rival North End gangs to arrange a truce and a "union feast" at the Green Dragon Tavern. John Hancock agreed to pick up the tab to celebrate the cessation of intergang violence. Yet the arrival of the stamps led the gangs to concentrate their aggression on a new, shared target. At a signal from Adams—and after consuming mugs of rum—the merged gangs joined a crowd in chasing the newly appointed stamp commissioner, Andrew Oliver, through the streets. After ransacking his home, they roared on to attack the mansion of his brother-in-law, recently appointed lieutenant governor Thomas Hutchinson. With blocks and tackles, they pulled down his mansion. Hutchinson and his family managed to escape.

John Hancock was apparently unaware of Adams's true intentions behind the feast. He abhorred violence. He had every reason to fear a similar attack by a mob on his mansion or his businesses. Oliver, like him, was a Harvard graduate; he was also the son of a wealthy merchant, an elder of the Boston church whose roots ran back to the founding of the colony. Hancock decided he must now openly declare his support for the protest movement in part to protect himself. He wrote to his London agent a letter that he shared with Samuel Adams; in it, he declared that he was preparing to join other Boston merchants in a boycott of English goods. If his ships returned from Britain before November 1, he would unload them, fill them with whale oil and send them back to England, but if they arrived after November 1, he would empty their holds, haul the ships ashore and, for the second year in a row, cancel his orders for all spring goods.

"The people of this country will never suffer themselves to be made slaves by submission to the d—— Act," he wrote. "A thousand guineas, nay, a much larger sum, would be no temptation to me to apply for a stamp, for such is the aversion of the people to the stamps that I would be sure to lose my property, if not my life." Nothing but repeal could secure America's trade with England, Hancock insisted. If Parliament persisted in enforcing the Stamp Act, he would "sell my stock in trade and shut up my warehouse doors. In case the Stamp Act is not repealed my orders are that you will not ship me one article." He was not alone: "The principal merchants not only of this town, but of those of other trading towns of this province" would join him in a boycott "which I am determined to abide by." Two hundred fifty Boston merchants followed Hancock's lead. A few days later, merchants in New York and Philadelphia also followed Hancock's example.[10]

On Hancock's desk as he signed the boycott's articles of agreement lay a demand for payment from his London agent. But now, Hancock wrote to him, he could not legally transmit any funds: All remittances required stamps, and he could not buy one. All the stamp agents had resigned. Now publicly attacking the stamp tax, Hancock protested that he already paid more taxes than an Englishman of his means. "Not a man in England, in proportion to estate, pays the tax that I do. I now pay yearly £300 sterling [$45,000 today] besides all the duties, imposts, ministers and many other additional taxes. I will not be a slave."[11]

On November 1, Boston's bells tolled all day. The newly formed Sons of Liberty, now including bankrupt shopkeepers and artisans, gathered at the Liberty Tree with effigies of the prime minister and other members of Parliament. They put the effigies in a cart. With thousands marching behind it, they wheeled it past the Town House, where the Massachusetts General Court was in session, and on to the gallows on Boston Neck, where they hanged the effigies. All business came to a standstill; the courts and customs house closed. But only a few days later Bostonians resumed their activities, completely ignoring the Stamp Act. The customs house reopened, and when Hancock's ships arrived at his docks, he filled them with whale oil and sent them off to London.

As the boycott took hold, the withholding of £4 million ($600 million) in payments and the loss of colonial merchants' custom cut deeply into the British economy. Exports from Britain to America dropped fourteen percent overnight as goods piled up in British warehouses. Hancock's agent had no choice but to join other merchants facing bankruptcy and demand Parliament repeal the tax.

When Parliament reconvened on January 14, 1766, Prime Minister George Grenville threatened to use troops to enforce the levy. But former prime minister William Pitt, calling for repeal, praised Americans for disobeying a tax framed by a body in which they were not represented. When colonial agents were called to testify, Benjamin Franklin of Pennsylvania warned that using troops to enforce the tax could lead to an open rebellion. A bill for full repeal by the House of Commons passed 275–167; under pressure from the king, the House of Lords passed the repeal bill on March 18, 1766.

London merchants, who considered John Hancock to be the most important American merchant, sent the good news racing toward Boston aboard the *Harrison*, one of Hancock's ships. It took two months for the message to arrive on May 16. Hancock convened the Select Board and made the official announcement. Sam Adams and the Sons of Liberty had apparently unofficially known the news for weeks, possibly learning about it from the captain or crew of a faster ship. Coordinating with Hancock and the Select Board, he had already prepared an elaborate celebration.

At one in the morning on May 17—what became known as Repeal Day—all of Boston's church bells began pealing, starting with the one in the steeple nearest the Liberty Tree; one hour later, after sermons of thanksgiving, marching band music filled the serpentine streets. At one o'clock in the afternoon, with the Union Jack flapping from every building, all the ships in the harbor fired cannon salutes and hoisted their colors. Bostonians poured from their houses, firing their guns in the air, many of them shouting Hancock's name.

That evening, all Boston seemed aglow. Bonfires dotted the town and candles illuminated windows. An "Extraordinary" printing of the *Massachusetts Gazette* reported that its four upper stories were "ornamented with the figures of their majesties and fourteen worthy patriots who have distinguished themselves with their love of liberty." On the Common, the Sons of Liberty constructed a pyramid illuminated by two hundred eighty lanterns:

> On the top of the pyramid was fixed a round box of fireworks. About one hundred yards from the pyramid the Sons of Liberty erected a stage for the exhibition of their fireworks, near the workhouse, in the lower rooms of which they entertained the gentlemen of the town.[12]

Samuel Adams gathered the Sons at the Liberty Tree for a parade; then they trailed John Hancock's carriage to the debtors' prison, where Hancock's cash bought the release of all its inmates.

On that balmy spring evening, Bostonians crowded the Common and gravitated toward Hancock's illuminated mansion for the fireworks display he had prepared on Beacon Hill. When the gates swung open, the crowd surged in to find that Hancock had laid out rows of tables in the yard in front of the mansion, where he offered to share a cask of 125 gallons of Madeira, barrels of cider and plates of food. From a stage he had erected, Hancock waved to the cheering crowd, then went inside to the feast his aunt Lydia had prepared for "the genteel part of the town."[13]

At eleven p.m., Hancock's fireworks exploded at the same time as the hundreds of fireworks launched from the wheel atop the obelisk, signaling a dazzling end to the day's celebration. For some Bostonians, the party went on. The next day, Hancock entertained twenty-nine merchants at the Bunch of Grapes; each guest offered a toast.

A few weeks earlier, while the news of repeal was still sailing toward Boston, members of the Long Room Club—the secret society founded by James Otis, Joseph Warren and Sam Adams—had honored Hancock. Adams opined that Hancock, New England's most important merchant, had demonstrated his loyalty to the nascent anti-royalist movement. Hancock's addition to the club's membership introduced a new element—the wealthy merchant—to a society that included ministers, lawyers and physicians.

Forerunner of America's first political party, the club was able to support candidates for town- and colony-wide office with writings published by the *Gazette*. By aligning himself with the Whigs, Hancock believed he was taking a stand for free trade. He joined forces with Adams and Boston's leading radicals. In the May 6 election for the General Court, the Boston Caucus delivered 437 of a possible 500 votes for Boston's seat to Hancock, securing his election. After one Long Room Club meeting, Sam Adams told his younger cousin John, "This town has done a wise thing today. They have made that young man's fortune their own."[14]

CHAPTER FIVE

"The Idol of the Mob"

The successful repeal movement encouraged John Hancock to capitalize on his popularity and expand both his business enterprises and his political engagements. To increase his exports to England, he launched a growing fleet of ships to transport goods in both the transatlantic and the Caribbean trade. He continued to outbid rivals on the Nantucket market for whale oil, built more retail stores and ordered £8,000 ($1.2 million) in stock to fill them.

"He changed the course of his uncle's business, and built, and employed in trade, a great number of ships," wrote Thomas Hutchinson, "and in this way, building at the same time several houses, he found work for a great number of tradesmen, made himself popular, was chosen select man, representative, moderator of Town Meetings, etc."[1]

When a fire broke out in the bakehouse of one of his tenants and destroyed twenty buildings, including many of his own, Hancock ignored his own losses and made provision for the fifty families left homeless. When the General Court appropriated £400 ($60,000) for their relief, Hancock matched the grant. In the winter of 1766–67, one of Boston's coldest, he bought and distributed a hundred fifty cords of firewood to the city's poor. Riding around the town in his red carriage, he sought out opportunities for largesse, including donating food and cash gifts to the ministers of every church to distribute among their needy parishioners. In their sermons, clergy lauded him for his humanitarian aid.

At the same time, invariably following the example of his uncle and aunt, he assumed the mantle of benefactor of Harvard College. With his aunt Lydia, he rode out to Cambridge on May 22, 1766, for the installation of the first Hancock Professor of Hebrew and Other Oriental Languages, during which he unveiled Copley's portrait of his uncle in the college library. There, he added his own homage to his alma mater: "a set of the most elegant [Oriental] carpets to cover the floors of the Library, the Apparatus and Philosophy Chambers" and a thousand books to fill its shelves.[2]

By the time he marked his thirtieth birthday with a sumptuous dinner on Beacon Hill, Hancock had emerged as spokesman for the town's merchants, shopkeepers and tradesmen, building a solid political base. Running for a seat in the province's House of Representatives, he outpolled both Samuel Adams and James Otis, the candidates endorsed by the Boston Caucus, and then he joined them as Boston's representatives. At the same time, he handily won reelection to the Boston Select Board. In the General Court, he served on no fewer than thirty committees, administering virtually every aspect of the province's affairs and earning a reputation as a mediator.

After the repeal of the Stamp Act and the end of boycotts, even as American merchants rushed orders to England for goods to restock their empty shelves, anti-tax riots broke out in London, forcing Parliament to cut domestic land taxes. As a result, government revenues fell sharply. Infuriated by mobs on both sides of the Atlantic, King George reshuffled his Cabinet in July 1766. He replaced tired, old, moderate William Pitt's administration with a high-Tory regime intent on abridging colonists' rights to those stated in the colonies' venerable seventeenth-century charters. The king approved Charles "Champagne Charlie" Townshend as the new Chancellor of the Exchequer. Townshend was a bibulous nobleman who preferred to stay on his rural estates, experimenting with fertilizing his turnip fields with manure.

The size of the national debt horrified Townshend, who was intent on introducing a new tax scheme that would strip the colonial assemblies of their power to control provincial governments. He initially expected revenue from the stamp tax in the American colonies to help offset the cost of garrisoning troops in the American colonies. Townshend took his Cabinet colleagues by surprise when, in June 1767, he devised new duties on glass, lead, paint, paper and tea to defray the salaries of judges and civil officers in America. Townshend also reorganized the customs service under an American Board of Customs with commissioners headquartered in Boston, which he considered the cauldron of opposition to British tax measures.

Invoking his prerogative as Chancellor of the Exchequer, Townshend now empowered colonial courts to issue writs of assistance—enabling colonial customs officials to break into ships' holds and warehouses to apprehend smugglers and confiscate their property without waiting to obtain these warrants from London. To streamline enforcement, Townshend replaced the Admiralty court in Halifax with superior courts in Boston, Philadelphia, New Orleans and Halifax. Accused violators would be tried in these Vice Admiralty courts without juries. In addition, the acts took over the appointment and payment of judges and provincial governors by the Crown, making them independent of colonial legislatures.

News of the parliamentary crackdown arrived in Boston in August 1767. John Hancock had believed that repeal of the Stamp Act constituted a parliamentary mandate for merchants to expand their trade without further government interference. Infuriated by Parliament's expansion of Crown authority over the American colonies, Hancock summoned an emergency meeting of Boston's merchants. He urged them to reimpose a boycott of English exports, especially of highly profitable luxury goods. To his London agents, he railed, "It is surprising to me that so many attempts are made on your side to cramp our trade, new duties every day increasingly made on your side. We are in a fair way of being ruined." And then he warned, "We have nothing to do but unite and come under a solemn agreement to stop importing any goods from England."[3]

At a packed Town Meeting on October 28, 1767, the merchants approved Hancock's plan for a partial boycott of British luxury goods, including shoes, boots, silks and gold and silver thread. The boycott was to take effect on January 1, 1768. Newport, Providence and New York City immediately followed suit. Considered trendsetters in Boston society, Hancock and Dorothy Quincy toned down their wardrobes, John moderating his style to somber colors and plain waistcoats. Dolly, whose father served on the Boston Committee for Non-Importation, tossed her lovely ribbons and laces into a drawer, not to be retrieved until the boycott was over.

Hancock also pushed through a resolution urging colonists to reduce their dependence on other British manufactures and instead to produce their own clothing, jewelry, watches, sugar, cheese, malt liquors, rope and anchors—all recently restricted by British laws to prevent American competition. By adding nonconsumption to nonimportation, Hancock's radical program threatened an end to American dependence on trade with Britain. Normally, Britain exported fully one-third of its manufactured goods to its American colonies. Tens of thousands of English workers depended on the transatlantic trade. The anti-Townshend embargo hit British commerce even harder than the Stamp Act crisis. Imports plummeted forty percent in one year.

Boston merchants further tightened the sanctions to include almost all British goods, allowing only supplies for its Grand Banks fisheries. New York merchants canceled all orders sent to England after August 15, 1768, boycotting all British imports until Parliament rescinded the Townshend Acts. Tradesmen vowed not to deal with merchants who refused to join the boycott. Housewives vowed to stop serving tea imported from England and renounced fashionable silks and satins. By autumn, merchants in Philadelphia, Maryland, South Carolina, Georgia, North Carolina, Delaware and New Jersey had joined the embargo. Virginia further banned the importation of slaves. Stimulating wool production and encouraging a homegrown textile industry, planters pledged not to slaughter lambs weaned before May 8. College students pledged to stop sipping foreign wines. At the 1770 commencement of the newly founded Queen's College—today's Rutgers University—graduates showed up in homespun gowns instead of the traditional imported academic robes.[4]

~e~

When John Hancock learned that the Townshend Acts legitimized the use of writs of assistance by the newly created American Board of Customs, he vowed that he would never permit an English customs commissioner to board any of his ships. The act required these customs commissioners to move to America. Hancock refused to shake hands or speak with them, even in casual interactions. Anyone inviting this eligible young bachelor knew not to invite anyone connected with customs. Consequently, Boston society ostracized them.

The spurned officials did not have to wait long for an opportunity to retaliate. On April 9, 1768, three weeks after Hancock's reelection to the town's Select Board, when his brig *Lydia* tied up at the Hancock wharf with his spring orders from London, two customs officials, suspecting the cargo included tea and other dutiable goods, boarded the ship. Hancock charged from his office down to the wharf and, followed by a crowd that included the ship's captain, rushed aboard and blocked the agents from examining the hold.

That night, one of the agents returned and slipped belowdecks. Hancock was waiting with eight or ten crewmen. Shining a lantern in the agent's face, Hancock demanded to see his orders and writ of assistance. The orders were undated, Hancock pointed out; he had no writ. Hancock ordered his men to seize the man and carry him above deck. As the first mate and the boatswain dangled the man by his arms and thighs, Hancock demanded, "Do you want to search the vessel?" Then Hancock told his men to let the terrified agent go ashore but with a warning: "You may search the vessel but shall not tarry below."[5]

Indignant, the board of commissioners demanded that Massachusetts's attorney general prosecute Hancock. In his ruling, the attorney general noted that the crewmen who had carried the agent ashore had been unarmed and that the agent had boarded the ship illegally, without a writ or permission of the captain. Moreover, when Hancock had brought the agent topside and asked whether he wanted to search the vessel, the agent had said that he did not. The attorney general decided that "from what appears, it is probable that his [Hancock's] intention was to keep within the bounds of the law."[6]

Hancock's bold confrontation with a British customs commissioner constituted the first physical assault on Parliament's authority in the American colonies. In Boston, it elevated him to the status of a hero. Less than a month later, he handily won reelection to the province's House of Representatives, which then elected him to its upper house, the Governor's Council, along with Samuel Adams and James Otis. But the royal governor, Francis Bernard, refused to seat them. In response, Hancock informed the governor that he would not attend the governor's election day banquet if any customs officials were invited. In retaliation for the governor's refusal to seat him on his council, Hancock, in his role as selectman, used his authority to bar the use of Faneuil Hall for the banquet.

Within days of John Hancock's exoneration for assaulting a customs agent, two customs commissioners again approached Hancock's Wharf. A crowd greeted them with a hail of stones. In a report to the lords of the treasury in London, the commissioners blamed Hancock for the incident. Calling Hancock the "idol of the mob," they complained that "this infatuated man gives out in public that if we, the commissioners, are not recalled he will get rid of us before Christmas."[7]

~ℓ~

At sunset on May 9, 1768, Hancock's sloop *Liberty*, carrying a cargo of Madeira, glided up to his wharf. Acting on a tip from an informant and expecting a prize catch, customs commissioners waited to inspect the vessel until the next morning. They found only twenty-five casks (each holding 125 gallons), about one-fourth the ship's capacity. Reporting to the commissioners, the inspectors could not explain the partial load but insisted that they had not seen any cargo off-loaded overnight. Secretly, Hancock had had the Madeira unloaded and, having taken on a fresh cargo, was about to send *Liberty* back to London.

Like many merchants in America, Hancock had come to think of the customs service as unscrupulous, abusing seizure powers for personal gain. As historian Peter Andreas puts it, the American Board of Customs Commissioners was "ready-made for abuse and manipulation. Little oversight and accountability and the potential for high rewards from seizures made for an explosive mix. Officers typically took a sizable cut of the prize money. . . . Such 'customs racketeering' was, in the view of colonial merchants, essentially legalized piracy."

In June, a British man-of-war, the fifty-gun frigate *Romney*, tacked into Boston Harbor. Its captain, assigned to assist the customs commissioners in arresting smugglers, declared, "The town is a blackguard town and ruled by mobs. . . . [B]y the eternal God, I will make their hearts ache before I leave."[8]

Emboldened, the customs commissioners saw a chance to avenge Hancock's insolence. One of the agents who had inspected *Liberty* changed his earlier statement. He now insisted he had been forcibly held the night of May 9 and had heard the squeal of blocks and tackles hoisting goods and had been warned he would be killed if he told anyone. A customs official then painted a broad arrow on *Liberty*'s mast, the sign that the ship had been confiscated and now was government property.

The captain of the *Romney* sent marines to haul the ship to a mooring under the man-of-war's guns. As they tried to make fast their towropes, a crowd of about five hundred gathered and pelted the marines with paving stones pried up from the streets. An employee ran up Beacon Hill to tell Hancock, but he declined to join them.

After the marines towed the ship more than a stone's throw away, the crowd turned to attack the customs official and his aide, beating them as they fled toward their homes, catching one and dragging him through the street while pelting him with rocks and filth until his friends rescued him. Part of the crowd smashed the windows of the officials' homes while others hauled the customs boat out of the water and set it afire on the Common. One particularly despised official, Charles Paxton, narrowly escaped tarring and feathering, eluding pursuers by disguising himself as a woman and escaping through side streets. That night, the customs board fled with their families and rowed to the safety of the *Romney*.

Hancock regarded the seizure of the *Liberty* as a business loss: His cargo ship would sit idle for months until the case was resolved in Admiralty court. Sending a friend to negotiate the next day, he offered to post bond to guarantee the ship's availability until the court date in exchange for clearance to send the ship to London with its cargo. Fearing further mob action, the commissioners agreed, adding that they would not press charges for smuggling. Other merchants, worried, hurried up Beacon Hill to urge Hancock to accept the settlement. Hancock agreed to it.

For Samuel Adams, the seizure of the *Liberty* presented an opportunity to ratchet up resistance to Britain's heavy-handed regulation. Summoning the Sons of Liberty to their totemic tree, he challenged them: "If you are men, behave like men; let us take up arms immediately and be free and seize all the King's officers."

With James Otis, Adams stormed into Hancock's house and protested that accepting terms with the customs commissioners constituted conceding their right to make unwarranted searches and seizures. At that moment, Hancock decided to throw in with Adams, Otis and the Sons of Liberty. Risking the loss of his ship and cargo and his own arrest, he canceled the deal.

The trial of Hancock and his crewmen began in October 1768 and lasted until the following March. British authorities hoped the high-profile trial would set an example and restore their authority. Governor Bernard decided to accuse Hancock of smuggling; to avoid jail, Hancock posted a £3,000 ($450,000) bond, the value of his cargo.

Hancock's attorney, John Adams, was able to exploit the paucity of the customs board's evidence, which was based on the word of an informer who was never identified and therefore couldn't testify. Adams argued that Hancock's only violation was in not informing the customs house that he had added new cargo without entering it on the manifest, a common practice. The prosecution could not produce any eyewitnesses. Adams was able to turn the case around, pointing out that it was the seizure of the ship that was illegal. Finally, the Customs Board decided to drop the case.

For the British, the case was a total fiasco. John Hancock emerged as somewhat of a hero throughout the American colonies.

Before the trial began, to protect its agents from further attacks, the American Board of Customs Commissioners appealed to General Thomas Gage, commander in chief of British forces in America, to send troops. Two full regiments—twelve hundred soldiers—soon sailed from Halifax. Stunned by the news, delegates from one hundred Massachusetts towns crowded into Faneuil Hall to protest on September 22, 1768. Five days later, twelve troop transports, escorted by five men-of-war with their gunports open and cannon charged, crowded Boston Harbor. Scrambling out of longboats, the Redcoats lined up in formation and, as a band struck up martial airs, quickstepped up Long Wharf toward the Common. Boston became an occupied town.

Silently, sullenly, the Sons of Liberty shadowed their march. One member, Paul Revere, sketched the scene; he would send a print to newspapers all over colonial America. From his balcony, John Hancock witnessed the spectacle. Soon, lines of white tents crowded what had been his front lawn. The bellowing of commands and the stench of latrines infuriated him.

His dinner parties and evening social gatherings vanished and were replaced by tense meetings in which the Select Board heard accounts of the latest atrocities in the town and of harassment of ships' captains by Royal Navy officers. Under a new rule intended to stiffen the revenue laws, the Admiralty court had charged Hancock and four of his officers with illegally loading *Liberty* before clearing customs, formerly a minor infraction but now potentially ruinous to Hancock if he had to pay a fine of triple the £9,000 value of the cargo. Again retaining John Adams as his attorney, Hancock endured four months of legal proceedings while Crown lawyers interrogated scores of witnesses, some secretly. In the end, they dropped the case for lack of any evidence but that of one paid informer.

Nonetheless, the customs commissioners again confiscated *Liberty*. Renaming it the *Gaspee*, they armed the now Royal Navy vessel as a revenue cutter to chase down suspected smugglers. Four years later, on June 10, 1772, the cutter would run aground on the shoals at Namquit Point in Narragansett Bay, seven miles below Providence, while pursuing a suspected smuggling packet. After dark, a wealthy merchant named John Brown organized eight boatloads of men and attacked the schooner. After seriously wounding Lieutenant Dudingston, the ship's commanding officer, the crowd put him and his crew ashore, ransacked the vessel and set it afire. Moments later, it exploded and burned to the waterline.

Thoroughly alarmed, Governor Hutchinson of Massachusetts warned that if Britain "shows no resentment against that colony [Rhode Island] for so high an affront," it would encourage colonists to adopt measures to "obtain and secure their independence."[9]

His appeal to London prompted the ministry to offer a £500 (about $75,000) reward and appoint an investigating commission made up of royal governors and chief justices to identify the rioters and send them to Britain to stand trial for treason. But no witness came forward and the commissioners eventually gave up and left town. No arrests were ever made, and Brown would later boast in writing of his exploit.

Despite his success, John Adams would later write of the drawn-out legal battle over Hancock's schooner, "I was thoroughly weary and disgusted with the Court, the officers of the Crown and the Cause."[10]

For Hancock, his continued resistance to Britain's harsh new policies won him high praise in England. John Wilkes, a radical member of Parliament, sent him "best compliments." His "late persecutions I consider as a consequence of his known zeal to the cause of his country which our common enemies desire to punish when they cannot suppress it."[11]

The irony of Hancock's position must have struck him. The fortune of the House of Hancock had been made from British government contracts, yet now he was using his wealth to pay lawyers to oppose government policies in court. He was still able to export whale oil and potash to England, but his ships returned with empty or half-filled holds for lack of luxury goods. To reinforce the boycott, he advanced credit and lent money to other merchants. With Aunt Lydia adding her cash, the Hancocks lent out £21,000 (about $3.1 million today). Determined to support and extend the import ban, Hancock began to travel to seaports in New England, New York and Pennsylvania to persuade other merchants to hold out until Parliament totally repealed the tariffs.

The persistence of the new American boycott against the Townshend Duties thoroughly alarmed the Board of Trade. The death of Chancellor of the Exchequer Townshend in September 1767 provided the king with an opportunity to appoint a new prime minister, Lord North. While North hesitated to rescind all the Townshend Duties for fear of appearing weak, when he called for partial repeal, the Cabinet supported him five to four. Then the House of Commons approved North's plan to repeal all but a token tax on tea while promising to impose no new taxes on the American colonies. John Hancock took pride in his prominent role in the success of the colonial boycott.

CHAPTER SIX

"A Singular Dignity and Grace"

Tensions between Bostonians and the British occupiers finally boiled over on the frigid night of March 5, 1770, the date immortalized as the Boston Massacre. On March 2, a soldier was walking past a Boston rope yard when a voice called out, "Soldier, will you work?" "Yes," the soldier replied. "Then go and clean my shithouse," the man responded. The soldier struck the rope maker, who retreated after being beaten and returned with his comrades. The brawl resumed the next day as more and more men on both sides arrived, wielding cutlasses and clubs. The fighting briefly subsided on Sunday, March 4. But that night, as bands of soldiers and civilians roved the ice-crusted snow in full moonlight, they collided at the customs house. An apprentice insulted a British officer, who cuffed him. A sentry, Private Hugh White, hit the apprentice again.

As word spread, a score of men and boys arrived. One shouted at White, "You Centinel, damned rascally Scoundrel Lobster Son of a Bitch." When White threatened to bayonet him, hard-packed snowballs and chunks of ice pelted him. Someone yelled, "Fire!" and church bells began tolling. The signal to come and put out a blaze drew a crowd; some were equipped with buckets to carry water, but others brought swords and clubs.

For an hour, Captain Thomas Preston, officer of the day, watched nervously. When the crowd only grew, he called out the guard, six privates and a corporal. In a column of twos, bayonets fixed to muskets, they pushed through the crowd. Preston deployed his men in a semicircle with their backs to the customs house wall, facing out, and he ordered them to load. More men crowded in. Some shouted, "Kill them, kill them"; more ice and snow struck the sentries, who lowered their half-cocked muskets menacingly. A chunk of ice struck Private Hugh Montgomery. In pain, he fell; when he got up, he fired. After a short pause, the other soldiers fired, reloaded, and fired again, hitting six men. Three dropped dead, and two died later; six, wounded, survived.

As at least a thousand Bostonians raged through the streets, Royal Governor Thomas Hutchinson jailed the soldiers for their own protection. Courageously, John Adams, risking losing his standing with his peers, agreed when Hutchinson asked him to take on Preston's defense. When the case finally came to trial after long delays, Adams won Preston's acquittal. Two soldiers, convicted of manslaughter, pleaded benefit of clergy and were branded on their thumbs. All over America, colonists talked of the Massacre.[1]

With his windows closed, Hancock might not have heard the volley that left five protestors dead or dying in the snow on King

Street. But the next morning, a specially convened Town Meeting elected Hancock the head of a delegation to march from the Town House to the residence of Governor Hutchinson and demand that the troops be removed. Bluffing, Hancock warned the royal governor that there were "ten thousand men armed and ready to come into town upon his refusal."[2] Hutchinson acquiesced. He ordered the troops removed to Castle Island in the harbor. Hancock carried the news back to the Town Meeting to the cheering of a crowd. After such a terrible night, it had become a great day for the town—and for John Hancock.

Hancock received further recognition with his election to the highest and most prestigious post in the province's General Court—moderator of the Boston Town Meeting. Already a selectman and Boston's delegate to the House of Representatives, Hancock emerged as Massachusetts's most popular leader.

~ℓ~

In London, the prime minister, Lord North, took notice. He urged Governor Hutchinson to find some way to separate Hancock from his increasingly radical confreres, especially Samuel Adams. The relationship between Hancock and Hutchinson, a fellow Harvard alumnus and merchant, had become stormy. When the speaker of the House of Representatives became ill, the House elected Hancock to replace him; Hutchinson rejected him. In defiance, the House again voted: Hancock received 511 of 513 ballots. Hutchinson again rejected Hancock and prorogued the assembly, shutting it down.

Lord North continued to press Hutchinson to find some way to placate Hancock. Still a loyal Crown subject despite his staunch opposition to British trade restrictions, Hancock had been a member of Boston's ceremonial Corps of Cadets for six years. The corps, made up of leading citizens of the town, acted as the royal governor's honor guard. When its members unanimously elected Hancock colonel and commander, an appointment requiring the governor's confirmation, Hutchinson acquiesced in April 1772.

Hancock borrowed a British army sergeant to teach the manual of arms and conduct weekly drills for the volunteer cadets. Absentees were to be fined. He purchased fifes and advertised for master fifers and paid their salaries. He bought four field artillery pieces—all merely to escort officials such as Hutchinson to ceremonies. He began signing his correspondence "Colonel Hancock." Flaunting his newfound role, he ordered magnificent uniforms, replacing the standard British crimson: tricorne hats with rosettes trimmed in beaver fur, scarlet jackets embellished with buff lapels and cuffs and brilliant white gaiters to be fastened over boots with black buttons.

Some of Hancock's public largesse backfired. When the congregation of Brattle Square Church decided that they needed a better edifice, two congregants, Hancock and merchant James Bowdoin, competed in generosity. Hancock proposed renovating the old church. He pledged £7,500 (about $1.1 million today) to completely rebuild the church, with pews, deacon's benches, a communion table and a pulpit in Honduran mahogany as well as an ornate Bible and a three-hundred-pound bell for the new belfry. And he proposed that portrait painter Copley act as the architect—a fairly common arrangement at the time—and Hancock would pay him. Bowdoin proposed moving the church to a plot of land he owned and pledged a much smaller cash gift. The congregation voted overwhelming for the Hancock plan. John Hancock had made an enemy.

When renovation was completed, John sat with Aunt Lydia and Dolly in a prominent pew to hear Dr. Samuel Cooper's sermon celebrating the consecration of the newly built church. The church bell rang out. Hancock had dictated the bell's inscription: "I to the church the living call / And to the grave I summon all."[3] And the church elders had provided an engraving for the cornerstone of the new church: JOHN HANCOCK. This testament of thanks would be seen by everyone who walked by, including James Bowdoin. As both continued in town and provincial politics, they would become rivals.

Directing some of his time and money to his alma mater, Hancock agreed to serve as Harvard's treasurer and maintain its account books and invest its funds. Some of his other beneficence might have appeared to have been self-serving. As one of Boston's principal property owners, Hancock suffered heavy losses from fires. At the May Town Meeting, Hancock presented a fire engine. In gratitude, the selectmen allowed him to select the master of the engine and allowed it to be parked near Hancock's Wharf, declaring "in case of Fire, the Estate of the Donor shall have the preference of its service." The fire engine was to be christened the *John Hancock.*

On March 5, 1770, the very day of the Boston Massacre, Parliament had eliminated all but a nominal customs duty on importing tea, Americans' favorite libation. Their intent was to rescue the bankrupt East India Company, Britain's second-largest financial institution. The company's stockholders had each paid £1,000 ($150,000 today) for shares in the tea monopoly; many of those shares were held by members of Parliament. In 1773, the share price plummeted to £160, all but wiping out their investments.

From London, Benjamin Franklin, agent for several American colonies, wrote to his son William, the royal governor of New Jersey, that Americans' refusal to take British-taxed tea was bringing the company "infinite distress."

When the British East India Company became unable to pay its debts or any dividend, its plunging value annihilated £3 million ($450 million today). It was the worst British credit crisis in fifty years, touching off bankruptcies and massive layoffs in British manufacturing firms; thousands of English workers were starving or existing on charity.

In an attempt to shore up the flagging economy, Parliament voted to amend the tea laws. Parliament had already been allowing the company a substantial "drawback," a refund of sixty percent of the twenty-five percent import duty it paid when the tea came from India to England before transshipment to the American colonies. Now, under the revised Tea Act of 1773, Parliament allowed a hundred percent customs drawback on tea exported to America, amounting to a twenty percent price cut, undercutting both legitimate Boston merchants and smugglers. Hancock's nonimportation boycott had left his warehouse bulging with unsold tea he had purchased in England.

Britain's recent attempts to crack down on smuggling had misfired: As Governor Hutchinson complained to the Board of Trade, eighty percent of the "prodigious" amount of tea consumed by Bostonians was smuggled from Holland through the Dutch Caribbean colony of St. Eustatius to avoid paying the threepenny customs duty. Still, Lord North insisted that the threepence-a-pound import duty be paid: Americans must pay a duty on every cup of tea as a reminder of the supremacy of Parliament.

When news of the repeal of the major provisions of the Townshend Acts reached Boston, it set off a buying spree by merchants. Hancock's warehouses filled with goods. Owners of small village stores streamed into Boston to replenish their own stocks. Because these aspiring store owners had little cash and no track records in business, there were few merchants who would sell to them. Hancock decided to extend credit to anyone who expressed to him a sincere desire to work hard. In his role as Boston's leading merchant, he helped other warehouse owners get their businesses running again after the years of boycott. He reasoned that the most important thing was to build up a strong colonial business class to respond, when necessary, in a unified voice against the overreach of British politicians and merchants.

Hancock's celebration of the revival of his businesses was cut short when he suffered an especially severe bout of gout. Hancock recognized the symptoms: His uncle Thomas had long suffered from this excruciatingly painful form of inflammatory arthritis. As early as 1768, when he was only thirty-one, John had written a friend, "I am very unwell."[4]

By 1772, his doctor, Joseph Warren, confirmed the diagnosis of gout. Today identifiable as congenital gout, the disease's symptoms included swollen ankles, knees and feet as well as skin the color of sea thrift in brilliant pink rings of pain. The gout came and went; sometimes the flare-ups lasted for weeks of chronic pain, while at other moments Hancock suffered from briefer bursts of violent pain. Increasingly, the diagnosis meant Hancock could barely leave his bed to attend Town Meetings or fulfill his duties as its moderator. He would resort to being carried by two stout servants in a sedan chair, but even the slightest jostling of his swollen limbs against its wooden frame produced a sharp stab of pain.

Hancock tried to maintain his busy schedule of political and social obligations. With great difficulty, he would get out of bed and, with the help of his servant Cato, dress appropriately to attend Town Meetings, gatherings at the Bunch of Grapes, and even Aunt Lydia's dinner parties. Each bout ended as abruptly as it had come on. When one flare-up ended, he wrote a friend, "I am so surprisingly recovered that I have plunged myself into the business of life again." When one particularly severe flare ended in July 1772, he celebrated with several of his male friends on a two-week coastal cruise aboard *Boston Packet*, his sleek square-sailed, two-masted brig, which he had stocked with plentiful food and wine to be poured by his servants.[5]

On November 5, 1773, after Hancock was reelected moderator of the Boston Town Meeting, the members resolved that anyone who supported the Tea Act was an "Enemy to America." Hancock and leaders of the Sons of Liberty tried to force the resignations of the agents who had been appointed to receive the tea shipments. Only three weeks later, on Sunday morning, November 28, 1773, three transports owned by the Rotches—the Hancocks' longtime rivals in the annual race to transport whale oil from Nantucket to London—glided into Boston Harbor. Each was laden with lacquered chests of British East India Company tea consigned to Governor Hutchinson's sons.

That night, Hancock and his men volunteered for guard duty to make sure none of the tea was unloaded. The next morning, so many Bostonians crowded into Faneuil Hall that the meeting had to be moved to Old South Church. There, by roaring voice vote, the crowd demanded that the consignees resign and the tea be shipped back to England.

Under a technicality of British law, once a vessel entered the harbor, all duties had to be paid within twenty days or its cargo would be seized by customs and sold to pay the tariff. The *Dartmouth*'s time would be up on December 17. As the sale of pistols spiked, the Hutchinsons fled Boston for their country estate. On the fifteenth, Francis Rotch tried and failed to get the ships out of Boston. At an emergency meeting of the Select Board, Hancock swore that "he was willing to spend his fortune and life itself" to block the tea from being unloaded.

On the sixteenth, an estimated seven thousand people—in a population of fifteen thousand—filled Old South Church and overflowed into the surrounding streets. Acting as an unofficial Town Meeting, they shouted approval to a resolution that the tea must not be landed. At six o'clock, Rotch returned from a final desperate appeal to Governor Hutchinson to allow the tea ships to return to England without paying customs duties, but, Rotch reported, Hutchinson remained adamant: The tea must be unloaded. Silencing the call for "a mob! A mob!" from the high pulpit, Hancock intoned gravely: "Let every man do what is right in his own eyes." Then, as if as a signal to the Sons of Liberty, who were dressed as Mohawks, Samuel Adams exclaimed, "This meeting can do no more to save the country." While some two thousand Bostonians watched, the "Mohawks" pried open and jettisoned 342 chests of tea from all three ships into Boston Harbor.[6]

Hancock went home exhausted, stricken with a severe bout of gout. Bedridden for much of the winter, he dreaded the news that inevitably must come with spring: just how severely the British would respond to the brazen destruction of property worth an estimated £10,000 ($1.5 million today). Hancock let it be known that, as his own protest, he was shipping his entire inventory of tea back to England and he would return any other merchant's as well gratis.

Early in February 1774, Britain's attorney general formally charged John Hancock, Samuel Adams, Dr. Joseph Warren and Dr. Benjamin Church with treason, holding them accountable for the Tea Party. They were to be tried in Massachusetts by an Admiralty court or in England. Defiant, Adams invited Hancock to deliver the fourth annual Massacre Day speech. Hancock accepted. On the March 5 anniversary, dressed in a scarlet velvet coat, he climbed the stairs to the high pulpit of Old South Church and, with every pew and gallery packed, riveted the crowd—including a number of British officers—for more than an hour with the most important speech of his life.

Emphasizing his devotion to "righteous government," Hancock asked, "Is the present system which the British administration have adopted for the government of the colonies a righteous government? Or is it tyranny?"

"Tyranny!" the audience roared.[7]

Challenging the British Parliament's "mad pretension" to power, he described the troops stationed in Boston as "an unfeeling ruffian," "murderers" and "parricides." Hancock denounced the presence of British troops in Boston; he said they had been sent there "to enforce obedience to Acts of the British Parliament, which neither God nor man ever empowered them to make." He conjured up a bloody vision of the day of the Massacre, the day when the British "polluted our land with the dead bodies of her guiltless sons." He called on patriots to arm themselves and prepare "to fight for their houses, their lands, for their wives, their children" so that those "noxious vermin will be swept forever from the streets of Boston." Predicting even more harsh new laws from "our inveterate enemies," he urged, "let us . . . be ready to take the field whenever danger calls" by forming militias.[8]

Hancock exhorted his auditors to be the first Americans to call for a union of colonies by summoning a "general congress of deputies" from all the assemblies on the continent to lay "a firm foundation . . . for our rights and liberties" under a new system "for our common safety." Paying singular tribute to Samuel Adams for committing to a "righteous cause," the wealthiest man in Massachusetts urged his audience to "despise the glare of wealth" and follow an "honest upright man in poverty." After descending from the pulpit as the crowd cheered, John Hancock shook hands with Samuel Adams.[9]

Hancock's stirring oration, the product of a collaboration with Samuel Adams and the Reverend Samuel Cooper of Brattle Square Church, was more than a statement of the sentiments of one man—it was a statement on behalf of the entire community. While it was written by a committee, most Bostonians considered it Hancock's handiwork alone. Even the often critical John Adams, in his diary, pronounced it "an elegant" and "spirited performance" before "a vast crowd" with "rainy eyes":

The composition, the pronunciation, the action—all exceeded the expectation of everybody. They exceeded even mine, which were very considerable. Many of the sentiments came with great propriety from him. His invective, especially against a preference of riches to virtue, came from him with a singular dignity and grace.[10]

Hancock's speech singled him out as the leading public figure in Boston. Reprinted in several colonies, it became one of the best-known polemics of the Revolutionary era. To celebrate his triumph, Hancock commissioned Copley to paint new portraits of both himself and Samuel Adams. Hancock placed them side by side in the foyer of his mansion, announcing his alliance with Adams to his many visitors.

As Boston waited in dread for the response from Britain, Hancock had little else to celebrate: Retail sales tumbled as the nonimportation boycott tightened, stifling trade. Hancock's ships returned empty from London, and the brigantine *Lydia* ran hard aground. It could not be freed with its cargo of whale oil, making it a total loss.

In London, an angry Parliament voted six to one to punish Boston by a series of Coercive Acts. On June 1, under the Boston Port Act, the Royal Navy would close Boston Harbor until the city repaid the East India Company and the government for the tea and the lost customs duties. Before the act could take effect, Hancock decided to close the House of Hancock and clear his credit in London by sending off consignments of goods with instructions to sell the vessels. With no remaining debts, he became free to devote himself entirely to politics.

On May 13, 1774, Major General Thomas Gage, commander in
chief of British forces in North America, landed at Castle William
in Boston Harbor with instructions from London to prosecute
John Hancock and Samuel Adams for treason. Advised by the
colony's chief justice to defer the arrests to avoid riots, Gage crossed
to Long Wharf with his personal flag flying. There, Colonel Hancock boldly received him, his cadets mustered to escort Gage to the
Town House for his official induction as royal governor. From
there, they were to escort Gage to his official residence. But Hancock did not salute Gage and he had not ordered the cadets to salute him as he passed between their lines—a stunning refusal of
Gage's authority. And the next evening, Hancock boycotted the
official welcome dinner at Faneuil Hall.

On June 1, Gage closed Boston Harbor to all commerce except
food and fuel. Somehow, Hancock got word to the captain of his
last ship unloading in London and ordered him to fill the vessel
with gunpowder and sail it to Salem, where Gage had moved the
General Court away from Boston protests. Gage expected to pro-
mulgate to the legislature two more Coercive Acts. The first allowed for the trials of customs officials in England—rather than in
America—for crimes committed while collecting taxes or quelling
riots. Even harsher was an act annulling Massachusetts's charter
and eradicating its self-government. Limiting Town Meetings to
once a year, the edict gave the Crown sole power to appoint and
dismiss the council, the attorney general and all judges.

When Gage did not appear in Salem, the delegates resolved
themselves into a convention and transformed themselves into a
provincial congress, unanimously electing Hancock as its first

president before Gage could dissolve the assembly. Pledging their unanimous support for Boston's citizens, the House then voted to send five delegates to the First Continental Congress: four merchants—James Bowdoin, Thomas Cushing, Robert Treat Paine and Samuel Adams—and a lawyer, John Adams.

When the latest Coercive Act arrived from Parliament, it permitted Gage to quarter his troops in private homes; he chose instead to have barracks built and paid for by the province. But he could find no willing civilian laborers. He turned to Hancock for help with recruitment. Hancock refused. In retaliation, Gage fired Hancock as colonel of the cadet militia for failing to salute him on his arrival. The enraged cadets responded by returning Gage's official standard to him and resigning en masse.

Before the congressional delegation could depart for Philadelphia, Bowdoin asserted he was too ill to join the others. He pleaded with Hancock to take his place. But on the advice of Samuel Adams, Hancock demurred. Someone must stay in Boston to preside over the provincial congress and provide military preparedness.

In addition to his other duties, Hancock insisted that Sam Adams dress appropriately for his new role. His usual scruffy appearance would strip the delegation of dignity. Cobbling together a secret committee of Adams's friends, Hancock arranged for him to depart in more suitable attire. A procession of Boston's best couturiers—a tailor, a shoemaker, Boston's best hatter—appeared at Adams's door on Purchase Street. A few days before their planned departure, a large trunk arrived on Adams's front step. It contained, according to William V. Wells, his great-grandson, "a complete suit of clothes, two pairs of shoes of the best style, a set of silver shoe-buckles, a set of gold knee-buckles, an elegant cocked hat, a gold-headed cane, a red cloak."

The benefactor of Adams's sartorial transformation inspected it at a farewell dinner on Beacon Hill before the delegates clambered into Thomas Cushing's coach-and-four and, with armed drivers, rolled past British guard posts on Boston Neck en route to the First Continental Congress in Philadelphia.

CHAPTER SEVEN

"Remove Immediately from Boston"

When the Massachusetts Provincial Congress moved to Concord for its March 1775 session, Hancock's cousin Lucy and her husband, the Reverend Jonas Clarke, invited Hancock and Samuel Adams to live in the Lexington manse where as a boy Hancock had resided for seven years with his grandfather, the Bishop.

As rumors began to fly in Boston of the departure of troopships from England, Hancock, as chairman of the Committee of Safety, became de facto commander in chief of the Massachusetts militia. He ordered cannon to be seized from Boston's Loyalists, spirited away and hidden in Concord. In addition to ordering six more companies of artillerymen to be ready, he ordered medical supplies, canteens and knapsacks "for an army of 15,000 to take the field."[1]

It had become apparent to Hancock that Boston was no longer safe for his family. On April 16, the warships *Falcon* and *Nautilus*

arrived filled with troops and horses—and with orders from Secretary of State Lord Dartmouth. Gage was to delay no longer in arresting Hancock and Samuel Adams, "the principal actors and
abettors in the Provincial Congress." He was to seize hidden weapons and put down the incipient rebellion.

Hancock arranged for his aunt Lydia and his all but formally
betrothed fiancée, Dolly Quincy, to join him in the Lexington
manse. Hancock stuffed personal papers, ledgers, cash, notes—all
his negotiable wealth—and the records and treasury of Harvard
College into a large trunk.

Covered in leather and studded with nails, with a curved top
and strong brass fastenings, the trunk was four feet long, two and
a half feet wide and two feet high. Filled with deeds, notes and
sacks of coins, it took two strong servants to hoist it into Hancock's
coach.

The group rolled out of Boston just in time. On April 18, Dr.
Warren learned from an informant at the headquarters of the British that Gage was preparing a large-scale military operation. He
fired off orders for the removal and dispersal of the weapons from
Concord. When Hancock arrived in Lexington, he posted the
town's minutemen outside the manse. Shortly after midnight, Paul
Revere galloped up and warned that at least eight hundred Redcoats were quick-marching toward them on the turnpike. Hancock
sounded the alarm; the town bell clanged all night. While Dolly
and Aunt Lydia looked on in horror, Hancock cleaned his gun and
his sword. He wanted to go out and personally lead the fight. As
chairman of the Provincial Congress's Committee of Safety, he
believed himself commander of the provincial militia and that it
was his duty to lead armed resistance to the British force. Dorothy
Quincy would later remember that Samuel Adams finally clapped

Hancock on the shoulder and said to him, "That is not our business. We belong to the Cabinet."

Worried about her aged father, Dolly wanted to go back to Boston. But Hancock objected: She was known to be romantically involved with him. He feared the British would use her as bait to capture him. "No, madam, you shall not return as long as there is a British bayonet left in Boston," he declared. Dolly retorted, "Recollect, Mr. Hancock, that I am not under your control yet. Tomorrow I will go to my father." At that point, Dorothy later recounted, she "would have been very glad to be rid of him."

Revere warned that there was no more time—Hancock and Samuel Adams must leave immediately from Lexington. But Dorothy Quincy would remember that "it was not till break of day that Mr. H. could be persuaded." Finally, Hancock was "overcome by the entreaties of his friends, who convinced him that the enemy would triumph indeed if they could get him and Mr. Adams in their power."

After driving off in Hancock's coach—Samuel Adams had an aversion to riding a horse—Hancock and Adams were on the run all through the British attack on Lexington and Concord and the British retreat, with heavy casualties, to Boston. Revere led the men first to Woburn, where Hancock parked his distinctive carriage in front of the Congregational parsonage; Hancock and Adams took refuge in the basement. Hancock sent a messenger back to Lexington to instruct Dolly and Lydia to join him. Hancock asked Lydia to bring with her the large, fresh-caught salmon that he had seen on the manse's kitchen table. When the women arrived in Woburn in Lydia's dust-covered red coach, Hancock ordered servants to hide it in dense woods by covering it with a mound of hay. Aunt Lydia started to cook the salmon, but she was interrupted by a terrified refugee from Lexington yelling, "The British are coming, the British are coming." Hancock and Adams instantly hid in a swamp until the alarm was over. Then they rode on, mud spattered, to a farmhouse in Billerica, a small village north of Concord.

As fragmentary reports reached them of the mayhem around Boston, Dolly agreed to go with Hancock, Lydia and the others west toward Worcester, where they expected to rendezvous with the other delegates and receive a detailed report on the fighting from the Provincial Congress. Hancock found neither. Adams and he had left Lexington so precipitously that no one knew where to find them. Hancock felt abandoned.

He complained in a note to the Provincial Congress: "How are we to proceed? Where are our Brethren? I beg by the Return of this Express to hear from you and pray furnish us with Depositions of the Conduct of the Troops." The next day, the Congress responded with a military escort, not only to protect the delegates, but so that Hancock could, as he insisted, "travel in reputation."[2]

It would be weeks before Hancock was able to piece together a picture of the momentous events that had transpired so near to them while he and Adams had remained on the run. What actually happened that spring day would become shrouded in folklore, transformed into a story repeated by poet, parent and teacher to child and new citizen ever since.

~•~

At three on the cool, windy morning of April 18, 1775, seven hundred elite British light infantry and grenadier guards marched to the south end of Boston Common and boarded launches from men-of-war that took them up the Charles River to Cambridge. There, they stepped off, without rations or bedrolls, for an expected twelve-mile sortie to Lexington, where, according to Loyalist informants, patriots were stockpiling munitions. But Gage's primary targets were John Hancock and Samuel Adams.

When Major John Pitcairn encountered Lexington's militia formed up on the town's green, he rode up and ordered them to disperse. By not immediately heeding his command, the militia crossed an invisible line that made them rebels in arms against the king. While wheeling his horse and giving a command to his men to surround and disarm the militia, Pitcairn saw a gun in the hands of "a peasant" behind a stone wall "flash in the pan without going off." But two or three more guns, also fired from cover, did go off. Instantly, without orders, "a promiscuous, uncommanded but general Fire took place," Pitcairn later recounted, insisting he could not stop it even when he swung his sword downward, the signal to cease firing. When the British did stop firing, eight Americans lay dead; ten more, badly wounded, were carried to nearby houses. The Regulars regrouped and dogtrotted toward Concord to seize the fourteen cannon and upward of a hundred barrels of gunpowder reportedly concealed there.

When hundreds of patriots refused to retreat and continued to fire on the Regulars, any veneer of civility between occupier and colonist vanished. Guided by Loyalists, grenadiers battered down doors with the brass-jacketed butts of their heavy brown Bess muskets in a targeted quest for concealed weapons. The Regulars ransacked and looted houses, dragging terrified families into Concord's streets, shooting and bayoneting anyone who resisted.

As the British column re-formed to countermarch to Boston, a swelling mass of well-officered militia galled them from rooftops, firing accurately out of windows, from trees and from behind stone walls. Four thousand men in moving rings of skirmishers swirled around the retreating Redcoats, firing into their thinning ranks, sometimes with long guns meant for duck gunning. Riders with saddlebags bulging with a seemingly limitless supply of poorly shaped bullets resupplied clumsy muskets rarely able to hit anything beyond one hundred yards. Some historians estimate only one in three hundred lead balls hit anyone.

By the time the Regulars reached Menotomy, fifty-five hundred militiamen had joined the melee in what was fast developing into the first major battle of the American Revolution. Outnumbered six to one, the Regulars responded savagely, giving no quarter even at undefended buildings, putting to death everyone they found inside. More than one hundred bullet holes riddled one tavern where grenadiers shot and bayoneted the proprietor and his wife and bashed in the skulls of two topers. In a bloodlust saturnalia, marauding British soldiers carried away anything they could cram into their knapsacks, even communion silver; set fire to buildings; and slaughtered livestock. One young boy responded to the carnage by scalping a wounded Redcoat with a hatchet and hacking off his ears. In all, seventy-three British soldiers died and two hundred more suffered critical wounds before, reinforced, they fought their way back to their boats and the men-of-war.

Overnight, an estimated sixteen thousand militiamen swarmed from all over New England. Trained by the British in the French and Indian War, militia officers laid out siege lines and organized work parties that built a thin sixteen-mile line of earthworks. The dozen-years-long clash with neophyte British imperial officials seemingly incapable of designing legislation had only provoked American colonists, precipitating ever more repressive—and equally unenforceable—British edicts. Years of British bungling now culminated in a mass of infuriated New England militiamen. Abandoning their spring planting, their families, their shops and their shipyards, they rushed to avenge the decades of British arrogance, escalating taxes and overbearing government regulation.

~e~

When the other Massachusetts delegates—John Adams, Thomas Cushing and Robert Treat Paine—still hadn't arrived at the delegation's rendezvous in Worcester after five more days, Hancock and Adams decided they had to leave without them. They were anxious about losing too much time and being late for the convening of Congress. With an armed escort now, the men rolled on to the small town of Lancaster, where they stayed overnight with Dolly's sister Sarah. Her husband, William Greenleaf, a member of the assembly, was the captain of the militia. Together, they decided that Dolly and Lydia should accompany the men as far as Fairfield, Connecticut, to stay with the family of Thaddeus Burr. Burr, a member of the Connecticut General Assembly, was a friend and longtime business associate of the Hancocks. To expose the two women to danger all the way to Philadelphia was out of the question. John and Dolly's formal engagement—and wedding—would have to wait.

After following the Connecticut River south through Brookfield to Springfield, Hancock and Adams and their military escort crossed Connecticut, making stops at Hartford and New Haven. At a dinner party years later, Dorothy would tell General William H. Sumner and his guests that the Burrs' cousin Aaron was there, too. Sumner, then adjutant general of the Massachusetts militia, wrote in his diary that Dorothy attested that "Aaron was very attentive to her and her aunt was very jealous of him lest he should gain her affection and defeat her purpose of connecting her with her nephew." Burr, she said, was "a handsome young man of very pretty fortune, but her aunt would not leave them a moment together."[3]

~~

On May 6, with an armed escort of Connecticut militia, the Massachusetts delegation made a triumphal entry to New York City. Crowds lined the streets to see them. Hancock's carriage was given the place of honor, where it led the parade and, as Hancock immediately wrote to Dorothy, raised "the greatest Cloud of Dust I ever saw."

Recounting the scene, he reported that the crowd had unhitched the horses and pulled the coach along. "We were met by the grenadier company" and the city's militia "under arms, gentlemen in carriages and on horseback and many thousands of persons on foot, the roads filled with people." Hancock estimated that a throng of some seven thousand—one-third of the city's population—turned out to cheer on the delegates. Hancock personally greeted a stream of visitors until ten o'clock when finally he had time for a late dinner of fried oysters. At eleven o'clock, he rode to the home of Captain Isaac Sears, a leader of the Sons of Liberty, for a short night's sleep. But he found time to send a letter to Dorothy. "I beg you to write me with every circumstance relative to that dear aunt of mine. Write often and lengthy."

As the delegation traveled south, Hancock experienced a new and severe form of gout and reported it to Dorothy: "My poor face and eyes are in a very shocking situation, burnt up and much swelled and a little painful. I don't know how to manage with it."[4]

On May 10, after three weeks on the road, Hancock's carriage finally rolled into Philadelphia, where the Second Continental Congress was already convening. At the same time, British major general Sir Henry Clinton was installing himself in Hancock's Beacon Hill mansion. Hancock had managed to bring with him large amounts of gold and silver and letters of credit as well as Harvard's treasury. As the college's treasurer, he had been entrusted to invest its endowment, and he had brought it along with him to Philadelphia.

Once again, the Massachusetts delegates were greeted by hundreds of people. All the city bells chimed a welcome as people poured out of their houses and businesses to see the New Englanders. The city's elite First Troop Philadelphia City Cavalry, with sabers drawn, led some three hundred militiamen as Hancock and Samuel Adams, seated side by side, made their grand entrance.

~ー~

As the delegates to the Second Continental Congress assembled, both the Adamses and John Hancock quickly assumed conspicuous leadership roles. Taking their seats in Windsor chairs at a green-baize-covered table in the upper chamber of the Pennsylvania State House, the Massachusetts men, all Harvard graduates, were among the best-educated delegates, John Adams noted. He was surprised to find men he considered to be of marginal education. One Connecticut delegate had been a shoemaker; two Pennsylvanians were plain farmers, another a country doctor. The

Massachusetts delegates were considered too radical for more conservative delegates, who kept their distance from them.

However, John Adams would soon discover that the majority of delegates were among the wealthiest men in America. They included nine plantation owners and five merchants, men of hereditary landed estates and mercantile fortunes. There were a former royal governor and a judge. There were no Quakers, who refused to take oaths, or Jewish delegates, and their absences precluded many of the wealthiest Americans from serving in the Congress.

Many of the delegates had been trained in the law even if they did not professionally practice it; five had been trained as barristers at the Inns of Court in London. Collectively, the delegates had served in provincial legislatures and on high courts and had written the charters of hospitals, colleges and counties; these were men not easily intimidated by the idea of writing a new constitution for a new form of government. Almost all were graduates of American colleges: Yale, the College of New Jersey (today's Princeton), Harvard, William and Mary, the University of Pennsylvania and King's College (now Columbia). But the men still exhibited a range of education and experience: One delegate, a self-employed retired printer from Pennsylvania, had attended school for only a single year. In contrast, Benjamin Franklin had received honorary doctorates from Oxford and St. Andrews and was a fellow of the Royal Society of England.

In a letter to Abigail at home in Braintree, John Adams characterized his newfound colleagues. James Duane of New York, a collection lawyer turned king's counsel, had a "sly, surveying eye"; John Dickinson of Delaware, a lawyer and leading radical pamphleteer, was merely "a shadow . . . pale as ashes."[5]

When Congress reconvened, its presidency had been left vacant by the illness of Peyton Randolph of Virginia. In choosing his successor, delegates divided along sectional lines. Samuel Adams mustered support for the candidacy of a New Englander over another Virginian. To more moderate delegates, the Adamses could tout John Hancock's qualifications. Conservatives from the Middle Colonies favored Hancock because of his long experience as moderator of Boston's Town Meeting and his conciliatory reputation while serving on thirty committees of the Massachusetts House of Representatives, as well as his wealth and business acumen.

Many had already come to know Hancock from his travels as the organizer of boycotts against English imports. His reputation as the most popular politician in Boston had preceded him. Samuel Adams's more radical Popular Party backed Hancock because of his outspoken resistance to the British occupation of Boston. On May 24, unopposed, Hancock won unanimous election as president of the Continental Congress.

～ℓ～

Many conservatives were horrified to learn of the New England radicals' seizure of the Crown forts on Lake Champlain inside New York province on May 10, 1775. Until then, the First Continental Congress had preserved the appearance of acting only on the defensive. Seizing £2 million (about $300 million today) of royal property and taking Redcoats and their families as prisoners complicated affairs. At the New York delegation's insistence, Congress almost immediately voted to remove the cannon captured at Fort Ticonderoga to Fort Edward at the southern tip of Lake George and to take an "exact inventory" so that they could later be "safely returned" to the British. The weapons had been seized by

Ethan Allen and Benedict Arnold under orders from Connecticut. New England delegates wanted them shipped to forces surrounding Boston.[6]

While there seemed to be an informal consensus about establishing a continental army and creating a union of colonial governments, there was no agreement on how hard a line Congress should take against Parliament and the Crown. Hancock appointed George Washington to chair a committee to examine the defenses in New York. Washington was the only delegate with serious military experience—he had achieved the brevet rank of British brigadier general after five years of active duty in the French and Indian War. Hancock also appointed him to chair the defense committee.

The only delegate in uniform, Washington made a vivid impression. Silas Deane of Connecticut described his "easy, soldier-like air and gestures" and his method of speaking "very modestly and in a cool but determined style and accent." John Adams, writing to Abigail, admired Washington's "manner."[7]

After Washington conducted a thorough review of each colony's military preparedness, his report triggered six days of debates over general defense preparations, recruitment bounties and a final attempt at reconciliation with Britain. Congress voted to approve Washington's recommendations to fortify King's Bridge on the Harlem River, erect batteries on either bank of the Hudson and enlist three thousand volunteers. Washington's oral report focused Congress's attention on the uniformed delegate as the most experienced soldier in Congress.

Washington's experience as a logician led to Hancock's next appointment of the Virginian as chairman of the committee on military supply. Each week brought Washington more duties.

Next, President Hancock appointed him to the board of financial estimate. All the other board members were merchants, but Washington had extensive logistical experience from frontier wars that the others lacked.

Hancock assigned to John Adams the task of nominating a commander in chief of a continental army. Adams was reluctant to name a New Englander: He believed someone from the South should be chosen to secure the support of the more populous colonies. Thirty years later, he would write in his memoirs that, when he nominated "the gentleman from Virginia," Hancock flushed bright red as if he had expected the honor.[8]

One of the durable myths of the Revolutionary era was born. None of the other fifty delegates ever corroborated Adams's account of Hancock's "mortification and disappointment," which Adams did not publish until after the two had fallen out politically and Hancock was dead and unable to refute it. It isn't very likely that Hancock, already hobbled with gout, would have accepted a position that would have required long days on horseback. In fact, to all other observers, Hancock appeared pleased to support George Washington as commander in chief. Writing to Joseph Warren, now president of the Provincial Congress in Boston, Hancock described Washington as a "gentleman you will all like." He was to be given a "suitable residence" and treated with "great respect."[9]

CHAPTER EIGHT

"A Shadow as Pale as Ashes"

John Hancock's duties as president of the Second Continental Congress kept him at his desk at the Pennsylvania State House or in committee meetings six days a week, reading and writing from dawn until late at night. Congressional committees began their deliberations at seven in the morning; Congress convened at ten and sat until five, taking only a short lunch break. After supper, they returned for more committee meetings, often continuing until late at night. Hancock presided over every session of Congress and participated ex officio on all committees. He had to persuade every colony to contribute men, supplies and money. In addition, he had to greet every visitor to Congress, listen to them, then send them to the appropriate committee member.

Hancock had to sign every document issued by Congress and he generated much of its correspondence. Even when exhausted, he threw himself into the work, making it a more personal role than merely presiding over meetings. His growing responsibilities seemed to exhilarate him. He seemed to be everywhere. When he wasn't attending committee meetings, he was summarizing their recommendations and disseminating the decisions of the whole Congress. He kept the Revolutionary leaders of each colony abreast of troop movements by sister colonies and forwarded intelligence of enemy movements.

No sooner had Hancock presided over lengthy debates over a resolution favoring independence than he had to write to the New Jersey Assembly that, as Washington had advised him, General Sir William Howe was expected to attack New York in ten days. He needed New Jersey militia replacements "with all dispatch." Then he wrote to the General Court of Massachusetts: The Continental Army, which had been "reduced by illness" and was without reinforcements, would be "obliged to flee before an army of vastly superior numbers. . . . The intelligence received this day from General Washington points out the absolute, the indispensable necessity of sending forward all the troops that can possibly be collected to strengthen the armies in New York."[1]

As president of the Continental Congress, Hancock issued circular letters to provincial congresses. It had become apparent that Britain had no intention of negotiating but instead would resort to force to crush colonial resistance. In emotional language, Hancock appealed for more militia:

> The Militia of the United Colonies are a Body of troops that may be depended upon. . . . They are called upon to say whether they will live Slaves, or die Freemen—they are quested to step forward in Defence of their Wives, their Children, and Liberty, and every Thing they hold dear. The Cause is certainly a most glorious one, and I trust that every

man . . . is determined to see it gloriously ended, or perish in the ruins of it.[2]

Hancock's language was formal yet intense and personal, conveying urgency. He rushed off each circular letter by dispatch riders for every colony's congress to send to their newspapers.

As Howe evacuated Boston, Hancock intimated to Washington how he chose to handle the delicate family matter of a fellow delegate—Benjamin Franklin. Hancock reported that General William Alexander, Lord Stirling, had crushed a Loyalist counterrevolution in New Jersey and arrested its leader, Franklin's son William, the royal governor. Stirling wrote from Elizabethtown, "I thought it most prudent to secure him and bring him to this place. . . . I have provided good, genteel, private lodgings for [him] . . . where I intend he shall remain until I have directions from Congress what to do with him."[3]

Hancock met privately with Franklin *père* before passing along Congress's decision to order Franklin *fils* imprisoned in Litchfield, Connecticut.

Hancock's gout flares seemed to coincide with periods of heightened stress. In his new position as president of the Continental Congress, the stress was unrelenting. His soon-to-be brother-in-law Edmund Quincy wrote to Dolly that Hancock's gout symptoms included eyestrain, "especially serious that it should affect his eyes since the clearest sight of every American patriot is [so] critical . . . and more so [for Hancock] than any other member of the most important council now existing on the globe."[4]

Even as Hancock urged on other leaders, he did not ignore his own family matters. His younger brother, Ebenezer, after failures in three business ventures, asked Hancock to find him a job in the Continental Army. Hancock recommended him to William Palfrey, his former chief clerk in the House of Hancock now serving as paymaster general of the army—a post Hancock had also arranged. When Congress approved Ebenezer's hiring, Hancock wrote his brother that he had been approved as assistant paymaster general for the Eastern Department, which included all of New England. He was to follow Washington's orders and must be sure to post a sentinel at his door day and night. Hancock then sent off the $150,000 payroll and the paylist with a reminder of procedure: "Be careful to make your monthly returns regularly to me."

A hint of Hancock's lifestyle in Philadelphia comes through in his personal correspondence with Washington. When Congress requested that Hancock write to the commander in chief to ask him to come to Philadelphia to lay out for Congress his plans for defending New York, Hancock invited Washington to "honor me and my lady's company at my house, where I have a bed at your service." Well aware of the city's stifling heat and humidity in June and the paucity of suitable accommodations in the crowded town, he described his lodgings as "a noble house in an airy open place. . . . The house I live in is large and roomy. . . . Mrs. Washington may be as retired as she pleases while under inoculation." Hancock shared the house with other Massachusetts delegates.

Hancock was perplexed when, inexplicably, Washington twice failed to respond. He seems to have taken it as a personal slight. He did not know that Washington rarely stayed at the home of a government official, preferring the informality and comforts of a good inn. When Washington came to Philadelphia to brief Congress and prepare to return to New York, Hancock declined to deliver Congress's resolution of goodwill to him in person, making the excuse that he was "deprived of that pleasure by a severe bout of the gout."[5] In reality, it's likely that Hancock did not attend because he felt snubbed.[6] If the two met to go over the plans, it appears to have been in Congress.

Hancock extended hospitality to other members of Congress in dinner parties. His most frequent guests were Robert Morris, John Dickinson and James Duane, all wealthy men. That tendency was noted disapprovingly by Samuel Adams, who preferred to dine in taverns in the company of more radical companions, such as Dr. Thomas Young and Charles Thomson.

~e~

Hancock hired secretaries at his own expense, but he needed more assistance in handling the voluminous congressional correspondence. To that end, Hancock supported the reappointment of the newly wealthy Philadelphia merchant Charles Thomson as secretary of Congress. Born in County Derry, Ireland, Thomson had been brought to America by his father, who died on shipboard within sight of Cape May, New Jersey. Young Thomson became a bound servant to a blacksmith but came under the tutelage of Francis Alison in New London, Pennsylvania; he provided him with a home and a classical education. Benjamin Franklin persuaded Thomson to teach Latin and Greek at his Academy of Philadelphia. Franklin provided a house for him as his next-door neighbor, and the two became trusted friends. When the academy dismissed him during a factional fight, Thomson became a merchant and made shrewd investments, including in a clandestine ironworks in the New Jersey Pine Barrens that produced bar and pig iron despite a British law that all iron products be imported from England.

On September 1, 1774, on the eve of the First Continental Congress, Thomson, a widower, married Hannah Harrison, a cousin of the wife of John Dickinson, a wealthy lawyer delegate from Delaware who was famous for his incendiary pamphlet *Letters from a Farmer in Pennsylvania*. The new Mrs. Thomson brought to the marriage a £5,000 dowry (about $750,000 today) and a fine country house in Bryn Mawr.

An organizer of the Sons of Liberty, Thomson recruited other radical merchants, artisans and laborers to protest every new British colonial policy. Here he no doubt met Hancock during the boycott movement. He protected Franklin's house against a mob that believed Franklin had authored the Stamp Act. When Paul Revere brought news from Boston that Parliament had closed down the Massachusetts port in retaliation for the Tea Party, Thomson called a mass meeting that drew eight thousand Philadelphians, nearly one-third of its population. By voice vote, they passed a resolution to set up a Revolutionary committee of correspondence; to send food and money to Boston; and to convene a continental congress in Philadelphia.

When the delegates to the resultant First Continental Congress arrived, Thomson worked behind the scrim with Samuel and John Adams to switch the site of its meetings from the Pennsylvania State House, still the official royal capitol of the province, to the newly constructed Carpenters' Hall, a symbolic victory for the radicals in the Congress. The Adamses then maneuvered to have Thomson elected secretary of the Congress. It would be his duty to prepare all schedules and safeguard all documents. And it turned out to be a controversial job. John Adams would at first call Thomson the "Sam Adams of Philadelphia," but he was among the delegates who would later protest Thomson's peculiar method of note-taking, complaining of "extraordinary liberties taken by the secretary to suppress, by omitting in the journals, the many motions that were disagreeable. . . ."[7]

These motions ought to have been inserted verbatim in the journals with the names of the people who had made them. When Thomson couldn't write "Resolved unanimously in the records" because there had been opposition, he simply stopped with the word "Resolved," and if a motion was tabled or defeated, he didn't record it at all.

It would emerge years later that Thomson actually had kept two sets of records: One was made up of his own personal working notebooks, in which he jotted down pretty much everything that everybody did; the other, the official journals, contained the expurgated version of events that Adams complained about. Thomson subsequently declined to write a history of the congresses despite the importunings of numerous delegates who assumed he would write one, given that Thomson had gathered vast numbers of state documents and private papers from members, saying that he was going to use them to write a history. But he wrote to Benjamin Rush, "No, I ought not. . . . Let the world admire the supposed wisdom and valor of our great men. Perhaps they may adopt the qualities that have been ascribed to them, and thus good may be done. I shall not undeceive future generations."[8]

With only two dozen warships to patrol the entire thousand-mile Atlantic coastline of the North American colonies, the British navy could not enforce the blockade mandated from London in the first year of the Revolution. Instead, Royal Navy ships based in Boston—where seven rode at anchor—raided and intimidated New England towns. On October 7, 1775, Captain James Wallace of the Royal Navy frigate *Rose* led a squadron of sixteen ships—four warships, four tenders, two transports, three schooners and three sloops—toward Bristol, Rhode Island. Earlier that day, Wallace had sent ahead a lieutenant to take to the townspeople a list of demands, including three hundred sheep. The citizens refused. Wallace instantly responded by ordering a cannonade. The bombardment lasted more than an hour, with cannonballs crashing into homes, shops and the town church. On Friday the thirteenth, Wallace sailed into Newport; in exchange for "Beef Beer & necessarys for his Ships," he pledged, "he would not fire upon the Town without giving the Inhabitants sufficient warning."

That same day, a committee of revolutionaries stood anxiously in the driving rain on the town dock of Falmouth (now Portland), Maine, as the British squadron sailed past. Four days later, Captain Henry Mowat of the *Canceaux* sent a longboat into Casco Bay with an ultimatum: "After so many premeditated Attacks on the legal Prerogatives of the best of Sovereigns" and "the most unpardonable Rebellion" of the town's citizens, he intended to "execute a just Punishment." After frantic negotiations with terrified town leaders, Mowat agreed to hold his fire if the town surrendered its cannon and muskets and gave hostages. Falmouth sent only a handful of muskets and pistols.

The next morning, villagers fled with wagons and carts piled high with their belongings as three ships opened fire. While panicking oxen broke their yokes and stampeded through the throng, Mowat ordered hot shot fired on the town. Fanned by high winds, the flames engulfed the entire village.

Washington rushed news of the raid to Congress, describing the attack on Falmouth as a "horrid procedure" and warning that "the same Desolation is meditated upon all the Towns on the Coast." President Hancock had the dispatch read aloud along with a report from Washington that Parliament was sending reinforcements to Boston, including five regiments of Scottish Highlanders and Irish Catholic Regulars in a new fleet, including six ships of the line and a thousand marines.

Less than a week earlier, Congress had given birth to the Continental Navy.

⁓

On August 1, 1775, the Second Continental Congress recessed for a month. Hancock left the sweltering humidity of Philadelphia to hurry north to Fairfield, Connecticut; life without Dolly had become unendurable. Dolly and Aunt Lydia were attending to the final arrangements for a simple Puritan wedding in the home of Thaddeus Burr. Hancock wrote to Dolly that he would attend to some essential congressional business en route but then would "ride on to Fairfield as quick as I can . . . as I am very desirous of being with you soon." As he went, he was surprised that he was greeted by adoring crowds. Newborn babies were held up to him. Many had been named John Hancock. Dolly's sister Sarah had named her newborn son John Hancock Greenleaf in April; Dolly's father wrote to her that family friends had named their twins John and Dorothy.

Hancock first dashed north to Watertown, Massachusetts, to confer with leaders of the Provincial Congress, then delivered half a million dollars in cash to Washington in Cambridge so that he could pay army salaries. (The money came from taxes collected by the colonies and from Hancock's own coffers.) His last stop was in Worcester to pick up Dorothy's trunks, which she had left as she fled Lexington with Aunt Lydia.

It was August 28 before the long-anticipated wedding between John and Dorothy took place in Thaddeus and Eunice Burr's home. Neighbors stood by the garden fences to catch a glimpse of the Quaker ceremony. One reported seeing that "silver buckles, white silk stockings, knee breeches of various hues, scarlet vests and velvet coats with ruffled shirts and broad fine neckwear adorned the masculine fraternity, while the ladies were radiant in silks and laces, lofty head-dress, resplendent jewelry and the precious heirlooms of old families."[9]

The day after their wedding, the Hancocks set off for their honeymoon in Philadelphia, where they settled into comfortable rented rooms in the home of an "agreeable lady." But the stress of Hancock's duties and his dashes over bad roads to bring his bride to Philadelphia seemed to have triggered a flare-up of his gout. Dolly had to devote much of her time to trying to provide Hancock with some relief. She had to leave her trunk and furnishings— and apparently her bridegroom—untouched as she sought new doctors. But there was little they could do to help Hancock endure the severe burning and swelling of his joints but advise him to stay in bed.

The pain became so acute that for the first weeks, although he tried to hide the severity of the attacks, Hancock could not attend every meeting of the Continental Congress. "Mr. Hancock having a touch of the gout there was no President in the Chair," wrote Richard Smith, a delegate from New Jersey. Yet, Smith noted, the support for Hancock's presidency continued to be strong. Most of the delegates were content to await his return to good health. But not all: John Adams wrote to James Warren in Boston that "our new [president] continues in the Chair without seeming to feel the impropriety."[10]

To assist her husband, Dolly pushed aside any thought of a honeymoon and went to work as Hancock's unpaid clerk. All the time she was in Philadelphia, she was busy packing up commissions to be sent off to officers appointed by the Congress. It wasn't until some time after this that Hancock kept a clerk; until then all the business of Congress was done by the president. She herself was for months engaged with her scissors in trimming off the rough edges of the bills of credit issued by the Congress and signed by the president and packing them up in saddlebags to be sent off to the various quarters for the use of the army.[11]

In addition, Dolly sent out the officers' commissions signed by her husband and took notes of the daily meetings dictated to her by Hancock late at night.

John Adams, her neighbor in the Arch Street mansion that housed the Massachusetts delegation, reported approvingly to Abigail that Dolly "lives and behaves with modesty, decency, dignity and discretion I assure you. . . . She avoids talking about politics. In large and mixed companies, she is totally silent, as a lady ought to be."

While failing to comment on Dolly's work as a clerk, Adams wrote that he appreciated the socializing she initiated, breaking up the ten-hour days, six days a week, with "after-hours caucusing and conversation."[12]

~⟞~

Despite his chronic fatigue, Hancock only added to his presidential duties by appointing himself chairman of the Navy Committee, on which he felt he could employ his experience in the House of Hancock in building and outfitting ships. At first, Congress only chartered or purchased vessels. Hancock generously donated a brig, renamed *John Hancock*, to Washington's fledgling "navy." Hancock then pursued congressional approval to build Congress's own navy. In this, his pet project, he launched a program to construct thirteen armed, fast frigates in Massachusetts. When his ally Thomas Cushing was defeated for reelection to Congress, Hancock appointed him Continental naval agent for New England and put him in charge of the enterprise.

Hancock gave Cushing very precise instructions to build two frigates. With Boston still occupied by the British, Cushing had to search for skilled shipwrights and found them in Newburyport. He signed a contract with Jonathan Greenleaf and the Cross brothers for one frigate of thirty-two guns and another of twenty-four. Hancock wrote to Cushing in early 1776 more than to anyone else. He directed the naval agent to "spare no expense." They were in a race with Philadelphia shipwrights to launch the first Continental Navy ships; the honor of Massachusetts and the honor of Hancock were at stake. And Hancock wanted not only to be the first; he also wanted the frigates to be the most beautifully made, with "neatly carved" heads and galleries.

Cushing was to take pains to "let ours be as good, handsome, strong and as early completed as any" being built in any colony. Hancock even insisted on choosing the captains and officers. A former captain for the Hancock fleet, his friend Captain Isaac Cazneau, took the helm of the twenty-four-gun *Boston*. The larger, thirty-two-gun frigate, described by Cushing as "a very fine ship," was named the *Hancock*. While his ships did not win the race to be first to go to sea, Hancock was delighted when the Navy Committee ordered that all Continental vessels and their prizes, when they came to Boston, were to tie up at Hancock's Wharf. As Boston proved to be the busiest port for the Continental Navy, Hancock's enhanced prestige and revenue compensated him for the disproportionate amount of time and effort he lavished on his pet project.

~e~

Again drawing on his long experience in shipping, Hancock championed the conversion of merchant vessels into an auxiliary navy of privateersmen. By an overwhelming vote, Congress authorized the creation of a squadron reporting to its Navy Committee. Congress commissioned Esek Hopkins, a slave trader and the younger brother of Congressman Stephen Hopkins of Rhode Island, to serve as the Continental Navy's first commodore. In October 1775, Congress appropriated £100,000 (approximately $15 million today) "to fit out for sea the first fleet" of four ships. The committee purchased two of the vessels from a member, Robert Morris. The first was the newly launched two-hundred-ton, one-hundred-forty-foot merchantman *Black Prince*. Its captain, John Barry, called it "the finest ship in America." Refitted with thirty guns and renamed the *Alfred*, it would serve as the flagship of the embryonic Continental Navy.

A second vessel, another brig, was renamed the *Columbus*. Its captain, Abraham Whipple, the commodore of the Rhode Island navy, who was married to Esek Hopkins's niece.

Soon, four ships crowded the shipyard, undergoing conversions. John Adams, busily rewriting the Royal Navy's Articles of War into "Rules for the Regulation of the Navy of the United Colonies," listed them: the *Alfred*, the *Columbus*, the *Cabot* and the *Andrew Doria*. Hopkins's son John was given the helm of the *Cabot*. From Rhode Island came the sloop *Katy*, renamed the *Providence*. Two more schooners, the *Wasp* and the *Fly*, and a sloop, *Hornet*, were the last of those that composed the first American fleet.

The ships refitted and armed on the Philadelphia waterfront were to act essentially as privateers; their mission was to capture enemy shipments of commercial goods and military supplies. By January 1776, when Congress formed the Marine Committee to supersede the Navy Committee, eight ships made up the Continental Navy, forerunner of the U.S. Navy.

American privateers proved effective at slowing the British war effort. In little more than the first year of the war, according to the registry kept in Lloyd's Coffee House in London, American privateers captured 733 British merchant vessels valued at £1.8 million ($270 million today), putting them under the auctioneer's gavel in French, American and Caribbean ports.

Eleven states would create their own de facto navies. Governor Jonathan Trumbull signed letters of marque for two hundred Connecticut-based privateering ships. As many as seventy thousand men served aboard privateering ships and shared in the loot. By the end of the war, many crewmen owned their own privateers. The Royal Navy lost one hundred ships in 1778 and more than two hundred in 1779 to the intrepid privateers. The British were eventually forced to build a fleet of frigates just to escort their merchant vessels in slow-sailing convoys.

In the eight-year course of the war, the Continental Navy would capture some two hundred British vessels valued at £6 million (about $900 million today), while American privateers captured more than five hundred vessels, their cargoes valued at an astonishing £66 million ($9.9 billion today). In all, Lloyd's listed 2,208 British vessels captured between 1775 and 1783.

~·~

In March 1776, Hancock received a letter from George Washington, who had just forced the British to evacuate Boston by placing in Dorchester Heights cannon dragged from Fort Ticonderoga by oxen. There, they could bombard the town and the Royal Navy ships in the harbor. Washington had negotiated with Gage, the British commander. Gage promised that the British would spare Boston from flames and evacuate peacefully if Washington held his fire. On March 17, 1776, a fleet carrying the British army, their artillery and twelve hundred fleeing New England Loyalists, including nearly all of the merchants in Boston, sailed for Halifax.

In the same letter, Washington reported to Hancock that his Beacon Hill mansion had been spared and was left intact by its temporary occupant, General Sir Henry Clinton: "I have the particular pleasure of being able to inform you, Sir, that your house has received no damage worth mentioning. Your furniture is in tolerable order, and the family pictures are left entire and untouched. Captain [Isaac] Cazneau takes charge of the whole until he shall receive further orders from you."[13]

But many of Hancock's properties, Cazneau wrote to him a few days later, had been badly damaged and his stores and warehouses plundered. "The town is shockingly defaced, especially the places of public worship," Cazneau reported. Old South Meeting House had been stripped of its pews; Old North Meeting House had disappeared entirely. The looters had obliterated Hancock's name wherever they found it on a building. "Your name on the cornerstone of Dr. Cooper's [Brattle Square] church is mangled with an axe." Hancock had lost much of his fortune.

One month later, in April 1776, Hancock suffered an irreparable loss: His beloved aunt Lydia died of a stroke. Fortuitously, her demise replenished Hancock's coffers: After freeing her slaves, donating a manse to Brattle Square Church and distributing £5,000 ($750,000) to relatives and to charities, she left the bulk of her estate, including extensive real estate, to her nephew. Hancock received £4,000 ($600,000 today) in cash.

At the same time, Hancock received bad news from Boston: For the first time in a decade, he had not been elected to the House or reelected to the council. Hancock was stunned. He wrote to Thomas Cushing, "I find I am left out of both House and Council. I can't help it, they have a right to do as they please. I think I do not merit such treatment."[14] Hancock seemed to have failed to grasp that there was growing resistance to his holding so many offices simultaneously: delegate to Congress and its president, major general of the militia, member of the House and selectman of Boston. Samuel Adams had gathered support for his viewpoint from other delegations from Massachusetts to Virginia, and now the first rift in Congress appeared. Hancock was apparently unaware of the developing split and its potential impact, but when he did learn of them, they shocked him.

CHAPTER NINE

"Why All This Haste?"

On Friday, June 7, 1776, a courier arrived in Congress with word that the Virginia Convention had resolved unanimously to instruct its delegates to vote to declare independence. President Hancock recognized Richard Henry Lee, who rose and read, "Resolved, that these united colonies are, and of right ought to be, free and independent states, that they are absolved from all allegiance to the British Crown, and that all political connection between them and the state of Great Britain is, and ought to be, totally dissolved." John Adams seconded the Virginian's motion.

Royal governments still functioned in New Jersey, Pennsylvania and New York; they had given no authority to their delegates to vote for a change of government. Conservatives strenuously resisted the motion. James Duane of New York demanded to know, "Why all this haste? Why all this driving?" James Wilson of Pennsylvania objected, "Before we are prepared to build a new house, why should we pull down the old one?" John Dickinson warned the New England delegates they would have "blood on their heads" if they precluded the possibility of peace.[1]

On June 11, at an impasse, Congress decided to postpone the vote for twenty days to allow reluctant delegates to write home for new instructions. Meanwhile, to avoid further loss of time, Hancock appointed a five-man committee to draft a declaration of independence: Thomas Jefferson, John Adams, Benjamin Franklin, Robert Livingston of New York and Roger Sherman of Connecticut. Attempting to strike a balance between the North and the South, Hancock chose delegates who were well-liked and respected for their abilities in making legislation in their own colonies. Hancock did not appoint Samuel Adams, who was stunned by the omission.

~ℓ~

It was years before most people knew that Thomas Jefferson wrote the Declaration of Independence, so carefully was the secret locked up in the anonymity of a Revolutionary committee. According to a letter Jefferson wrote to James Madison in 1823, when he finished his rough draft, "before I reported it to the committee, I communicated it separately to Dr. Franklin and Mr. Adams requesting their corrections." Franklin and Adams made minor changes of a word here, a word there, interlining them in their own hands. On July 2, Congress, after voting in favor of the resolution on independence, sat as a committee of the whole. For two and a half days, the representatives debated every line and provision, with Hancock moderating the discussion. No one took notes except for a few details Jefferson himself wrote down.

Throughout the ordeal, Jefferson remained silent in his humiliation at the number, extent and importance of the changes, disgusted by the timidity of conservative members and their slashing deletions. In his notes, he derided "the pusillanimous idea that we had friends in England worth keeping terms with. . . . For this reason, those passages which conveyed censures on the people of England were struck out, lest they should give them offense."

One such instance involved Scottish mercenaries. A shipload of Scots Highlanders bound for Boston to reinforce the British had been blown off course and had fallen into American hands. And in Virginia, Scots under Lord Dunmore had burned Norfolk. According to Jefferson, "The words 'Scotch and other foreign auxiliaries' excited the ire of a gentleman or two of that country." So all mention of Scottish mercenaries was suppressed. In addition, in his draft declaration, Jefferson, owner of a hundred forty enslaved people, charged that King George was personally to blame for the slave trade. Jefferson wrote in 1818 that his antislavery "expressions were immediately yielded" by the North and the South. The same "gentlemen," especially John Rutledge of South Carolina, were encouraged by this easy victory to continue "their depredations"; in all, they made eighty-nine emendations. Throughout the brutal editing process, Jefferson sat beside Franklin, "who perceived that I was not insensible to these mutilations." He said that Franklin tried to reassure him by whispering a parable to him:

> I have made it a rule . . . whenever in my power, to avoid becoming the draftsman of papers to be reviewed by a public body. . . . When I was a journeyman printer, one of my

companions, an apprentice hatter, having served out his time, was about to open shop for himself. His first concern was to have a handsome signboard, with a proper inscription. He composed it in these words, "John Thompson, hatter, makes and sells hats for ready money," with a figure of a hat sub-joined. But he thought he would submit it to his friends for their amendments. The first he showed it to thought the word "hatter" tautologous, because followed by the words "makes hats," which showed he was a hatter. It was struck out. The next observed that the word "makes" might as well be omit-ted because the customers would not care who made the hats; if good and to their mind, they would buy, by whomsoever made. He struck it out. A third said he thought the words "for ready money" were useless, as it was not the custom of the place to sell on credit. Every one who purchased expected to pay. They were parted with, and the inscription now stood, "John Thompson sells hats." "Sells hats?" says his next friend. "Why, no one will expect you to give them away. What, then, is the use of that word?" It was stricken out, and "hats" fol-lowed, the rather as there was one painted on the board. So his inscription was reduced ultimately to "John Thompson" with the figure of a hat subjoined.[2]

Jefferson never wrote of the editing, but he did send to Richard Henry Lee in Virginia the approved version and a copy "as origi-nally framed." "You will judge whether it is better or worse for the Critics." When he wrote his autobiography at age seventy-seven, he included in full "the form of the Declaration as originally re-ported" with "the parts struck out by Congress" underlined in black. And in 1776, he requested to be replaced by Virginia as one of its delegates. He was reluctant to serve again in Congress, and only did so after his wife died in 1782. After his term ended in 1784, he never again agreed to serve in Congress.

⁓

John Hancock is primarily remembered for his large, flamboyant signature on the Declaration of Independence. According to a story that originated years later, he said that he signed his name large and clear so that King George III could read it without his spectacles. Contrary to legend, there was no ceremonial signing on July 4, 1776. After Congress approved the text on July 4, Hancock signed the approved copy as president of Congress before sending it to the printer John Dunlap, who produced the first published version to be widely distributed as a broadside. Hancock was the only delegate whose name appeared on it. His iconic signature appears on a sheet of parchment carefully printed two weeks later and signed by Hancock and all the delegates present on August 2, although the location of this version was originally kept a secret. (Now this document is on display at the National Archives.)

Until a second broadside with all the signers' names listed was issued six months later, Hancock was the only delegate whose name was publicly attached to the treasonous document as it was disseminated to governors, troop commanders and newspapers that took it to England and the capitals of Europe. His signing alone, affixing his name to the document that would become his death warrant if he were captured by the British, can be described only as heroic.

After signing the Declaration on July 4, President Hancock ordered it read aloud to a crowd in the Pennsylvania State House yard as dispatch riders hurried printed copies throughout the new states. In New York City, General Washington welcomed its rhetoric as a badly needed tonic for his troops.

Since driving the British out of Boston at cannon point three months earlier, Washington had been amassing Connecticut and New York militia in anticipation of an imminent counterattack. A British armada composed of a hundred fifty troop transports and thirty men-of-war had dropped anchor in New York harbor; thirty-two thousand Regulars, including nine thousand German mercenaries, had pitched their tents on Staten Island.

By the time the Declaration arrived on July 9, Washington's inexperienced militia faced the largest fleet and biggest army Great Britain had ever sent from its shores. Washington had the document read aloud to his troops and then ordered them back to their billets. Some joined the mob surging through the streets and breaking the windows of prominent Loyalists. Reaching Bowling Green at the tip of Manhattan, they vaulted the fence surrounding the equestrian statue of King George III. The largest statue in America, it had been dedicated only six years earlier to celebrate the British victory over France. Looping ropes around the horse and its royal rider, they pulled the fifteen-foot statue to the ground. One man sawed off the king's head; the rest was carted off to Litchfield, Connecticut, where women converted it into 42,088 bullets.

On August 27, after being outmaneuvered and soundly defeated at the Battle of Brooklyn, Washington managed to evacuate most of his army under cover of a storm. His troops were rowed to Manhattan Island by fishermen from Gloucester, Massachusetts. Retreating first north, then across New Jersey, and surviving a series of rearguard actions, Washington led his army, made up of twenty percent of the force he had assembled in New York, across the Delaware River. On Christmas Day 1776, he counterattacked, surprising a groggy garrison of Germen mercenaries in Trenton. Ten days later, he routed the British at Princeton. As a steady drumbeat of Washington's dispatches reached President Hancock to be read aloud to Congress, delegates found little time to debate a new form of government.

Months earlier, on the day that Congress created the committee to draft the Declaration of Independence, they also created a second panel made up of a delegate from each colony and chaired by John Dickinson to prepare a written constitution for a confederation of states. When Benjamin Franklin had returned to America a year earlier, he proposed a government similar to his 1754 Albany Plan of Union, but Congress never debated it.

One week after Congress promulgated the Declaration, the Dickinson committee presented draft Articles of Confederation and Perpetual Union to the full Congress. But it would take fully five years and two defeats in Congress before the nation's first constitution was finally ratified. No state or combination of speculative investors was willing to relinquish its claim to a bonanza in western lands. All that could be settled immediately was a name for the new entity: the United States of America. A fourth draft of the Articles, not debated until November 1777, would finally be presented for congressional approval and submission to the states for ratification.

The confederation was to be "a firm league of friendship" of states for their "common defense, the security of their liberties and their mutual and general welfare." With a unicameral congress as the confederation's central institution, each state would have one vote; the delegates were to be elected by the states' legislatures. The states would remain sovereign and independent, with Congress serving as the last resort on appeal of disputes. Congress would have the authority to make treaties and alliances, maintain armed forces and coin money but would lack the authority to levy or collect taxes and regulate commerce. Any revenues would come from the states, each contributing according to the value of privately owned land within its borders.

The root cause of American financial insecurity, Alexander Hamilton would write to his future father-in-law, General Philip Schuyler, in 1779, lay in the states' refusal to grant the power to tax to Congress, leaving the body and its armies at the mercy of requisitions that the states either could not or sometimes would not honor. For instance, Pennsylvania's Conestoga wagons were vital to supplying the armies and transporting war matériel, but Washington had to plead for them each year, and the state rarely met its quotas. Virginia manufactured cannon and gunpowder, but then Governor Jefferson insisted that much of its output go to support Virginia's own garrisons in the Illinois country while providing little support for Continental armies north or south.

With no power to tax, Congress continued to print continental dollars and, its quotas unheeded at home, borrowed heavily in Europe until its credit had been exhausted. It then resorted to the expropriation and confiscation and forced sale of Loyalists' property. Paper money issued in 1777 purchased goods valued at $16 million; by 1779, it took $125 million in continental paper to purchase $6 million worth of supplies. By this time, the nation's worsening financial condition was primarily blamed on an insufficient supply of stable currency.

The Articles would not take effect until every state ratified them. A president, until the federal constitution of 1787 superseded it, could serve only one year over a period of three years. In effect, John Hancock became the first president of the confederated United States of America.

In December 1776, as Washington's dwindling army, reeling from
its crushing defeat at the Battle of Brooklyn, retreated across New
Jersey, he wrote to Hancock to advise Congress to evacuate Philadelphia, the presumed target of the British. Hancock opposed the
move, confident that Washington could stop the British advance.
And he believed that for Congress to flee prematurely would de-
moralize the troops. Only when the British were within twenty
miles of Philadelphia, and the majority of congressmen voted to
adjourn and reconvene in Baltimore, did Hancock acquiesce. He
packed Dolly—still recovering from the birth of their month-old
daughter, Lydia Henchman Hancock—and all his personal papers,
ledgers, cash and letters of credit into his coach. Then he followed
the rutted, winter-hardened hundred-mile road to the temporary
capital to preside over meetings until it became safe to return to
Philadelphia. In the meantime, Robert Morris was to remain in
Philadelphia to conduct minimal congressional business.

A thriving port for exporting Maryland's tobacco, Baltimore
was a ramshackle collection of docks, warehouses and rat-infested
shanties with a scant handful of mansions, with no suitable building for congressional meetings and few rooms to rent—and those
available went for exorbitant prices. William Ellery, delegate from
Rhode Island, described the town as "the dirtiest place" he had
ever seen. Other delegates complained that Baltimore cost double
their expenses in Philadelphia, then considered the priciest place in
America. Samuel Purviance, a merchant with business ties to Hancock and acting as the Continental agent for Baltimore, welcomed
the Hancocks to his home until they could find suitable quarters.

Hancock finally had to settle for a small, run-down, £25-a-month

($3,750) house in a neighborhood considered too unsafe for Dolly to take a walk in. Hancock complained loudly to Robert Morris in January 1777, "I have got to housekeeping, but really, my friend, in a very poor house. . . . I have only two rooms below, and one of them I am obliged to let my servants occupy." Two days after the Hancocks moved in, thieves broke in and stole trunks loaded with books, linens, papers and cash.

To add to his discomfort, Hancock received a most unwelcome visitor from Harvard College. In July 1773, Hancock had been elected to the prestigious post of treasurer of his alma mater. The Board of Overseers chose Hancock in part because of his business acumen, in part because of his growing political influence and undoubtedly in part because of his generosity and that of his friends, which they hoped to encourage further. Hancock could hardly refuse the honor; he took charge of the college's books and its entire treasury of £15,449 (about $2.3 million today) and securities.

Early in April 1775, as Hancock prepared to travel to Philadelphia, the Overseers had requested he return the books and the treasury to the college before he left town. But when Hancock learned a week later from his father-in-law, Judge Quincy, that General Gage had received orders from London to arrest him and Samuel Adams for treason, Hancock had scooped up the Harvard papers and treasury along with his own cash and securities and packed them in a massive trunk with the obvious intent of spiriting the trove out of reach of the pursuing British.

Hancock would have little time or opportunity to return the treasury as he fled during the chaotic days of the British attack on Lexington and Concord. He had concealed the coach in thick brush while he hid in Woburn; then he virtually sat on the trunk during the long journey to Philadelphia and again during the hundred-mile flight of Congress to Baltimore. There, with even less room, time or inclination, he'd put off attending to faraway Harvard's financial affairs. So Hancock was dumbfounded when Harvard tutor Stephen Hall—a member of the faculty—appeared in Baltimore with a written demand for the college's treasury.

In December, the finance committee of college Overseers, with James Bowdoin acting as its chair, had instructed Hall to go to Philadelphia to confront Hancock. En route, he had learned that Congress had taken flight to Baltimore. There was no question that the college needed the account books and the money and the treasurer closer to campus. The college had been shut down and badly needed repairs after American militia occupied its dormitories during the siege of Boston, peeling the tin roof off one dorm and stripping all brass fixtures from its walls and doors to melt and mold into bullets.

When Hall showed his instructions, Hancock was perturbed. He rightly surmised that the Overseers wanted his resignation but were reluctant to come right out and request it. Hancock immediately turned over to Hall £15,000 (about $2.2 million in cash and negotiable securities), virtually all of the funds entrusted to him two years earlier, but he would have no idea of the exact amount of interest the securities might have ordinarily earned until he had the time to examine more than two hundred accounts that had remained in Boston. And he was offended by the idea that he should pay interest on money he had protected. He sent Hall away with the money but no letter of resignation.

Hancock then requested that William Bant, who was in charge of his Boston affairs, write a letter and deliver it in person to the Overseers at their next meeting. The Overseers' response was a seven-thousand-word letter demanding a complete accounting of the treasury and the payment of compound interest. It would not be until July 1777, when the Overseers elected a new treasurer, that the affair would appear to come to a conclusion, although the Overseers had not received any resignation, accounting or accumulated interest. (By then the Overseers were demanding triple interest.) In September 1777, Hancock accounted for £16,442, but he still refused to pay any interest.

~℮~

In early December 1776, Hancock received word that the Massachusetts General Court had reelected him as a delegate to the Continental Congress. When the full Congress elected him to a second term as its president, Hancock accepted. Before the year 1776 ended, Hancock received even more welcome news: When Washington crossed the Delaware River into Pennsylvania with the remnants of his battered army, the British commander, Sir William Howe, pulled back most of his forces from New Jersey into winter quarters in New York City, leaving only small outposts in a handful of towns.

Washington struck back, responding with his pair of surprise attacks at Trenton and Princeton. In Baltimore, the news of the twin victories heartened Hancock and the other delegates to Congress. Just days before he celebrated his fortieth birthday, on January 31, 1777, he finally received the final copies of the Declaration of Independence, listing all the signers. His had been the only name affixed to the treasonous document for six months. Meanwhile, Congress voted to return to Philadelphia.

The Hancocks decided that when travel conditions improved in the spring, Dolly and the baby would go to stay with the Burrs in

Fairfield, Connecticut, while John and a pair of servants returned to the capital. The voyage from Baltimore to Philadelphia took two weeks, during which time Hancock learned that some Americans were not very impressed by the presence of the president of the Continental Congress. While waiting for a ferry to cross the ice-floe-clogged Susquehanna River, Hancock stayed in a country inn whose keeper decided that the only double bed should go to a married couple rather than to President Hancock. He was relegated to a crowded single room with his servants and other unimpressed travelers.

CHAPTER TEN

"Constant Application to Public Business"

It would be more than a year after the promulgation of independence in July 1776 before Congress could again pause to debate confederation. Despite Washington's stunning twin victories, the Continental Army remained weak, ill-equipped and poorly armed. Hancock and his mercantile colleagues worked six days a week arranging clandestine purchases of gunpowder from the Dutch—at six times the going rate in Europe—and of surplus weapons from French dealers.

Until France could be coaxed by Benjamin Franklin to abandon official neutrality and sign a treaty of alliance, Hancock had to keep pressure, often unsuccessfully, on the individual states' congresses to meet annually negotiated arms and recruiting quotas.

In the meantime, the portents of a massive invasion from Britain only heightened Hancock's sense of personal isolation, made acute by Dolly's going to Connecticut with the baby and her sister. She liked Philadelphia little more than Baltimore, despite

Hancock's expectation that she would remain with him. While she had written to him constantly before their marriage, Dolly rarely wrote him now. When she finally did in the summer of 1777, the letter brought the sad news that their infant daughter had become ill and died. In her own grief, Dolly wrote to him even less, and Hancock felt more alone than ever. To alleviate his loneliness, at least once a week that summer, he and several friends in Congress met for an evening of eating and drinking. But some other members complained about his expensive lifestyle. Hancock, who received no salary or expense allowance from Congress, responded to their finger wagging with "I have expended my own money [and] in that case had a right to drink wine if I pleased."[1]

Throughout the summer of 1777, as a massive British expeditionary force under General John Burgoyne invaded from Canada, General Howe sailed with his army from New York into the Chesapeake. Once again, Washington warned Congress to leave Philadelphia and move to a temporary capital. This time, Congress packed up and moved sixty miles to the small town of York, Pennsylvania, west of the Susquehanna.

In a cramped rented house, Hancock stubbornly steered Congress's attention back to the task of crafting a permanent government by finishing the drafting of the Articles of Confederation. Six coastal states—Pennsylvania, New Jersey, Delaware, Maryland, New Hampshire and Rhode Island—proposed that Congress be empowered to limit the western boundaries of states. These states' colonial charters confined their land to a few hundred miles from the Atlantic. Prospects for approval appeared dim: Virginia, the

Carolinas, Georgia, Connecticut, and Massachusetts claimed that their territory extended to the "South Sea," or Mississippi River, according to their colonial charters granted by Britain. They had no incentive to limit their boundaries.

The motion failed, but two months later Congress voted to add to the Articles a clause providing that no state could be deprived of western lands for the benefit of the United States. But American Indian tribes could cede their lands, and in a series of treaties they did. Pressure from investors in land companies—including the Illinois Company and the Grand Ohio Company, organized by the Franklins, and the Mississippi Land Company, founded by Washington—led Virginia to nullify all such purchases in the so-called Northwest Territory.

In October 1777, after presiding over Congress for two and a half years, Hancock was suffering from intensifying bouts of gout. He was exhausted from the work of moving legislation through an endlessly bickering Congress, and his wrists ached constantly as he signed hundreds of commissions and documents. Amid jubilation over the news that the American army had defeated Burgoyne at Saratoga, Hancock wrote to Jefferson in Virginia that he needed a rest: "My constant application to public business both in and out of Congress has so impaired my health that some relaxation has become absolutely necessary and tomorrow morning I set out for Boston with the leave of Congress to be absent two months."[2]

Hancock's request set off a rare display of rancor that revealed a growing rift in Congress. He asked permission of the delegates to deliver a long farewell address. At its conclusion, a delegate moved that the "thanks of Congress be presented to John Hancock." That was too much for Samuel Adams and some other fellow New Englanders, who objected that it was "improper to thank any president for the discharge of the duties of that office."[3]

A vote on the objection was divided, with every member of the Massachusetts delegation except Hancock supporting the objection; the vote for the original motion of thanks passed by a margin of only two votes, six to four.

Well aware that his post as president of Congress and his role as signer of the Declaration of Independence made him a prized target for capture by the British, Hancock asked Washington for a military escort for his trip around British lines to Boston. Samuel Adams led the Massachusetts delegation in voting against it. Ignoring the fracas, Washington sent a troop of twelve dragoons to escort Hancock and his family home.

Hancock wrote to Dolly to request that she meet him at Hartford with a light carriage, servants and his chief clerk, Bant. His foot wrapped in gauze and propped on a seat, Hancock led a caravan of wagons carrying all his possessions on a slow journey that had to take a long detour to the north to avoid British patrols before crossing the Hudson at Fishkill, far north of New York City. He wrote again to Dolly, who was already waiting for him in Hartford, about his "many difficulties on the road" but added, "I shall not mind. The remembrance of these difficulties will vanish when I have the happiness of seeing you."[4]

~ℓ~

On November 19, 1777, after an absence of two years and six months, John Hancock returned to Boston. With his escort of

Continental dragoons, his carriage crossed the Neck and entered the town. He was welcomed by a cheering crowd, and the Corps of Cadets turned out to honor their former colonel.

"His arrival here was made known by the ringing of bells, the discharge of thirteen cannon on the Common, the cannon from the fortress on the hill, and the ships in the harbor," reported the *Independent Chronicle*. The owners of the Newburyport-based privateer *Civil Usage* presented him with a handsome yellow carriage captured as it was en route to British headquarters in New York City "as a token of respect for that gentleman which has so nobly distinguished himself in the present contest with Great Britain."[5]

Riding around the town in his new carriage, taking in the impact of the flight of the Loyalists, Hancock found that the city's population had declined by one-third: Now a town of only ten thousand, it was no longer the largest in colonial America. Stopping at nearly every corner, Hancock talked to everyone. He ordered lumber at his own expense to repair homes and shops. Learning of the acute need "for providing for the aged and infirm persons in the almshouse who are provided with wood and clothing," he purchased a hundred fifty cords of firewood for distribution to the poor. He also provided assistance to widows and orphans, helping to support the children of Dr. Joseph Warren, the hero of Bunker Hill, and he advanced money to cash-strapped friends and colleagues. Deciding to overlook their recent contretemps, he magnanimously included Samuel Adams.

The defeated British-Hessian army that had surrendered at Saratoga was being billeted in dormitories at Harvard College while awaiting the approval of Congress to be shipped back to Britain. A paroled Hessian officer free to go into Boston wrote that "President Hancock is so frank and [kind] to the lowest that one would think he was talking to a brother or a relative. He visits the coffeehouses of Boston where are congregated the poorest of the inhabitants—men who get their living by bringing wood and vegetables into the city." The Hessian saw in Hancock's generosity a political strategy: "He who desires to advance in popularity must understand the art of making himself popular. In no country does wealth and birth count for so little as in this."[6]

Hancock's rambles around Boston showed him the full extent of the devastation. Leaving a trail of destruction, the troops had looted virtually every house. They chopped down most of the trees—including the Liberty Tree—tore up all the fences and pulled down many wooden buildings for firewood. The mansions of the North End had been spared only because professional British officers had been billeted in them.

In Hancock's home, Cazneau had put "the best furniture . . . in the chamber back of the great chamber"—the master bedroom— and kept the key until about three weeks before General Clinton left the house. Cazneau was then "sent for and they demanded to search for papers. . . . When we came to open the door, the key would not open. On this [Clinton] seemed much displeased and said he would break it open. He kept the key and wished me good morning."

A few days before Clinton sailed for Halifax, he summoned Cazneau again and "desired I would look about and see if anything was wanting. I told him the great settee was not in the house." Clinton ordered it returned. The backgammon table in the library was also missing; it could not be found and never was replaced. "The china and the glassware was found out, unpacked and put into the great room. . . . Mr. Clinton was very angry that I did not acquaint him that it was secreted. . . . Said I had not used him well.

If his servants had been dishonest it might have been sold and given suspicion that 'twas done by his orders."

While Clinton had spared Hancock's house, the British had caused Hancock's other properties an estimated £4,732 ($700,000) in damages, according to an inventory taken by Bant. His accounting enumerated barrels of cider and choice vinegar, bushels of charcoal and cauldrons of sea coal, six muskets and "rent of the house for one year." Among the losses was one inflicted by one of Hancock's own relatives. Hancock's wine cellar, one of the finest in Boston, had been ransacked by his cousin William Bowes, a Loyalist. With the aid of a sheriff, Bowes had taken £350 ($50,000) worth of the best wines, including Hancock's prized Madeira, and fled to London.

Five houses had been pulled down; British soldiers who had lived in seven small brick apartment buildings had left them so damaged, they would have to be rebuilt. The British had used Hancock's Beacon Hill stables and coach house as hospitals. A fire on Hancock's Wharf had burned down a number of stores. The British had stolen anchors and sails from his ships' chandlery and "100 hogsheads of salt which these scoundrels threw into the [harbor]." They had destroyed a large scow and badly damaged a new ship under construction, sawing off her stern.[7]

The loss of income from rent on damaged properties left Hancock in a cash bind. Bant, a former Son of Liberty, was also a merchant and lawyer, and one of his duties as Hancock's business manager was bill collecting. Shortly after Hancock's homecoming celebration, the two men huddled for several hours, taking inventory of the remnants of the Hancock empire. Bant had just returned from twice traveling from Portsmouth, New Hampshire, to Cape Cod, attempting to collect overdue debts and rents. He reported that the people he had dunned either didn't have any cash or had paid in badly depreciated currency that Hancock, as a high government official, was honor bound to accept at a great loss.

On his first trip in 1776, when Hancock was far away in Philadelphia, Bant had been able to glean only £500 ($75,000) and saddlebags stuffed with excuses and promises. On the second round in 1777, in the wake of Hancock's triumphal return, Bant came back with £1,500 (about $225,000). In Hancock's absence, Bant had decided it was necessary to sell off his remaining ships for ready money. Laid up in docks in Boston and Salem, they were only deteriorating; converting them to cash made more sense to Bant than keeping them. Bant sold them for £1,000 ($150,000). Hancock's dream of a revived House of Hancock fleet had to be postponed.

Yet Hancock was still a wealthy man. He could rely on rents from the intact shops on Hancock's Wharf and other properties in eastern Massachusetts as well as the interest on loans and his increasing speculative ventures in real estate. He decided it was time to shift his main effort from business to politics.

At the beginning of 1778, the Massachusetts House of Representatives resolved to pay Hancock £2,335 ($350,000) for his years of service as Massachusetts's representative in Congress, in effect compensating him for his losses. And Hancock's immense popularity with the general population came in part at least from his thoughtful generosity.

Many Bostonians could remember that, before the Revolution, Hancock had built a bandstand on Boston Common and installed walkways that crisscrossed the park and rows of trees around its perimeter. He donated three hundred white globes that burned whale oil to provide street lighting, and at his own expense he organized a band to give free concerts. But some of his fellow citizens less able or willing to match his openhandedness—particularly other politicians—were suspicious of Hancock's motives. Men like Samuel Adams and James Bowdoin saw it merely as a means to attaining greater political power.

But Hancock's resumption of his conspicuous philanthropy prompted most Bostonians to reciprocate, reelecting him to the House of Representatives as moderator of the Town Meeting—its highest honor—and to a fourth term in the Continental Congress. Hancock accepted his election in Congress so he could cast his vote for final approval of the Articles of Confederation.

But he was in no hurry to leave Boston again and return to York. Hancock wrote to Congress to ask for an extension of his already overextended leave as president. Dolly was pregnant, and he needed to stay with her during the remaining weeks before the birth. Using the time to win back control of the House, Hancock used his influence to unseat James Warren, protégé of Samuel Adams, and install his ally, Timothy Pickering, in the speaker's chair. Warren wrote to his mentor, "The cunning of a party" had "set up an idol they are determined to worship. The plan is to sacrifice you and me to the shrine of their idol."[8]

On May 17, 1778, Dolly Quincy Hancock gave birth to their son. Three days later, their close friend Samuel Cooper baptized John George Washington Hancock at Brattle Square Church, which John and Aunt Lydia had rebuilt. John was jubilant that his son was the fourth John Hancock born in America and that, while the others were British subjects, this John Hancock was the first born an American.

Two weeks later, on June 3, 1778, after a leave of seven months, Hancock finally left for York. Even his departure stirred controversy. James Warren wrote to Samuel Adams in Congress in York, describing Hancock's farewell to the House of Representatives:

> General Hancock took pompous leave of the House by going up to and shaking hands with the Speaker after moving for leave to return soon if his health would not admit of his tarrying long [in York]. I suppose a cavalcade will attend him, subscriptions for that purpose having been circulated for a week. . . . You will provide for his reception as you see fit.[9]

Making all he could of his exit, Hancock used the bully pulpit of his reelection as moderator of the Town Meeting to announce the signing at Versailles of a Treaty of Amity and Commerce with the United States.

Hancock finally left Boston for York accompanied by Dr. Samuel Holten, a new delegate to Congress elected to replace John Adams, who was departing to join Franklin. Holten noted in his diary that, as Warren had predicted, "a large number of gentlemen, with their servants and carriages, accompanied us to Watertown, where an elegant dinner was provided," along with toasts, the firing of salutes and cheering.[10]

As the carriage rattled over bad roads during the two-week journey, Hancock suffered great pain. John Adams described Hancock's appearance when he arrived in York: His "face and eyes are in a most shocking situation, burnt up and much swelled."[11]

Hancock learned en route that the British had already begun to evacuate Philadelphia. Hancock and Holten arrived in York without fanfare and took their seats with the other Massachusetts delegates to vote in favor of the latest draft of the Articles of

Confederation. But the upheaval of the renewed British invasions and the flight to yet another temporary capital once again delayed the vote. And, spurred on by speculators eager for western lands claimed by Virginia, Maryland refused to ratify the Articles until every other state ceded to Congress its claims to western lands.

Even when Virginia offered its western lands exclusively to soldiers, Maryland remained adamant. Virginia remained a point of controversy when Governor Patrick Henry approved sending a small army to seize the Illinois country from the British and their Loyalist auxiliaries, which would enable Virginia to claim the territory by right of conquest. Now, as Hancock signed the latest draft, several states still would not ratify the Articles of Confederation and they would hold out for three more years.

Presiding over the 1778 vote was Henry Laurens of South Carolina. When Hancock had written from Boston to ask for an extension of his leave, Congress had refused and instead voted to make Laurens, who had been filling in for Hancock, president pro tem to fill out the remaining year of Hancock's term. A South Carolina plantation owner, Laurens was closely aligned with the slave-owning Lees of Virginia, who were now allied with Samuel Adams. Hancock was stunned when Laurens refused to yield the chair. Laurens, in effect, became the second president of the United States, and power shifted to the South. Hancock did not put up a fight. He was already weary of life in the small town and the increased factional infighting he found that had taken hold in Congress.

CHAPTER ELEVEN

"Too Precious a Keepsake"

Hancock returned to Congress too late to participate in peace negotiations with Parliament. Fortified by the arrival of the news from Paris that Benjamin Franklin and the American diplomatic mission had signed a treaty of alliance with France, Congress had asserted that the only peace terms it would consider were a complete withdrawal of British troops from the former colonies and recognition of American independence. The British had refused these terms and abandoned the talks. As Hancock began to unpack his baggage, he learned that the British army was beginning to evacuate Philadelphia and retreat to New York City, where they could be supported by the Royal Navy against the expected arrival of the French navy. Congress was to prepare to reconvene in Philadelphia.

Once again, Hancock's homesickness grew worse with the arrival of each mail pouch from Boston with no letter from Dolly.

I wrote you two letters the day before yesterday and this is my seventh letter and not one word have I heard from you. . . . I can by no means in justice to myself continue under such disagreeable circumstances. . . . The mode is so very different from what I have always been accustomed to, that to continue it long would prejudice my health exceedingly. . . . This moment the post arrived and to my very great surprise and disappointment not a single line from Boston. . . . I shall write no more till I hear from you.[1]

While scolding his wife, Hancock forgot the agreement of the Second Continental Congress that there was to be no personal correspondence to or from delegates. Did he know that fellow Massachusetts delegate John Adams had been freely violating the edict and exchanging letters with his wife, Abigail, in Braintree? It was Dolly and not Hancock!

Hancock was still on the road to Philadelphia when Congress reconvened in Philadelphia on July 2 to celebrate the second anniversary of the Declaration of Independence with street parades and fireworks. He celebrated later with delegates and other friends at an elegant banquet at City Tavern. They were entertained by an orchestra of clarinets, oboes, French horns, violins and bass violins. The centerpiece on the head table was "a large baked pudding in the center of which was planted a staff on which was displayed a crimson flag in the midst of which was this emblematic device: An eye, denoting Providence; a label on which was inscribed 'an appeal to heaven'; a man with a drawn sword in his hand and in the other the Declaration of Independency, and at his feet a scroll inscribed 'the Declaratory Acts.'"[2]

The rest of Congress and Philadelphians got to celebrate only four days later when a French fleet under the command of Vice Admiral Count d'Estaing arrived in Delaware Bay, ninety miles south of the city, with Conrad-Alexandre Gérard, the first foreign ambassador to the United States. Hancock led the congressional delegation that welcomed Gérard.

Months earlier, on February 6, 1778, the French foreign minister, Charles Gravier, Count de Vergennes, summoned American diplomats Benjamin Franklin, Silas Deane and Arthur Lee to Versailles. For two years, France had been surreptitiously supplying arms to the Americans to aid them in their fight for independence from France's ancient enemy, the English. French artillery had arrived in time for the Americans to defeat an invading force from Canada, so recently wrested from French colonization; George III's favorite playwright, General John Burgoyne, led the British army at the Battles of Saratoga.

The stunning victory convinced the French monarchy that, with its assistance, the Americans would force the British to recognize their independence. The signing of the United States' first international treaty created a military alliance against the British. The treaty required that neither France nor the United States agree to a separate peace with Britain. American independence was to be a condition of any future peace treaty. In addition, the treaty was intended to promote trade and commercial ties between the two allies.

The signing of the treaty gave Americans the opportunity for joint naval and land operations with the French. The French court chose Admiral Count d'Estaing to lead its first major attempt at coordination with the Americans: an expeditionary force made up of twelve ships of the line and four thousand marines. Sailing from Toulon in April, the force eluded a British attempt to bottle them up in the Mediterranean. After the French fleet escaped, the British were slow to respond, not launching Admiral John Byron (grandfather of the poet Lord Byron) with thirteen ships of the line until June. D'Estaing's orders were to trap the English fleet in Delaware Bay. But that fleet, commanded by Lord Richard Howe, had already sailed for New York City while his brother Sir William Howe evacuated Philadelphia on learning of the Franco-American alliance.

After putting Gérard, the first French *ministre plenipotentiaire*, ashore, d'Estaing decided to tack north to attack New York City after a council of war with Hancock and other congressional leaders. Washington recommended that, whether or not that attack succeeded, d'Estaing's naval and land forces should next attack Newport, Rhode Island, in a joint operation with Continental Army units and New England militia. The city was the British base in Rhode Island—and the last British bastion in New England. Excited at the prospect of finally joining the fight and frustrated by Laurens's succession to the presidency, Hancock decided to resign his seat in Congress and rush back to Boston to take up his post of senior major general of the Massachusetts militia.

In December 1776, General Howe had detached Sir Henry Clinton with a large supporting fleet to seize Newport and hold it with a garrison of three thousand British Regulars, Hessians and Loyalists. The fleet was under the command of Sir Robert Pigot, who had ordered the final bloody assault on Bunker Hill. Pigot's garrison included Edmund Fanning, commander of the Loyalist King's American Regiment and an honors graduate of Yale.

When d'Estaing's fleet found it impossible for his deep-draft ships of the line to cross the shallows at the mouth of New York harbor, he decided to proceed with the first test of collaboration between French and American forces. Washington had decided to rely on the Continental Army commander already in Rhode Island, Major General John Sullivan, to call on the New England states "in the most urgent manner" to raise five thousand militiamen to reinforce his thousand Continentals.

Washington detached two of his most experienced Continental brigades. John Glover's Marblehead fishermen had already proven themselves when they helped Washington's battered army escape entrapment after the debacle on Long Island. James Varnum's brigade included the only all-Black regiment in the Revolutionary army, the First Rhode Island Regiment, which had repulsed Hessian assaults on forts along the Delaware River, slowing the British occupation of Philadelphia. For the Newport campaign, Varnum would lead the First Rhode Island Regiment.

Washington assigned his twenty-year-old protégé, Major General Marie-Joseph Paul Yves Roch Gilbert du Motier, Marquis de Lafayette, to command one division. Washington was well aware that Lafayette was the son-in-law of the Duke d'Ayen, who was head of the French navy and, as such, d'Estaing's commanding officer. Washington sent General Nathanael Greene, a Rhode Island native, to command the other division.

The overall commander of the Americans was to be the quarrelsome Sullivan, whose thousand Continentals were based in Providence. Washington well knew the risk. Sullivan had joined Benedict Arnold's ill-fated expedition to Canada and, after Arnold was wounded and his replacement, General John Thomas, died of smallpox, had assumed command: It had been his decision to abandon the invasion and retreat up Lake Champlain. When he was superseded by Horatio Gates, Sullivan, a delegate to the First

Continental Congress, formally complained to his connections in Philadelphia. They rewarded him by promoting him to the rank of major general.

Washington refused to relieve Sullivan, still considering him a useful officer. As one historian put it, this decision was "not because of any special fitness for the post but because he was more available than any other officer of appropriate rank."[3] But Washington cautioned Sullivan to be sure to defer to the advice of Greene and Lafayette.

~℮~

Arriving in Boston on July 16, Massachusetts's newly minted senior major general John Hancock set about recruiting militiamen. He aimed to exceed Washington's requisition of five thousand New Englanders by drawing on his experience as chairman of the Massachusetts Provincial Congress on the eve of the Revolution. Most of the volunteers were farmers who could afford to enlist for only fifteen days so that they could return to their farms in time for the harvest.

An expert on logistics who had helped the House of Hancock supply the British during two wars against the French, General Hancock managed to pull together provisions, supplies, weapons and ammunition in only three weeks. By August 7, he had crammed a caravan of wagons with supplies for his recruits as well as six carriages for himself with tents, clothes, bedding—and an ample stock of French wine and his favorite Madeira to share with his fellow officers.

Early on the morning of August 8, 1778, Hancock mustered his troops on the Common and mounted his coal-black charger. His

Corps of Cadets, outfitted in splendid new uniforms, stood at attention, awaiting his orders. His helmet plumes whipping in the
breeze and sunlight glinting off his gold epaulets, Hancock raised
his sword and lowered it, the signal to advance. Led by their fifers,
eighty cadets escorted Hancock out of town, followed by an army
of six thousand farmers shouldering their flintlocks. Sullivan
would now have ten thousand Americans to face the three-
thousand-man British force.

Glover's oarsmen shuttled the militia across the Sakonnet River
in eighty-six flat-bottomed boats to the American lines northeast
of Newport. But Hancock arrived with his escort of cadets too late
for the council of war. In any case, it is unlikely that the other more
experienced generals would have listened to the advice of such an
inexperienced militia commander. Without ceremony, Sullivan
brusquely assigned Hancock and his recruits to Lafayette's division.

Ten days earlier, on July 29, d'Estaing's fleet had arrived off
Point Judith, Rhode Island. After making contact with the American generals, d'Estaing welcomed them aboard his flagship for a
council of war to make detailed plans for the assault. Sullivan evi-
dently plunked down a sheaf of plans without allowing for discussion. The tone of exaggerated compliments by d'Estaing in later
correspondence reveals immediate friction between the two allied
leaders. Washington biographer Douglas Southall Freeman wrote,
"Where Washington or Greene would have suggested cooperation,
Sullivan had written in plain, direct words, 'I wish your Excellency
would make a show of landing your troops . . .' And again, 'You will
move your ships . . .'"[4]

The courtly French general turned admiral was unimpressed

by the Yankee country lawyer turned general's preparations. D'Estaing had been promised provisions and water for his thousands of men, who had been at sea for months. There were none. Many of them were suffering from scurvy and unfit for combat. Congress had pledged him thousands of militiamen: "We found that the troops were still at home," d'Estaing wrote in his final report. Lafayette was supposed to bring soldiers from the main Continental Army: "He appeared with nothing but militia."[5]

Yet the French admiral decided to acquiesce to Sullivan's plan. On August 8, d'Estaing's ships were to run the British defenses. The next night, Sullivan was to move his troops from Providence to the northeast tip of Aquidneck Island and prepare to attack to the south. Early the next morning, French marines were to land on the west side of the island, opposite the Americans, while d'Estaing's ships bombarded the British fortifications from the water and the ground troops assailed them. Their joint objective was to crush the British forces in a vise.

After the war council, d'Estaing delicately let Sullivan know he was not entirely enthralled with their relationship: "I fear that you left on my table a plan, which I have had the presumption to keep, because anything made by yourself is too precious a keepsake. . . . I beg you, Sir, to be kind enough to accept some pineapples and two barrels of fresh lemons."[6]

Meanwhile, a second French squadron under Admiral Pierre André de Suffren de Saint-Tropez had led two frigates up the Sakonnet River, causing the British to panic. Three British ships ran aground and were destroyed by their captains; two more frigates and several troop transports were scuttled to block the French fleet from entering Newport Harbor.

~e~

At noon on the same day that Hancock arrived in the American camp, all eyes were straining to see a British fleet commanded by Lord Howe arriving opposite Newport with reinforcements for its outnumbered garrison. Howe's fleet arrived at the worst possible time for the French: Their warships were high up the Middle Channel and their sick were languishing on Conanicut Island, where they could be cut off and destroyed by a British landing force.

Hancock and his militia were busily digging trenches to bottle up Pigot's force at the southwest tip of the island, besiege Newport and bombard the town. Hancock wrote excitedly to Dolly,

> Yesterday we opened one battery on the enemy. They cannonaded the whole day, with no other loss to us but one man killed and two wounded. As soon as the fog clears away this morning, we shall open another battery. We have a strong report that the French fleet has appeared off Newport. If they arrive, our business will soon be over, and hope we shall soon enter Newport.[7]

But when the fog finally lifted, it was to the chagrin of d'Estaing and the French: Twenty-five British ships of the line, the fleet of Lord Howe, had arrived overnight and threatened to bottle up the French fleet in Narragansett Bay before it could land its marines to support the Americans.

At that moment, d'Estaing heard the American siege guns open fire. A courier arrived from Sullivan with news that the British had withdrawn their troops from the northern end of the island and were pulling them back toward Newport to oppose the American siege. Without consulting d'Estaing and totally ignoring the allies' plan—Sullivan's own plan—Sullivan was leading his troops across the island to occupy the British works. To d'Estaing, this constituted a serious breach of military etiquette. But far worse was that the Americans were landing before the French without prior notification to d'Estaing. The punctilious d'Estaing now had to decide whether he should adhere to their original plan or turn to meet this new threat from the British.

The wind made the decision for him. A strong southerly forced the French to stay inside the bay while Admiral Byron's vessel and four more ships of the line, earlier hindered by the wind from arriving in time to join Lord Howe, overtook Howe's fleet. On the morning of the tenth, the wind shifted to the north. D'Estaing ordered his marines back aboard the ships and set sail with them, choosing to attack the British fleet before it could bottle him up in the bay. Howe, surprised, also made sail to keep the weather gauge. For the next twenty-four hours the two fleets maneuvered, seeking the advantage.

On the night of August 11, violent gusts of wind scattered both fleets. For two days and nights, a West Indian hurricane battered the ships. D'Estaing's flagship, the eighty-gun *Languedoc*, lost all her masts; her rudder was smashed. Two fifty-gun British ships closed in while the British man-of-war *Preston* attacked the eighty-gun *Tonnant*, which had only one mast intact. The leviathans battled inconclusively until darkness. Both sides intended to resume fighting the next day, but the damage to both left them unseaworthy. As more French ships arrived, Howe decided to withdraw and limp to New York to refit.

Drenched in their trenches through the forty-eight-hour storm, the Americans still expected reinforcement from the French.

Sullivan opened more siege lines, expecting the French to join him. But d'Estaing refused to disembark his marines and instead sailed off to Boston to make repairs, ignoring Hancock's and Lafayette's entreaties. News that the French were withdrawing set off whole-sale desertions in the militia. Overnight, Hancock became a general without an army.

Again consulting no one, Sullivan ordered complete with-drawal from the island. In a brilliant rearguard action protecting Sullivan's force, Varnum's Black troops repelled with "desperate valor" three "furious assaults" by Hessian Regulars. Overnight, Glover's fishermen once again averted catastrophe as they rescued five thousand militiamen and Sullivan's twelve hundred Continen-tals from a British counterattack.[8]

⌒₂⌒

After doing little damage with their weapons, the leaders of the armies now unsheathed their quills and attacked each other. In his general orders, Sullivan blamed the fiasco on the French. No sooner had the French set sail than Sullivan and his generals signed an offi-cial letter of protest to Congress alleging that d'Estaing's actions

> stained the honor of France, are contrary to the interests of His Most Christian Majesty, are most pernicious to the prosperity of the United States, and [are] an outrageous of-fense upon the alliance between the two nations.
>
> The General cannot help lamenting the sudden and unex-pected departure of the French fleet. . . . He yet hopes the event will prove America is able to procure with her own arms that [which] her allies refused to assist her in obtaining.[9]

Infuriated by Sullivan's undiplomatic assault, Lafayette, who had opposed d'Estaing's departure, nevertheless hotly defended his countryman against Sullivan's charge of desertion. He wrote to Washington that he had seen more fighting among the Americans than against the British: "I am more upon a wartime footing in the American lines than when I came near the British lines at Newport."[10]

Becoming aware that any illusions he might have ever harbored about being victorious on the field of battle were now at an end, Hancock steered clear of the shoals of vituperation. He returned to Boston, where he was welcomed like a conquering hero, with his Corps of Cadets riding through the city to the cheering of a crowd that soon was marching along with him.

Only in private correspondence did Hancock make known his views. When rivals in the Massachusetts General Court blamed him for the wholesale desertion of his militia and called for his censure, he wrote to Jeremiah Powell, president of the Massachusetts House of Representatives, that the blame

> must not fall upon us. . . . The expedition was undertaken in full confidence that the fleets and the troops would cooperate with us. . . . I am exceedingly mortified . . . and I could almost wish that I had not been here to undergo such feelings, which I scarce before experienced. . . . [T]he failure must center with the [French] fleet. . . .[11]

Little if anything about the debacle that d'Estaing put in writing has survived. A nobleman loyal to King Louis XVI until he, too, was guillotined in the French Revolution, he had misgivings about assisting revolutionaries but had probably been motivated by an inbred antipathy to the British, who had taken him prisoner in the intercolonial wars in India. Oddly enough, he had been paroled by the brother of General Pigot, the British commander at Newport. As for d'Estaing's relationship with Sullivan, he was clearly reluctant to take orders from a commoner. When he learned that Sullivan was a self-taught country lawyer, he would comment only that Sullivan must have had many unhappy clients.

The Rhode Island campaign and Hancock's role in it received little coverage in American patriotic newspapers but proved irresistible to James Rivington's Loyalist *New-York Gazetteer*, which lampooned the affair:

> In dread array their tatter'd crew,
> Advanced with colours spread Sir,
> Their fifes play'd *Yankee Doodle* do,
> King Hancock at their Head Sir.[12]

John Hancock
by John Singleton Copley, 1772

Thomas Hancock
by John Singleton Copley

Lydia Henchman Hancock
by John Singleton Copley

Dorothy Quincy Hancock
by John Singleton Copley

John Adams
by Gilbert Stuart

View of Beacon Hill from Boston Commons, 1768

Hancock House exact replica,
Ticonderoga, New York

Second Continental Congress, 1775,
by Robert Edge Pine

Signing of the Declaration of Independence
by John Trumbull

Declaration of Independence

John Hancock, George Washington, and Thomas Jefferson
atop the Declaration of Independence

John Hancock's signature

John Hancock, First President
of the American Congress
and Governor of Massachusetts

Gilbert du Motier,
Marquis de Lafayette

John George Washington Hancock
by Charles Willson Peale

CHAPTER TWELVE

"The Frenchmen Ate Voraciously"

Ignoring his critics, Hancock decided that the debacle in Rhode Island had caused far more damage to the independence movement than an initial failure at integrating French and American commands. While making no public statement, he wrote immediately to Washington to urge him to intervene. In turn, Washington wrote to d'Estaing to thank him for his efforts and to Sullivan to demand that he desist from any further contact with the French. Then he wrote to Congress to pass a resolution praising d'Estaing: Faced with a hurricane and superior British forces, he had "behaved as a brave and wise officer."[1]

Within two days of returning to Boston, General Hancock—mustering his wealth, his popularity and his wife's social connections—launched a sustained diplomatic campaign to salvage the fledgling Franco-American alliance. A lifelong Bostonian, he was well aware that for the past hundred fifty years New

Englanders had been weaned on hatred for the French and for Ro-
man Catholicism, their stories and sermons filled with black-robed
clergy accompanying scalping parties. In his own lifetime, he had
seen his neighbors twice board ships and sail off to Canada to fight
the French. His own family wealth had been built on the huge
profits from contracts to arm and feed the British defenders. The
sight of the uniforms of some fourteen thousand French sailors
and marines, who would have been the Bostonians' mortal enemies
only fifteen years earlier, jarred many of the now outnumbered ten
thousand townspeople who had not fled with the Loyalists to Canada and England.

When French procurement officers sought the skilled labor of
the town's shipfitters to repair their battered vessels, Bostonians
either flatly refused or said the work could take years, given how
busy they were. Brawls between townsmen and visiting sailors were
part of everyday life in a port, but even the sound of the French
language set off violent confrontations. When a French crew member attempted to come ashore, he risked bodily harm. And when
the French set up a bakery to produce their own distinctive loaves
for French sailors, the baker tried to bar Bostonians, triggering a
riot that left many French wounded. A young French nobleman,
the Comte de Saint-Sauveur, tried to intervene and was killed.
Hancock's arrival on the scene and his promise, as commanding
general, to officially honor the ill-fated count with a monument
cooled French tempers.

The sight of French officers laying out artillery batteries at Hull
across the harbor from Boston led to a formal protest to the General Court. When defending his countrymen, d'Estaing recounted
common beliefs among the Americans:

That the troops of his most Christian majesty burn and destroy the fences of the inhabitants of the town. . . . That they take from them their wood, their hays from the cocks, open their barns and waste their grain. That they take up their spread flax and convert it to beds. That they take their cooking utensils from their houses take from them their fruit and poultry. That they destroy their potato yards and their cornfields . . .[2]

Gradually, frequent visits to worksites by the ever more popular Hancock resulted in shipfitters agreeing to aid the French. They set to work measuring and cutting masts, and cordwainers strung miles of hemp in the ropewalks of the North End to replace shredded rigging.

It took even less time for the Hancocks to decide to deploy their own particular form of diplomacy, beginning with an invitation to Admiral d'Estaing and Lafayette to a formal dinner atop Beacon Hill. Dressed in purple velvet, Hancock was piped aboard the *Languedoc* to deliver the invitations personally. Hancock sent his carriage to bring the admiral and the young general to the Hancocks' glittering new banquet hall. As they entered, Lafayette paused before a portrait of Washington that Hancock had commissioned a year before, probably by Charles Willson Peale in Philadelphia. Lafayette asked Hancock if he had a copy. Hancock did, but he already intended to present it as a gesture of friendship to d'Estaing.

At this awkward moment, Hancock promised to have a copy made for Lafayette and went on to present the original to the admiral. Lafayette later attested that he had never seen "a man so glad to possess a sweetheart's picture as the admiral was to have this one of Washington."[3] As the portrait was hoisted aboard his flagship, d'Estaing ordered a royal salute. He placed the painting above the fireplace in his cabin and draped it with laurel wreaths.

As her contribution to the couple's diplomacy, Dolly deployed culinary skills learned at the elbow of Aunt Lydia; she commenced with the banquet for d'Estaing and Lafayette. Eventually, she hosted virtually every officer in the fleet for either breakfast, dinner or *petit souper.* In his barn, Hancock kept a flock of a hundred fifty turkeys. On days with dinner guests, Hancock's servants killed an average of four of the fattened birds, then cleaned and plucked them before cooking them in a large oven. One day, an unplucked bird caught fire. To the amusement of the French, the quills exploded loudly; the guests politely remained silent about the attendant stench.

Another day, Hancock invited thirty officers for breakfast.

The Count brought up almost all the officers of the fleet, midshipmen included. Mr. H sent word for her [Mrs. H] to get breakfast for 120 more, and she was obliged to prepare it as they were coming into the house. They spread twelve pounds of butter onto bread and sent to the guard on the Common to milk all the cows and bring her the milk. She sent to all the neighbors for cake. The Frenchmen ate voraciously, and one of them drank seventeen cups of tea at the table.

The midshipmen made sad destruction of the fruit in the garden. Count d'Estaing, however, politely said he would make it up to her and told her she must come down to the fleet and bring all her friends with her. True enough, Dolly did—and carried a party of five hundred with her. They were "all transported in the boats of the fleet and stayed all day. The Count . . . asked me to pull a string to fire a gun," which, half frightened to death, she "did, and found she had given a signal for a *feu de joie* to the fleet, the whole bunch of which immediately commenced firing, and they were all enveloped in smoke and stunned with the noise. Such a noise she never heard before, nor wishes to again."[4]

Having decided to devote his fortune to cementing relations with the French if necessary, Hancock sponsored in Faneuil Hall late that September a gala reception at which the admiral could meet five hundred of the leading citizens of Boston and surrounding towns. In his general's uniform, Hancock presided and offered thirteen toasts to the United States and thirteen to the king of France, each one accompanied by a thirteen-gun salute. When someone lifted his glass to the Continental Congress, an aide-de-camp looked at Hancock. Hancock shook his head. After the banquet, James Warren, increasingly aloof as a Samuel Adams partisan, came up to Hancock and demanded to know why he had done so. Hancock replied that the Congress had been subsumed in the toast to the United States.

Not satisfied, Warren pursued his objection, insisting to friends that Hancock had deliberately insulted the Congress to suggest that he wanted the military exalted over the civilian. Angered when he heard the allegation, Hancock declined when the House of Representatives invited him to its next session, replying that while a flare-up of gout prevented him, "I confess my indisposition has been increased by the reflection which Malice has circulated against me since the entertainment of Friday last."[5]

At the same time, Warren acknowledged Hancock's achievement with the French in a letter to Adams, who was attending Congress in Philadelphia:

> [Boston's] disposition at first appeared to cause an odium on the Count and to discredit our new allies [but] seems to have entirely subsided and has been succeeded by the most perfect good humor. . . . General Hancock has made the most magnificent entertainments for the Count and his officers, both at his own and at the public houses.

But Warren qualified his compliment. He lamented that "all manner of extravagance prevails here in dress, furniture, equipage and living amidst the distress of the public and multitudes of individuals. How long the manners of the people will remain uncorrupted and fit to enjoy that liberty you have so long contended for I know not. I fear you have lost your labor; they will soon be fit to receive some ambitious master."[6]

The growing rift between the Hancock and Samuel Adams factions now broke into the open. This violation of the old Whig principle of unity, which until then had papered over many differences of opinion among the revolutionaries, worried Samuel Phillips Savage, an old friend of both men. As the French departed, he wrote to Adams in an attempt to restore peace between them:

> I most sincerely value you as my friend, but as much as I value you my country lies nearer my heart, and I greatly fear the differences now subsisting between you and your once strong friend Mr. H. may greatly hurt her interest: the effects are already visible; the enemies of America triumph in the

strife and are taking every measure to increase the flame. The friends of their country cannot stand by idle spectators. They see the increasing contest with weeping eyes and aching hearts and wish a reconciliation.

Permit me my friend to attempt (however inadequate to the task) a restoration of friendship between two who once were dear to each other and who now perhaps from mistakes and misapprehensions seem so distant.[7]

Samuel Adams's response to Savage made it clear that there would be no reconciliation anytime soon:

You call upon me by all that is sacred to forgive him. Do you think he has injured me? If he has, should he not ask forgiveness? No man ever found me inexorable. I do not wish him to ask me to forgive him: this would be too humiliating. If he is conscious of having done or designed me an injury, let him do so no more, and I will promise to forgive and forget him too or, I would add, to do him all the service in my power. But this is needless; it is not in my power to serve him. *He* is above it.[8]

⁓

Abigail Adams, a more placid than usual invitee at the farewell for the French, reported to her husband, John, in Paris that Hancock's grand reception for the town and for the fleet was the finest affair ever held on American soil. "Comte d'Estaing has been exceedingly polite to me," she wrote. As a consequence, she added, "I have been more desirous to take notice of them [the French] as they have been neglected in the town of Boston."[9]

At the end of October 1778, as d'Estaing and his fleet prepared
to set sail for warmer waters, Hancock sponsored a grand ball in
the concert hall he had helped to build for the town. He invited
some two hundred leading citizens. Samuel Adams's adherents
mostly refused to attend, regarding the ball as an amoral extravagance given at the expense of the sufferings of the troops. Hancock
paid for the evening, as he did for all the other entertainments he
had sponsored. He considered these events an investment in the
independence of the new nation. There seems to have been at least
one long-term dividend: In public, before he sailed, Admiral
d'Estaing pledged to Hancock that the French fleet would never
again fail the United States.

Hancock's informal diplomacy, undertaken ten years before the
United States created a formal Department of State, paid an immediate dividend as well. Gold and silver coins—so long a rare
sight in cash-starved New England—revived Boston's economy.
The French fleet's procurement officers bought provisions for the
fleet—along with the timber and rigging to repair the ships—
and all ranks shopped for clothing, souvenirs and paper for
letters home.

The next summer, when another French fleet paid a call on Boston, Lafayette returned with a new ambassador, the Chevalier de
La Luzerne. Hancock entertained once again, this time aboard the
frigate *Hermione*. But the Hancocks' larder was bare, and finding
enough food on short notice proved difficult. Feigning despera-
tion, Hancock wrote to his brother-in-law Henry Quincy, in
Braintree:

The ambassadors are to dine with me and I have nothing to
give them, nor from the present prospect of our market do I

see that I shall be able to get anything in town. I beg you to recommend to my man Harry where he may get chickens, geese, hams, partridges, mutton, etc. that will save my reputation . . . and by all means some butter . . . Is there any good melons or peaches or any good fruit near you? Can I get a good turkey? . . . I dine on board the frigate tomorrow.[10]

—⁓—

By this time, John Hancock had been reelected as a delegate to the Continental Congress, moderator of the Boston Town Meeting, senior major general of the militia and speaker of the House of Representatives. He enjoyed such popularity that he had the power to resolve, almost single-handedly, the thorniest political issues. As the war shifted south and allowed Bostonians a respite to rebuild their city, they faced vexing unresolved issues, among them the future fate of Loyalists who had fled with the British in 1776.

Besieged by a New England army of sixteen thousand, more than fifteen hundred Loyalists had crowded aboard British ships that took them to Nova Scotia; another four hundred Bostonians had since followed them, decreasing Boston's population by thirty percent. Among them were mariners and merchants, including Hancock's former business partner Charles Ward Apthorp; shopkeepers and distillers; doctors and lawyers. Notable exiled Bostonians included Thomas Hutchinson and his sons and cousins, the Olivers and Sir Francis Bernard and his family.

Former provincial officials who fled included Hancock's friend Jonathan Sewall and his wife, Esther, Dorothy Quincy Hancock's sister. As both attorney general of Massachusetts province and Admiralty judge of Nova Scotia, Sewall had been a high-ranking royal official who remained resolutely loyal to Parliament. The couple remained in Boston for the British occupation and the siege of Washington's army, but in September 1775, even before Evacuation Day in March, they boarded a ship that carried them to England and into exile. Since then, Esther's only link with her family in Massachusetts had been packages of food and clothing that Hancock and Company could deliver to her in London, along with longing letters from Dorothy.

A number of the Loyalists now petitioned to be allowed to return rather than face permanent exile in Britain or Canada. Many wrote directly to Hancock.

While many Bostonians protested their return as a matter of political principle, others thought that "the wealth they will bring will more than counter-balance the detriment." Presenting a resolution arguing for a law to bar their repatriation, Hancock adamantly opposed the return of

those professed enemies to our rights and liberties, the first fomenters of our present troubles who have left this country and aided the British tyrant in his worse than savage measures to deprive Americans of everything that ought to be held dear and sacred by any people.

Despite the pain it would cause both Dolly's family and himself personally, Hancock remained adamant. He urged his colleagues in the legislature to support a new law that would ensure that "such traitors could never return and enjoy in common the fruits of what our immortal patriots have bled and toiled to procure us."[11]

The legislature followed Hancock's leadership, delivering its answer on May 1, 1779. Massachusetts would adhere to the recommendation of the Continental Congress and seize the property of residents who had "forfeited the right to protection." Massachusetts's act authorized the appropriation of the property of every Loyalist "who did withdraw himself from the jurisdiction of the [Massachusetts] government and thereby deprive it of the benefit of his personal services." The confiscated property was to "escheat, enure, and accrue to the sole use and benefit of the government and people of this state."[12] The legislature subsequently published a blacklist of nearly four hundred Loyalists whose estates were to be confiscated and who would be arrested and deported if they set foot again in Massachusetts. If the proscription stood, Dorothy would never see her sister again.

CHAPTER THIRTEEN

"I Have Lost Many Thousands"

With each war involving the arrival of troops and sailors in colonial America from England, smallpox epidemics had followed. In their aftermath, more and more colonists in coastal towns had fled westward, establishing new settlements that became towns. But political power remained in eastern ports. To carry on any legal business in Massachusetts required long and costly trips and stays in Boston. In New Hampshire, colonists had to travel to Portsmouth.

A major cause of the Revolution had been Americans' objection to taxation without representation by the British Parliament. By mid-1777, farmers in western Massachusetts began to demand a state constitution that would give them a voice in the state's legislation equal to that of the merchants in coastal counties. According to western reformers, every incorporated town should have been entitled to send a representative to the legislature. Objecting, the more populous eastern towns insisted on proportional representation. In June 1777, over the objections of several towns, the General Court reorganized itself into a constitutional convention to draw up a new frame of government for Massachusetts.

A key component of any new form would certainly be a chief of state—a governor—and John Hancock had little doubt that he would be chosen. In fact, he believed he deserved to be. But the creation of a new Massachusetts government was sure to be a divisive fight, and he decided to remain aloof from the fray and leave the combat to surrogates. If the measure passed, he had no doubt he would receive the prize of the governorship; if it failed, he would not be accused of designing the office for himself.

In a joint session, the House of Representatives and the executive council formed a committee to draw up the document. Hancock remained on his usual committees in the House and left the infighting to his allies John Pickering and Thomas Cushing. By February 1778, the committee had worked out a compromise. To allay the fears of easterners that they would be outvoted in a legislature with equal representation for every town, they proposed that each town could send one delegate but that the town would have to pay his expenses, putting the office beyond the reach of many smaller, cash-poor settlements. And to satisfy westerners' suspicions of a strong executive, Pickering and Cushing proposed denying a veto to the governor.

On February 28, the convention passed the draft constitution and sent it out to the towns for ratification. It pleased no one; some thought it was too powerful, others too weak. The convention's failure to include a provision to make amendments doomed it, leaving the voters either to accept it entirely or reject it outright. In a counterconvention in coastal Essex County, delegates gathered in Ipswich and protested that the document included no bill of rights and was far too liberal on property qualifications. The draft constitution was overwhelming rejected by a strong majority.

The lack of a constitution continued to rankle westerners, who clamored for a more equitable form of government. In August, delegates from Berkshire towns demanded that the General Court call a convention to draft a new constitution. The Court at first ignored them, but by February 1779 it decided that citizens should be allowed to make their views known. Each Town Meeting was to put two questions to a vote: Did the citizens want a new constitution, and should there be another statewide convention to draft one? By a two-to-one margin, towns voted in the affirmative to both questions. In June, the Court called for the election of delegates. John Hancock was among the delegates selected from Boston.

Meeting for the first time on September 1, the delegates elected James Bowdoin of Boston as the convention's president. While drafting the document was assigned to a committee of thirty, the real work fell to a subcommittee of three. Once more, Hancock chose to remain aloof, wanting to appear disinterested even while he remained fully engaged in public affairs. He had been elected speaker of the House, a delegate to Congress, and captain of the castle, a paid ceremonial post that named him commander of the fortifications on Castle Island in Boston Harbor. He voiced no objection when Bowdoin appointed himself and John and Samuel Adams to the drafting committee. John Adams, home on leave from his diplomatic post in Paris, would write the constitution.

Beginning with "A Declaration of the Rights of the Inhabitants of the Commonwealth of Massachusetts," the document created a relatively conservative form of government adhering to Whig principles favored by radicals as well as by moderate easterners while holding off the demands of western reformers. In March 1780, the convention approved Adams's work and sent the constitution to all two hundred ninety towns. One hundred eighty-one towns responded. By June, enough had approved the document that the convention declared that it was ratified and that it would take effect in October. While an election ordinarily would not have taken place until the following spring, the convention decided to hold one in the fall.

No one was surprised when, on September 4, John Hancock was elected the commonwealth's first governor by a three-to-one margin in every county, winning a stunning victory over fifteen other candidates by receiving more than eleven thousand votes out of the total 12,281. Hancock's principal opposition came from Bowdoin, also a Harvard graduate ten years older than Hancock. A wealthy landlord and speculator in New England real estate, Bowdoin had inherited a fortune from his Huguenot merchant family and had enhanced his wealth through trade and shipbuilding. Bowdoin's reputation had been somewhat tarnished when he was too ill and had declined to serve after being elected to the First Continental Congress and then had held no public office during the war. Actually, Bowdoin might have been suffering from tuberculosis; moreover, his daughter was married to a Loyalist. In Maine, much of his undeveloped Kennebec lands had been taken over by squatters, leaving him with little sympathy for hardscrabble backcountry farmers. Most of his support came from the mercantile port towns of Essex and Suffolk Counties. Despite being supported by Samuel Adams, Bowdoin received a mere 888 votes.

The outcome of the election for a lieutenant governor was less clear-cut. No candidate received a majority. Under the new constitution, the selection was thrown into the House and the Senate.

They elected Bowdoin, who received the most votes, but he declined to serve under Hancock. They then offered the position to James Warren, also an ally of Samuel Adams, but he, too, declined to serve under Hancock. Placing third in voting was Hancock's close friend Thomas Cushing. He accepted. Robert Treat Paine, another of Hancock's allies and a signer of the Declaration of Independence, was elected attorney general. Hancock had made a clean sweep of all the executive offices—and his votes were drawn from every economic level, occupation and region.

As was his style, Hancock decided to assume the office with a flourish. At noon on Wednesday, October 25, 1780, a "remarkably fair and pleasant" autumn day, to the tolling of the town's church bells, Hancock climbed into his favorite yellow carriage for the procession to the State House. Forty-three years old and slender, Hancock wore a crimson velvet waistcoat with gold trim and matching buttons and an embroidered white vest. Escorted by one hundred mounted men of the Corps of Cadets with swords drawn, he paraded through streets lined with cheering well-wishers.

At the State House, the General Court dissolved itself and the members of the newly constituted state legislature took their seats. Lieutenant Governor Thomas Cushing administered the oath of office of the president of the Senate—the newly named upper house of the General Court—to his close friend and mentor. In a plain one-minute inaugural speech, Hancock pledged "to devote my whole time and services in my country's cause to the utter exclusion of all private benefits, even to the end of the war."[1]

The secretary of the assembly, Cushing's son-in-law, John Avery, stepped out onto a small balcony overlooking the site of the Boston Massacre where royal governors had once spoken. He introduced the new governor: "His Excellency John Hancock Esquire, Governor of the Commonwealth of Massachusetts." To the roar of the crowd, cannon on Fort Hill and Castle Island and ships in the harbor fired thirteen-gun salutes. Hancock, Cushing, Avery and dozens of their followers walked over to Brattle Square Church for prayers of thanksgiving. Hancock's close friend the Reverend Samuel Cooper delivered the first-ever election sermon. Then they marched on to Faneuil Hall for a celebration that lasted until dawn the next day—to the disgust of Samuel Adams. He denounced Hancock for presenting himself with

> more pomp and parade than is consistent with the sober republican principle. . . . Why should this new era be introduced with entertainments expensive and tending to dissipate the minds of the people . . . [and] promote superfluity of distress and ornament when it is as much as they can bear to support the expense of clothing a naked army? Will vanity and levity ever be the stability of government . . . ?[2]

Adams's political lieutenant, James Warren, echoed the complaint, accusing Hancock of introducing "a plague of feasts and entertainments more suitable to effeminacy and ridiculous manners of Asiatic slavery than the hardy and sober manners of a New England republic."

Despite the scolding, Bostonians, exhausted by five years of war and privation, went on celebrating with a "round of balls and glittering entertainments" that lasted long after weary, newly minted governor Hancock went to bed atop Beacon Hill.[3]

~e~

On October 31, 1780, John Hancock stood before the Massachusetts legislature and delivered the progenitor of the "state of the state" address. His longest speech was in itself a historic event. Just as no one in America had ever before been able to elect their own chief executive, no one had ever heard that executive address the people as the masters of their own government. Hancock was aware of the "distinction" of the moment, which had placed him "at the head of this Commonwealth by the free suffrage of citizens."

Hancock turned then to "the weighty business that lies before you," underscoring the new risks that came with self-government. Independence from British rule meant the absence of British laws or any other laws until new ones were enacted. He laid out a practical agenda, beginning with defense. While the war had moved south, its outcome was far from certain. Massachusetts must continue to contribute its share of men, arms, ammunition and tax revenues to maintain Washington's Continental Army. In addition, still acting as senior major general, he urged the state militia to expand to defend the western border and the legislature to create a naval militia to protect the ports and coastline from British raids.

Calling Massachusetts a "bulwark of democracy," Hancock emphasized the need to restore and improve the state's public schools, which had been devastated by the war. Even his alma mater, Boston Latin School, had been shuttered. As a British brigade had marched off to Lexington and Concord, the school's legendary Master John Lovell had proclaimed, "School's done; war's begun." Scores more schoolmasters had exchanged their ferules for muskets, their schools starved by lack of money. Many, like Lovell, were Loyalists who fled to Canada with the British.

Hancock would never forget how much he had benefited from the education his uncle and aunt provided for him. He urged the revival of Massachusetts Bay Colony's 1647 Old Deluder Satan law, which required that every town with more than fifty families maintain a common school to provide all its children—including servants—an elementary education, including how to read, write and calculate. Praising "our wise and magnanimous ancestors" for their care in establishing the "University at Cambridge" and grammar schools in several larger towns and noting that the schools had been "no small support to the cause of liberty," he asked the legislature to increase teachers' salaries.

Providing relief for widows and orphans must become a priority, Hancock declared, rather than having the population depend on the largesse of public-spirited citizens, an unmistakable reminder to many of his auditors that Hancock contributed large amounts of food, housing and firewood to distressed Bostonians. He also called for a law "for the suppression of idleness, dissipation and all those vices that are particularly inimical to Free Republics." Since a majority of Massachusetts's citizens still considered Congregationalism to be the official religion, Hancock asked the assembly to pass a law designating it as the official state religion and requiring "due observation of the Lord's Day." The lawmakers would soon respond by banning all vices and fining anyone who failed to attend church for three consecutive months a stiff ten shillings ($75 today).[4]

Deciding that his most pressing duty was to work vigorously to contribute to the continuing war effort, Hancock pushed the legislature to meet quotas for the men and supplies allocated by Congress. But his task was made more difficult by Britain's new strategy since France had entered the war. Making New York City their base in the North, the British carried the fighting to the South. Indeed, there had been no major battle in the North since the summer of 1779, when the Americans had tried unsuccessfully to dislodge the British from the Penobscot region.

Without an immediate threat to their homes, farmers were reluctant to abandon their families and fields to join the Continental Army despite increasingly generous recruitment bounties of land. Hancock instead focused on enlarging the state militia. He earned the praise of General William Heath, commander of the Northern Department, for seeing that Massachusetts's militia arrived "more punctually and are nearer complete than from any other state [New York excepted]."[5]

By autumn of 1781, the main British army, led by Lord Cornwallis, had become trapped on the Yorktown Peninsula of eastern Virginia. Washington had quick-marched his army, with reinforcements of French troops, around New York City. Under the command of Lafayette, the joint force of sixteen thousand besieged the British while a French fleet trapped and destroyed a British fleet in the Battle of the Capes. After Cornwallis surrendered his army on October 19, 1781, Washington shifted his army north to envelop the remaining British army in New York. He dispatched Lafayette to bring the news to Hancock in Boston. Lafayette arrived with Jean-Baptiste Donatien de Vimeur, comte de Rochambeau at his side and celebrated on Beacon Hill with a lavish dinner with the Hancocks.

While negotiations in Paris would take two more years, the prospect of peace encouraged Hancock to restore order in his business enterprises. He knew he was still rich, but he had been forced to neglect his affairs by the pressures of his official offices. Relying almost entirely on managers he had trained, he had lost track of taxes he owed on considerable real estate holdings in New

Hampshire. Late in 1781, he discovered that he and his partners had lost twenty thousand acres of land to confiscation for failure to pay taxes.

By this time, Hancock's two best friends, whom he had previously entrusted with the management of his affairs, had died. Before Hancock had gone off to Congress in 1775, he appointed William Palfrey, whom he had personally trained and promoted from managing Store Number 4 in Faneuil Hall, to become chief clerk of the House of Hancock.

After the rout of American forces on Long Island in 1776, Hancock, as president of Congress, had entrusted Palfrey to negotiate an exchange of prisoners taken in the Battle of Brooklyn with the British commander, Sir William Howe. Palfrey's success had led Hancock to recommend him to Congress to become paymaster general of the Eastern Department of the Continental Army. Hancock subsequently asked Palfrey to take on his feckless younger brother, Ebenezer, as an assistant paymaster. In both posts, Palfrey had performed so capably and scrupulously that, in 1780, Congress rewarded him with an appointment as consul general and commercial agent for Congress in France.

Hancock and Palfrey became so close that, in December 1780, just before Hancock's protégé sailed aboard the sixteen-gun sloop *Shillala*, Palfrey wrote to Hancock to ask him to continue to watch out for his wife and two sons. Palfrey had offered his wife the choice of making the perilous winter crossing of the Atlantic with him or remaining in Boston with their two sons. She decided to remain ashore. Palfrey wrote to Hancock, "Mrs. Palfrey will stand in need of every attention to make my absence supportable and I beg leave to solicit a continuance of your favours."[6]

The ship never arrived in France; it sank with all hands.

Devastated by the loss, Hancock honored Palfrey's entreaty and supported his wife and two sons, paying for the boys to attend Harvard.

Meanwhile, William Bant, a former merchant and Son of Liberty who had succeeded Palfrey as chief clerk in the House of Hancock and protected Hancock's businesses and properties during the British occupation, died while Palfrey was at sea. And then Reverend Samuel Cooper—Hancock's close friend, confidant and minister—also died, leaving Hancock deeply depressed.

Because he didn't have the help and support of his close friends and business associates and was focusing all his attention on politics, Hancock's financial affairs took a beating. In addition to his losses in New Hampshire and his taxes on real estate holdings in Connecticut, Hancock discovered that he was owed, by a conservative estimate, £12,000 (about $1.8 million). Short of cash, he decided he needed someone to help collect some of the debts owed to him. He hired William Hoskins, "a gentleman conversant in business" who was known to be skilled at dunning. Hancock asked Hoskins to visit Bant's widow in Groton, Massachusetts; there Hoskins discovered that Hancock's financial records were incomplete. With Bant's widow's help and the deceased man's own meticulous records, a clear picture of Hancock's finances slowly emerged.

Hoskins pursued and persuaded some of Massachusetts's leading citizens to begin to pay up in words that Governor Hancock could have hardly employed. To General Joseph Palmer of Braintree, he wrote:

> It is his Excellency's desire that as soon as your health and
> business will admit coming to Boston that you will call upon
> him at his Boston seat and inform him what has been done
> and what further is likely to be done toward accomplishing

and completing the long-labored affair between him and yourself.[7]

With Hancock's support, Hoskins dunned the elite debtors of illustrious political families. Firebrand patriot lawyer James Otis, drifting in and out of sanity, was asked to remit £400 (about $60,000 today). James Warren, close ally of Samuel Adams, resisted and attempted to strike a bargain: Would Hancock "throw aside the interest?" Hancock acquiesced to this "not entirely pleasing" accommodation after Warren made a payment, but Hoskins argued that "the governor thinks that this balance ought to have been immediately paid to him," since he had been patient "for years back" while Warren had "not availed himself of any consideration for [his] use of it."[8]

Hoskins hunted and hounded debtors beyond New England, writing to merchants from Nova Scotia (one merchant owed several hundred pounds) to London, where the House of Hancock's former agent owed £720 (more than $100,000 today). Hancock insisted that British merchants owed him more than he owed them, and as peace was restored between the two nations, Hancock intended to revive the lucrative trade between them with a clean ledger book. At the same time, Boston's gossips whispered that Hancock himself was notoriously slow at paying his own bills.

As the British began to evacuate their armies in November 1783, Hancock set about resuming trade with England. The majority of Boston's merchants were Loyalists who had departed with the British, leaving little serious competition in the city. Hancock wrote to James Scott, his friend and most trusted ship's captain, in London, where, after he had sold Hancock's last cargo of whale oil in 1775, he remained throughout the war:

I have lost many thousands sterling but, thank God my country is saved and, by the smile of Heaven, I am a free and independent man. . . . The return of peace gives a countenance to retire from public life and enjoy the sweets of calm domestic retirement and pursue business for my own amusement. I am determined . . . to resign my command of this Commonwealth and return to private life after the many fatigues I have gone through. . . .

Hancock told Scott he was sending a debt collector to London. He gave Scott his power of attorney and authorized him to make a trading arrangement with a new agent. Then Scott was to buy a ship and sail it to Boston. In addition to luxury goods to sell in Hancock's stores, its cargo was to include a new "stone yellow" coach lined with crimson velvet, with Hancock's coat of arms and the House of Hancock's motto, *Nul Plaisir Sans Peine*, on its doors. In addition, Hancock ordered six dozen of the "very best pewter plates . . . Oval or long dishes for Saturday's salt fish . . . My crest is to be engraved in each dish and plate." Finally, he ordered new furniture, including twelve "stuff-backed chairs" and a matching sofa to match one "much worn."[9]

CHAPTER FOURTEEN

"A Delicate Business"

John Hancock tried to avoid controversies, but one in particular continued to dog him. As the governor, he sat ex officio as president of the Board of Overseers of his alma mater, Harvard. According to the 1936 chronicle of the university, *Three Centuries of Harvard*, authored by another distinguished alumnus and later admiral, Samuel Eliot Morison, Hancock was "the wealthiest young merchant in the province" when he was honored with appointment as the college's treasurer. "Politics, and a desire to secure for the college a part of the fortune of which John was being rapidly relieved by his political friends, doubtless account for this appointment." As Morison recounted,

> He had given sundry books and subscribed £500 sterling [$75,000] toward the restoration of the library, carpeted the second floor of Harvard Hall, richly paneled the philosophy chamber and presented a "curious coralline on its natural

bed" to the new museum. In consequence of the "repeated demonstrations of his affectionate regards to Harvard College" he had been "invited to dine in the Hall" and "sit with the Governors of the College" at every "public entertainment" and sit for his portrait at the College's expense, for which Mr. Copley rendered a bill of forty guineas. . . .[1]

Appointed shortly after his Massacre Day speech singled him out as one of the leaders of resistance to Parliament, Hancock had taken the account books of the college, as well as the treasury, with him to Beacon Hill. After the massive reinforcement of the British forces and the closing of the port under the Coercive Acts, the college closed. By the time the Overseers requested that Hancock return the books and the treasury, Hancock, recently elected the first president of the Provincial Congress, had moved temporarily—or so he thought—to the parsonage in Lexington, a shorter commute to the Provincial Congress, then sitting at Concord.

Finally finding time to write to President Samuel Langdon, Hancock said that he "very seriously resented" the Overseers' demands. "If the gentlemen choose to make a public choice of a gentleman to the displacing of him, they will please to act their pleasure." In view of Hancock's power and influence, "they dared not do it as yet."[2] Instead, the Overseers authorized the college's president to act as interim treasurer and to receive rents, tuition, legacies and donations. Hancock's records show that he received no money on behalf of the college after November 1774, and he made no payments after March 1775.

Another year passed. Hancock was presiding over the Continental Congress in Philadelphia when he heard from Harvard again. "In language of humble supplication," President Langdon pleaded with Hancock to send him the accrued interest. But Hancock no longer had the college's account books with him. Hancock sent off a messenger in a light wagon to Beacon Hill to bring him all of the college's ledgers and papers—to Morison's horror—"at a time when New York, part of the Jerseys and half of the valley of the Hudson were in enemy hands!" President Langdon balked at "this untimely removal of valuable papers" and hinted that Hancock's resignation "would be acceptable."

Hancock next heard from the college in early February 1777. Congress, fleeing the British advance, had taken temporary sanctuary in Baltimore. Tutor Stephen Hall, dispatched by the Overseers to find the treasurer and the treasury, returned to Cambridge with "essential documents in his saddlebags," including a letter from Hancock "expressing his resentment at the Overseers' severe and unmerited censure of his dilatoriness."

On March 12, 1777, Hancock's attorney turned over to the college "bonds, notes, mortgages," worth £15,449 ($2.3 million). But, Morison notes, "his accounts were not settled, nor was the balance in his hands known to him, nor anyone else." A few days later, the Overseers chose a new treasurer. In effect, they had fired Hancock, the president of the Continental Congress. "Hancock chose to interpret this as a personal insult and political slight—an unforgivable offense to him," Morison noted.

To close the books on Hancock's years as treasurer, the college's Overseers voted to pay Copley for Hancock's portrait and requested that Hancock permit it to "be conveyed to the College and placed in the Philosophy Chamber, [beside] that of his late honorable uncle." Morison recounted that the gesture still "failed to move the former treasurer to square his accounts but he did turn over additional notes which he had forgotten to the face value of £624 [$94,000]."[3]

With James Bowdoin's support, history tutor William Gordon introduced a motion to sue Hancock for the full amount of the surety bond he had posted, but the motion failed; the Overseers were divided over the issue. When Hancock defeated Bowdoin to win election as governor in 1780, the board voted to send him a congratulatory address—and a renewed request for settlement. Governor Hancock received it "in silence." At the same time, he proudly began to deliver the annual commencement address to the college, speaking to new graduates and admitted students in carnival-like exercises where the public could see and hear him.

Hancock was presiding over the February 1783 Overseers meeting when a committee headed by Gordon reported that "it is not known what sums the late treasurer received and paid." Clearly more interested in embarrassing Hancock than in receiving the disputed payment, Gordon moved that unless Hancock rendered an accounting and paid triple interest before the next meeting, the college corporation would be advised to put Hancock's bond in suit for what would have been a ruinous amount.

At the subsequent meeting in June, Hancock was again presiding when Gordon, lecturing Hancock, accused him of trifling with the college. Gordon moved to immediately commence legal proceedings to recover the debt with triple interest. There was dead silence in the hall; no one dared to second the motion. In addition to all of Hancock's benefactions to the college, he was considered too powerful. The motion died.[4]

Hancock's only response was to absent himself from the next month's meeting, but he was clearly furious at the "indignity." He wrote to the college president, Joseph Willard, to complain of the "illiberal treatment" he had received, and he threatened to transfer William Palfrey's two sons to Yale. (He did not make good on the threat.)[5]

Hancock might have known that Professor Gordon had been seeking ways to discredit him. The history professor was aligned with the James Bowdoin–James Warren–Samuel Adams faction in the increasingly divisive politics of Massachusetts. As early as 1777, Gordon had written to ask John Adams if he had any documents bearing on the Harvard treasury "affair." Gordon said he was writing a history of the Revolution and wanted Adams to provide him with documents. On April 8, 1777, John Adams wrote back to Gordon, "The affair of the treasury of H.C. is a delicate business, and as I have no particular connection with it, I believe it will be most prudent for me to mind my own business, and give myself no trouble about that."

If Gordon intended to diminish Hancock's attachment to the college, he certainly did not succeed.

In private, Hancock bristled, but as governor, he continued to support legislation that benefited the college. His staunch new ally was the college president: Hancock himself had inaugurated the Reverend Willard in December 1781 in the college chapel, delivering a twelve-minute speech in perfect Latin. As historian Morison put it, Hancock "congratulated the university . . . which he considered in some sense, the parent as well as the nursery of the late happy revolution."[6]

At the next commencement exercises nearly a decade later, in 1792, Hancock received as close to an apology as he would ever get for his rough handling by Gordon: an honorary doctoral degree. Wearing a plain black academic robe and a lamb's-wool wig, he delivered an oration in Latin.

Finally, Hancock submitted his accounting of the treasury funds to the Overseers. According to his figures, he owed the college £1,054 ($158,000), most of it due to additional interest accrued on the unpaid interest. But he still did not send the money. He considered the repeated demands for money unreasonable; he had returned the money originally entrusted to him. The rest was interest that supposedly would have been earned in normal times. He had protected the treasury during the British invasion, and he had lost much of his fortune in the cause of independence. Why shouldn't Harvard absorb some of the loss?

In his first term as governor of Massachusetts, Hancock faced two major challenges: helping to win the war and paying Massachusetts's share for the cost of the victory. When Washington requested that the newly installed Hancock send him more men for the Continental Army, Hancock promptly authorized the conscription of 4,240 men. As he had found in the ill-fated Newport campaign, many among the large number of unemployed were willing to be conscripted, but they were accustomed to selecting the length of time they would serve. In response, Hancock pushed through the legislature a law imposing a mandatory three-year term of service.

It would prove easier to find recruits than to pay for them. Neither Massachusetts nor the Continental Congress had enough money to buy their weapons, ammunition and supplies. The state had already provided more men and money than any other state, and it had the highest taxes. By 1781, it was £11 million (about $1.65 billion) in debt; the new levy would add £944,000 ($141 million).

There were poll taxes to vote, sales taxes on liquor and consumer goods, import duties and property taxes. Farmers were paying fully one-third of their income in taxes on farmed-out land that could no longer produce surplus crops used to barter in a virtually cashless society.

Continental paper currency had collapsed, falling to a hundredth of its face value. Congress had issued $241 million in continental dollars that were "not worth a continental." Supposedly universally acceptable, a paper dollar would buy only an English penny's worth of goods. The states had issued another $210 million in thirteen different currencies, leading to a host of new issues. A New England dollar was more acceptable than a Virginia dollar; freshman congressman James Madison had to write home to his father for hard money when a Philadelphia livery would not accept Virginia's currency; Samuel Adams complained that it had cost him $2,000 in continental currency to buy a $20 suit.

As the commonwealth's Revolutionary War debts soared, the government was able to collect only one-fifth of all property taxes. Overriding Hancock's veto, the legislature increased customs duties—up to twenty-five percent on some luxury goods—to discourage imports and encourage domestic manufacturing. As a consequence, many citizens complained that taxes levied by the state had become even more oppressive than they had been under British rule. Even conservatives like John Adams thought the tax bite had become "heavier than people could bear."[7]

Cut off from foreign trade throughout the long war, Americans had learned to rely on local craftsmen to produce cloth, leather, iron and many other needs. But now the markets were flooded with cheaper, better-made imported goods, largely coming from Britain, that put many Americans out of work. In Boston, craftsmen, mechanics and manufactory workers marched in protests against imports and demanded higher tariffs to protect the jobs. Irate at payments in virtually worthless continental dollars, veterans took to the streets and joined the marchers, demanding long-overdue back pay. In western Massachusetts, farmers stopped paying their taxes. Instead, they began to organize conventions that demanded tax repeal in addition to an end to property confiscation and jailing for nonpayment of property taxes. The Confederation Congress, finally constituted a year before, searched for ways to ease the postwar debt crisis and encourage domestic manufacturing.

Since no new revenues could be expected by raising direct taxes, on February 3, 1781, the Confederation Congress turned to indirect taxation as the solution. The two possibilities, excise taxes and customs duties, had both proven unpopular and been among the causes of the break with England. Congress decided on a bold move that would increase the scope of its power and passed a resolution to create customs duties that would provide Congress an independent source of income by levying a five percent tax on all imported goods. Passed unanimously, it would have to be approved by all thirteen states to become law.

In March 1782, the proposal reached Hancock, who was well aware of Congress's lack of funds but, as an advocate of state sovereignty, worried about granting Congress more power, even a modest step toward a central government. He feared that Congress, like Parliament, might wield taxation as a weapon. Instead, he favored restricting imports, even if it hurt foreign commerce. He joined merchants in calling for a ban on British ships that would effectively compel importers and exporters like himself to use American vessels, expanding the shipbuilding industry and Massachusetts's merchant fleet and putting thousands back to work. But the General Court ignored Hancock's reasoning and passed the five percent impost bill.

But Hancock must have known that the bill would eventually pass. Just prior to recessing at the end of the session, Hancock, by telling the General Court that he had reservations and needed more time to consider the question, was able to postpone a public decision until spring.

When the Court reconvened, it sent the impost bill to the governor for his signature. Hancock knew the procedure: According to the constitution, he had five days to ponder the bill. But if he held the bill for more than five days, it automatically became law. For five days, Hancock said nothing. The bill became law without him commenting on the merits of the measure—except to argue that one of the days had been the Sabbath and therefore shouldn't have been counted as a business day. The General Court ignored his gambit and resolved that the bill had been with the governor for five days and therefore "constituted a law of the commonwealth."

Far from being embarrassed, Hancock was pleased that he had avoided taking a public stand on such a divisive issue. Those in favor of the new law were happy to have won; opponents couldn't blame Hancock.

~l~

Even though Hancock might have preserved his popularity, the victory came at a personal cost. While for the second time, he easily won election as governor, his victory was accompanied by a severe and sustained flare-up of gout. By November 1782 he was obviously a sick man; all through that winter, his health was the worst it had ever been. Bedridden, he was often unable to address the General Court in person. Once, when he did manage to attend, he had to be helped into the chamber and he delivered his speech seated.

As the summer of 1783 approached, Hancock, who had for the third time glided to election, began to talk about retiring. One hot day in June, eight-year-old William Sullivan accompanied his father—lawyer, legislator and advisor James Sullivan—when the man visited Beacon Hill. Decades later, Sullivan reminisced that Hancock had "the appearance of advanced age, though only forty-five." To the boy, Hancock appeared "nearly six feet in stature and of slender person, stooping a little and apparently enfeebled by disease. His manners were very gracious, of the old style of dignified complaisance. His face had been very handsome."

When the Sullivans arrived around noon, the governor

was dressed in a red velvet cap, within which was one of fine linen. . . . He wore a blue damask gown lined with silk; a white stock, a white satin embroidered waistcoat, black satin smallclothes, white silk stockings, and red morocco slippers. It was a general practice in genteel families, to have a tankard of punch prepared in the morning, and placed in a cooler when the season required it. . . . At this visit, Hancock took . . . a full tankard, and drank first himself, and then offered it to those present.[8]

But this effort must have exhausted Hancock; the visitor noted that the governor could no longer hold a pen.[9]

For much of the summer, Hancock remained bedridden for

days on end. Intense joint pain and swelling made the carriage ride over a rough road to the summer home he had built on Point Shirley across the harbor unbearable. He could see it through a spyglass but he could not accompany Dolly and their son, Johnny, now five, with their friends to the summer resort he had created. When he was able, he rode around town in his new yellow coach, stopping frequently to talk with workers, encouraging them and sometimes lending them money or paying for some of the projects outright with his own money. As Boston rebuilt after eight years of damage and neglect, he underwrote the planting of trees on the Common and formed a partnership to construct a new bridge across the Charles River.

His popularity grew with each civic gesture.

CHAPTER FIFTEEN

"*Perhaps* Restore Our Virtue"

In the summer of 1784, Beacon Hill welcomed a visitor who banished the malaise of Hancock House. The Marquis de Lafayette, now the youngest field marshal in the French army, arrived in a carriage accompanied by an entourage of two French aides and his liveried servants. In his first visit to Boston since the end of the war, Lafayette was making a celebratory tour that had begun with a long, affectionate reunion with the Washingtons at Mount Vernon.

Since landing in America, Lafayette had been amazed at the warmth of his reception in every town in Pennsylvania, New York and New England. He had thrilled at the throngs of veterans who turned out as he pranced by them in his splendid white uniform on his tall white horse. It was the first occasion since the end of the Revolution for veterans, politicians, women and children to celebrate and to add glory to the memories of suffering left by the long war. In addition to the lingering private dinners atop Beacon Hill that Dolly hosted for Lafayette, Hancock, in his position as governor, arranged a splendid civic welcome, with cannon salutes, pealing church bells and a banquet for five hundred guests at Faneuil Hall before Lafayette continued his tour. To some Bostonians, the Hancocks' openhanded hospitality at a time when many of their neighbors were suffering the effects of the postwar recession was indecent, even immoral.

At the same time, an alliance of Puritans was conducting a statewide campaign to halt what they insisted was a decline of public morals. They had set out to close private drinking clubs. When during that bitter-cold winter, a new kind of social club called the Sans Souci opened with card playing and dancing added to the usual tippling, it immediately came under fire from the alliance's principal supporters: Samuel Adams, James Bowdoin and Mercy Otis Warren.

In January 1785, the *Massachusetts Centinel* inveighed against the club with an article headlined "Sans Souci, Alias Free and Easy: Or an Evenings Peep into a Polite Circle—An Entire New Entertainment in Three Acts." The paper warned Bostonians, "We are prostituting all our glory as a people for new modes of pleasure ruinous in their expenses, injurious to virtue, and totally detrimental to the well-being of society." In the *Centinel*, Samuel Adams joined the attack, asking, "Why do you thus suffer all the intemperances of Great Britain to be fostered in our bosom in all their vile luxuriance?"[1]

By this time, Governor Hancock's gout had grown even more acute. During one evening ride in his coach, he was stricken with an especially severe bout. Servants had to carry him into his mansion and cut off his clothes before they could carry him upstairs to bed. To John Hancock, this latest outpouring of invective was more than he could endure. Seeing the Adams-Bowdoin campaign as a thinly veiled political attack reflecting on him and increasingly disenchanted with politics after five terms as governor, he decided to resign. On January 29, 1785, the five-time governor—the governor's term was one year at this time—sent his letter of resignation to the General Court:

> Sensible of my infirm state of health, and of my incapacity to render service and give that attention to the concerns of the public that is expected from a person of my station, justice to the public and myself loudly call upon me not to prejudice the community, but rather to promote its benefit, to effect which I am obliged, gentlemen, to inform you ... that I must at present give up all my attention to public business and pursue the means of regaining my health.[2]

In the spring 1785 elections, Bowdoin, backed by Samuel Adams, campaigned on the issue of moral decay and defeated Thomas Cushing by a two-to-one margin. However, Adams lost to Cushing in the race for lieutenant governor. Undaunted, he wrote to his cousin John, now the ambassador to Britain:

> You will have heard of the change in our chief magistrate. I confess it is what I have long wished for. Our new governor has issued his proclamation for the encouragement of piety, virtue, education and manners and for the suppression on vice. This with the good example of a chief magistrate and others may *perhaps* restore our virtue.[3]

～e～

At the end of the Revolutionary War, anticipating pent-up consumer demand, wholesalers like Hancock in Boston had seized the opportunity to import large quantities of English goods. This drained the region of gold and silver, and they took on immense debt. Normally, importers like Hancock would sell the imported goods on credit to storekeepers in interior towns. They, in turn, sold them on credit to farmers. Under the new constitution, wealthy Boston merchants were able to gain control of the legislature and pass a law that allowed landed interests to make loans to farmers at usurious rates that they could no longer repay. Hancock had floated to victory in five gubernatorial elections, but by 1785, when he decided to retire, he was facing increasing criticism from commercial interests for his inability to use his influence to solve the critical challenges facing Massachusetts.

Neither John Hancock nor any other member of the founding generation could have imagined that, even after the stunning American military victory over the armies and navy of the British Empire, the American Revolution constituted only the first phase of a far more protracted struggle to achieve true independence. The Treaty of Paris of 1783 had halted the overt conflict of war and granted political autonomy—but it did not guarantee American economic independence and agency. For fully three more contentious decades that ultimately led to another all-out war—the War of 1812—Britain continued to deny the United States' sovereignty.

In the second phase of the struggle, Britain made everintensifying attempts to stifle American trade and to starve her former colonies. Ignoring the military failure and the consequent

treaty of peace, the British Parliament ratcheted up efforts to elim-
inate American competition, first by re-invoking the colonial-era
Navigation Act of 1756, which required that all goods transported
between British possessions or to and from England be carried on
British ships—"English goods in English bottoms."

Embargoing long-existing trade between New England and the
Canadian Maritime Provinces, the Navigation Act also barred
long-flourishing commercial ties with British Caribbean colonies.
Moreover, Britain insisted that its treaty allies, Spain and Portugal,
also forbid American trade with any of their colonies. Further,
Britain prohibited their domains from receiving vital exports from
the United States, including sheep, wool and woolens. All the
while, in violation of the peace treaty, Britain refused to remove its
troops from fortified trading posts around the Great Lakes and
along the Canadian-American frontier on the grounds that Americans were refusing to honor the treaty by not paying off their prewar
debts to British merchants in silver or gold, not badly depreciated
continental currency, as they had been contracted to do.

⁓

When the British re-invoked the Navigation Acts and closed their
West Indian ports to American shipping, many wholesale merchants, suddenly finding themselves with no way to trade their way
out of debt, sued backcountry merchants. Hancock refrained from
this practice, allowing debtors of modest means to repay him in
devalued paper money—a move that cost him money—or to
pledge to pay when they could; he even extended them further
credit. But wealthy creditors, such as political opponents and even
erstwhile political allies—including ailing Revolutionary firebrand

James Otis—Hancock now dunned mercilessly. Hancock expected these creditors to pay him in silver or gold, as he must pay his creditors. In turn, the creditors sued farmers and refused them further credit. Hancock himself had slipped deeply into arrears on his property taxes: He owed a staggering £227,000 (about $34 million) by the time he began sending William Hoskins to collect from creditors as far away as Nova Scotia and London.

From Hoskins's reports and from Hoskins's brother-in-law, William Greenleaf, sheriff of Worcester County, Hancock learned of the worsening debt crisis in western Massachusetts. By mid-1786, nearly one-third of all farmers in western Massachusetts had been hauled into court in debt suits. They were especially bitter because the legislature had adjourned its 1785–86 session without heeding their petitions for "stay" laws to halt foreclosures of their homes and farms. Poor harvests had left farmers with scarcely enough to feed their families and nothing to pay property taxes. Creditors from Boston thronged the rural courts, filing thousands of lawsuits—two thousand in Worcester County alone—that led to sheriffs' sales or imprisonment for debt.

~∘~

The depression in trade in America in the mid-1780s caused growing political dissent as well as economic hardship. With public credit destroyed, currency free-falling, British and French gold scarce, unemployment as the army disbanded, widespread land speculation and the West Indian trade and the fur trade to Canada lost, the Confederation teetered on the brink of collapse. Every state attempted to save itself by some means of counteracting the general business distress, and all of them failed. In New York,

Governor George Clinton and his constituency, mostly upstate farmers, distrusted and resisted the calls for stronger national solutions to interstate problems coming from New York City merchants, most of whom they put down as too pro-British. Clinton, a populist, wielded considerable power. He stoutly refused the call of Congress for a special session to consider customs duties to support the Confederation.

Tensions between states grew sharp. New York demanded a customs duty on every boatload of firewood from New Jersey "as if they had arrived from any other foreign port." This wood was vital to fueling and heating New York City, whose trees had been cut down by British occupation forces. Pinched New Jersey boatmen put pressure on their legislature to tax New York for the lighthouse and the plot of land around it on Sandy Hook. Meanwhile, Connecticut exacted heavier customs duties on imports from Massachusetts than on those from Great Britain.

By the summer of 1786, the postwar depression had reached a critical stage, and no sector of the American economy remained immune. International trade had all but stopped. Farmers could not pay the taxes or their loans and faced widespread foreclosures. Scottish merchants who operated hundreds of country stores had cut off their credit, even refusing to supply seed for farmers, and they were suing to collect the debts on their books. Import-export trade once again moved between Britain and the United States, but imports had dropped off from £2.3 million in 1785 to £1.6 million in 1786, a thirty percent decline. Farm wages had fallen more than twenty percent in five years. Several states had passed "stay" laws and stopped the collection of debts to meet demands for relief from the vicious combination of a money shortage, high taxes and insistent creditors. Seven states were running their printing presses to produce ever less valuable currency. Only Rhode Island barred paying creditors with state fiat money.

~ℓ~

In June 1786, recognizing the need for a collective effort to address the crisis, a special committee of Congress debated a motion for a reorganization of the government. The committee's report revealed the delegates' acute awareness of the weaknesses of the Articles of Confederation. Proposals for reforms included the creation of a special federal court in which individual states could appeal state court decisions involving foreign nations. Another would have given Congress power over foreign and domestic commerce; others would grant Congress the power to requisition payment of state quotas fixed by Congress. (New Jersey had flatly refused to pay its share of the costs.) But under the Articles, any such action had to be approved unanimously by the states. The report was never distributed to the states, and the effort was abandoned.

In September, Virginia's congressional delegation invited all the states to an interstate commercial convention in Annapolis, Maryland; nine accepted. Oddly, Maryland was one of four states that declined. With John Dickinson of Delaware, principal author of the Articles, elected as its chairman, the convention opened but, after three days, only a dozen delegates from five states had bothered to arrive. The attendance was so poor, argued Alexander Hamilton of New York, that a comprehensive study of the nation's commercial problems would be impossible. Hamilton studied the instructions given the state delegates attending the convention. He argued in favor of writing a resolution declaring "that there are important defects in the system of the Federal Government." With

Dickinson and James Madison of Virginia supporting him, Hamilton urged that the convention prepare an address to all the states to send commissioners to a new convention in Philadelphia in May 1787 to discuss not only commercial problems but *all* matters necessary "to render the constitution of the Federal Government adequate to the exigencies of the Union." And then he recommended adjourning the Annapolis meeting before more delegates could arrive and block his resolution.[4]

—◦—

When the delegates to the Annapolis Convention gathered to continue their critique of the Confederation, there had been no question where George Washington stood. He had become firmly convinced that the nation's affairs were approaching a crisis. But other Americans, such as Benjamin Franklin, saw the 1780s as a period of unparalleled growth and prosperity. Even in distressed areas, the prospects seemed bright. Farmers lacked cash, but they had homes, abundant food, unlimited hunting and fishing rights, cash crops and almost no taxes to pay. Life was crude but good for many, prosperous for thousands more. The United States had only the population and economic status of a Third World country, but it was rapidly developing.

The Annapolis white paper sent to Congress declared that the middle states—the hub of commerce—believed that the Union was suffering from serious problems that warranted a convention. In addition to sending the resolution to Congress, the delegates sent the call for the Philadelphia convention to all the states.

The fragmentary dispatches that reached Washington's veranda at Mount Vernon led him to despair briefly that Americans could govern themselves. But when Congress approved the convention, the chances of a solid turnout of delegates from a majority of the states vastly encouraged him.

—❧—

Under its conservative 1780 constitution, Massachusetts had limited political participation to men who owned certain levels of property. The common Enlightenment belief was that property gave a man a stake in society. For town elections, the bar was set at £20 (about $3,000); in state elections, a minimum of £40 ($6,000) and in some instances £60 ($9,000). The qualifications for office holding were even steeper. To qualify to serve as governor, John Hancock had to document that he owned a freehold of £1,000 (about $150,000 today), which was not a problem for him. To become a member of the House of Representatives required landholdings valued at £100 ($15,000); to run for the state senate, £300 ($45,000) or an estate valued at £600 ($90,000). In many western towns, not one single citizen could meet the property qualifications to hold statewide office. Many in the western counties saw them as creating a ruling class favoring the mercantile and maritime eastern counties.

Two weeks after the Annapolis Convention ended, landowners in western Massachusetts—many of them veterans of the Revolutionary army—revolted. As the backcountry economy worsened, they protested that the state was only making it worse. For the past four years, scores of communities had petitioned the assembly to address their grievances. But on July 8, 1786, the legislature decided that its work for the year had been completed and adjourned until January 31, 1787.

Once again, the legislature adjourned without doing anything
to provide relief. How were farmers supposed to pay debts, taxes,
lawyers and court fees with hard money when none was available?
Why couldn't paper money be issued? And why was there a state
senate? Wasn't it just a waste of money, a source of privilege for
Boston's elite? And why was the state government in Boston instead of being more centrally located as in other states? Didn't distance and bad weather keeping representatives of western
communities from reaching Boston make it possible for the merchant elite to pass oppressive laws?

In the 1786 statewide elections, wealthy merchants from coastal
towns led by Samuel Adams supported Hancock's longtime rival
James Bowdoin, who won a bitterly contested special election so
close that it was thrown into the legislature. The Senate, controlled
by the merchants, insisted on Bowdoin as governor; the House at
first backed Thomas Cushing but eventually bowed to the Senate.

Under Bowdoin, fewer and fewer farmers could pay their debts
to storekeepers or tax collectors—instead, they faced imprisonment or eviction. Between 1782 and 1786, more than a hundred
men were sentenced to debtors' prison in western Massachusetts.
The number of court cases filed in western Massachusetts doubled;
in some counties, it quadrupled. In 1784, one-third of the farmers
in Hampshire County were in debt trouble. If a farmer had no
other property to settle his debt—often between only $60 and
$100 in today's money—court rulings frequently resulted in the
farmer being stripped of his land to satisfy back taxes, in some ex-
treme cases leaving him with no land at all. Seizure of livestock by
counties to satisfy back taxes was also becoming more widespread.

At this singularly inopportune moment, the state senate
pushed through a new law that shifted the burden of repaying

Massachusetts's huge Revolutionary War debt—£1,250,000 (about $187 million today)—from war bond holders (Bowdoin held £3,290, or nearly $500,000)—to property owners, allowing no exception for cash-strapped farmers eking out a living on land they had received in lieu of army pay. To landowners, the new property taxes echoed the abuses under British rule that had precipitated the Revolution.

CHAPTER SIXTEEN

"A Storm in the Atmosphere"

Tired of being put off by the legislature, the selectmen of the town of Pelham, near Amherst, called a Town Meeting. The town moderator, Dr. Nehemiah Hinds, and Daniel Shays, his compatriot through five years of active duty in the Massachusetts Line, wrote a letter to the selectmen of a dozen other Hampshire County towns calling for a convention in Amherst to seek "some method" to change the state constitution and replace it with a more responsive government.

Other towns quickly set up committees of correspondence; within a month, five other counties organized conventions. The largest was held in Hatfield: Fifty Hampshire County towns sent representatives, including delegates to the state legislature and members of the county's most prominent families. They adopted twenty-one resolutions, six calling for a radical change in the state's government. They demanded a new constitution, one that would abolish the state senate, provide affordable property qualifications for representation in the lower house and put the lower house in charge of the annual election of government officials and their salaries. And the capital *must* be moved out of Boston.

One week later, fifteen hundred well-organized protestors marched from Pelham through Amherst and Hadley toward Northampton. After crossing the Connecticut River, they were joined by hundreds of men from hill towns to the northwest and from the south and from West Springfield, site of the federal arsenal for all New England. At that moment, the arsenal housed several large fieldpieces, seven thousand new muskets with bayonets, hundreds of old muskets, thirteen hundred barrels of gunpowder and more than two hundred tons of shot and shells.

Some protestors carried muskets, swords and bludgeons; others were unarmed. Many of the men were veterans. Assembled into military formation behind fifes and drums, they marched to the Northampton courthouse. When three black-robed justices escorted by the county sheriff approached the courthouse, Shays, spokesman for a six-man delegation, strode up to the courthouse door, presented a petition and demanded that the judges cease all proceedings and adjourn without transacting any business. The justices, retiring to a nearby inn, decided to postpone "all matters pending" until November. The next week, crowds closed the courts at Worcester, barred judges and lawyers from entering courthouses at Concord and Great Barrington and, after chasing away the sheriffs, stopped the sheriffs' sales.

Four days after the Northampton protest, Governor Bowdoin issued a proclamation condemning Shays for introducing "riot, anarchy and confusion" and dispatched militia general William Shepard and eight hundred militiamen to guard the state supreme court in Springfield. Shepard had been a colonel and Shays's commanding officer in the Massachusetts Line. Shays assembled an equal number of armed men and, on September 26, 1786, confronted the state militia, forcing it to flee. The Supreme Court adjourned.

The "rebels," as Governor Bowdoin quickly denominated them, expanded their protests week after week. The Regulators, as the insurgents called themselves, evoked memories of a pre–Revolutionary War uprising on the North Carolina frontier against taxes and seizures of farms by a tyrannical royal governor.

The news of marches on courthouses from Worcester in the west to Concord in the east shocked Bowdoin and the leading merchants of Boston, who had expected no such well-organized armed resistance.

Bowdoin called an emergency meeting in Faneuil Hall to endorse a document, drafted by Samuel Adams, that sang the praises of the 1780 constitution and denounced the protestors. Adams insisted on harsh punishments: He argued that "in monarchies the crime of treason and rebellion may admit of being pardoned or lightly punished, but the man who dares rebel against the laws of a republic ought to suffer death."[1]

Like so many of his companions, Shays had fought throughout the long Revolution. And like several of the tax protestors, he was a former officer, a captain of the Massachusetts Line. After enlisting as a private, Shays had served in Rufus Putnam's Fifth Massachusetts Regiment, then worked his way up through the ranks to captain. He had fought in the Battles of Saratoga under Benjamin Lincoln, charged into Breymann Redoubt and seen Benedict Arnold shot and trapped under his horse. He had helped to build the fortifications at West Point. Considered Putnam's "best captain . . .

bold and kind," he had led light infantry in the bayonet attack on Stony Point under "Mad Anthony" Wayne.

When Washington announced Arnold's treason with British spymaster John André, it was Shays who was chosen as captain of André's guard. Shays was constantly in the room where this "fine looking young man" was confined; he even marched André to the gallows. In a print depicting "The Unfortunate Death of Mister Andre," Shays stands with a spontoon at the right of the gallows. Then Shays had, at last, gone home.

Before the war, Shays had started to buy up land in western Massachusetts. After selling off much of it, he had mortgaged the rest. By 1786, he owned 251 acres of rocky soil in hill towns. Shays had received his veteran's land grant in Pelham, where he held several town offices. Because his officer's pay in heavily depreciated continental currency had been so low, he was having trouble paying off small debts he had incurred in the service. Strapped for cash, he sold for £1 a sword presented to him by his commanding officer, the Marquis de Lafayette, during the French nobleman's celebratory postwar visit to Massachusetts. By the time of the protest movement, Shays was indebted to at least ten men.

Luke Day, who led the contingent of protestors from West Springfield, had been the first to arrive in Northampton. He was forty-three and the scion of a once wealthy family of landholders. As a militia lieutenant, he had led fifty-three men to Lexington in April 1775 and then joined in the siege of Boston. His battalion was chosen to join the Continental Army, and he volunteered to join Benedict Arnold on his ill-fated march to Quebec. Promoted to captain of the Seventh Regiment of the Massachusetts Line, he marched south with Major General Benjamin Lincoln and helped to defeat Cornwallis at Yorktown.

After eight years of active duty in the Revolutionary army, Day joined other officers in founding the Society of the Cincinnati and demanding half-pay lifetime pensions. When Congress promised to meet the request and then reneged, Day received a lump-sum pension in government bonds that had since depreciated to one-eighth of their face value. Day had been forced to neglect the family farms during the long war. His grounds deteriorated, while state and town taxes quadrupled. After two years of borrowing heavily, Day was deep in debt. He was arrested by his creditors and imprisoned in Northampton jail in July 1785.

As the protests continued, the Confederation Congress requested that Secretary of War Henry Knox investigate them. Knox, a major landholder, exaggerated wildly to Congress that the "wicked and ambitious" Shays commanded at least fifteen thousand men who were "determined to annihilate all debts public and private" and threatened "to overturn not only the forms but the principles of the present constitutions." Knox reported to Congress that Shays and his adherents were besieging the federal arsenal in West Springfield. Knox warned Congress that a civil war appeared imminent.[2]

In Virginia, after reading Knox's report, General Henry "Light-Horse Harry" Lee wrote to his mentor, George Washington, echoing Knox's warning. He urged Washington to use his "unbounded influence" to restore peace.[3] Washington refused: "Influence is no government."[4]

From Congress, James Madison wrote to his father that he thought the Shaysites "profess only to aim at reform of their constitution and certain offenses."[5] Both Madison and Washington were aware that Congress had no money to raise an army or pay troops.

But thoroughly alarmed at reports that armed rebels were about to seize cannon, Congress did the one thing it had clear-cut authority to do under the Articles of Confederation. It voted to raise an army, authorizing Knox to recruit 1,340 men. It also commissioned General Benjamin Lincoln, Washington's second-in-command at the end of the Revolutionary War, to recruit a Continental force from Massachusetts and Connecticut, ostensibly to serve against Native Americans in the Ohio Valley.

Certain that Congress could do nothing expeditiously, Governor Bowdoin decided to raise £2,000 ($300,000) privately from fellow merchants—he himself contributed £250 ($37,500)—to pay a militia. Made up largely of unemployed Bostonians, it constituted the largest military force mustered since the Revolution. Of the 135 merchants and bankers who contributed to Bowdoin's fund, more than half were speculators who held more than forty percent of the state debt. They had served in the state legislature or they had close relatives who did. William Phillips, president of the Massachusetts Bank, put in the largest donation, £300 ($45,000), enough to pay a hundred fifty recruits for a month. Collectively, merchants and bankers contributed enough for Bowdoin to hire 155 troops. No attempt was made to conceal the fundraising. Appalled, John Hancock, the wealthiest merchant in New England, made it known that he refused to contribute to any scheme to finance an army of mercenaries to fight against their fellow veterans of the Revolution.

～ℓ～

As snow blanketed the Berkshires, Captain Shays gathered his own force of about twelve hundred men. The day after Christmas 1786, he led a march to Springfield to join forces with other insurgents under the command of Luke Day, aiming to intimidate Shepard's militiamen guarding the arsenal. Their march thoroughly alarmed Governor Bowdoin, who now placed forty-four hundred men—the largest armed force mustered in the United States since the Revolution—under Benjamin Lincoln's command.

Rushing to scatter the arsenal's guard before Lincoln could reinforce it, Shays and Day made the classic mistake of keeping their forces divided. When Shays proposed a joint attack on January 25, 1787, Day, on the opposite shore of the Connecticut River, replied that he would not be ready to attack for another two days. His message was intercepted. Shays pressed on and attacked the arsenal in West Springfield, still believing that Day would attack simultaneously.

The Shaysites marched up to within one hundred yards of the arsenal before Shepard, who had placed two cannon to be charged with grapeshot, ordered a warning shot above their heads. When the attackers still pressed on, Shepard ordered his gunners to aim at waist level and fire a volley of grapeshot. Four Shaysites dropped dead; twenty more were wounded. Among the dead was Jabez Spicer, a Revolutionary War veteran. The rest broke and ran. For several days, Lincoln and his force pursued the Regulators. Then, after pushing two thousand recruits all night, Lincoln overtook Shays, who was encamped for the night at Petersham, and attacked him at dawn on February 4, 1787. After a running battle on snowshoes in waist-deep snow, Lincoln captured a hundred fifty insurgents. Day fled to the hills of New Hampshire.

Shays and his aides disappeared across the Vermont border to seek sanctuary. At Arlington, the provisional capital of the independent republic, they camped in Governor Thomas Chittenden's yard.

Shays had offered command of his movement to Ethan Allen, a major general of Vermont's militia, but Allen, who had recently led the republic's militiamen in quelling a taxpayer revolt, rebuffed the offer.

Instead, Shays and his core followers retreated to build a fort near Sunderland in Vermont's mountainous southwest corner. (Its ruins were discovered in 2014 in an archaeological dig by a local high school science class.) The Shaysites traded with neighboring towns in Vermont and New York for the next quarter century. Shays never surrendered to Massachusetts authorities. By the time the Massachusetts Supreme Court reconvened, some four thousand Shaysites and their families, facing arrest for treason and seizure of their properties by the state, had sold their belongings and fled to Vermont.

In mid-February 1787, the Massachusetts legislature passed the Disqualification Act and laid down peace terms. After dividing the insurgents into two groups, rank-and-file rebels—the privates and the sergeants—and their leaders, it established separate levels of punishment. The first group had to surrender their arms, confess to a justice of the peace that they had rebelled against the state, take an oath of allegiance (and pay the justice of the peace for administering the oath), then pay the justice an additional fee of nine pence. For three years, they were to be disqualified from voting, holding office, serving on juries, teaching school, working in inns or taverns or selling liquor.

In what amounted to a plea bargain, the law stipulated that if they could prove to the legislature that they had adhered to these restrictions and behaved as good, law-abiding citizens for one year, their restrictions would be lifted on May 1, 1788. They would avoid prosecution and the possibility of being fined, whipped or hanged. In all, seven hundred ninety took the oath of allegiance.

The legislature excluded Daniel Shays, Luke Day and Eli

Parsons from the possibility of pardon. In addition, it would not pardon any insurgents who had held state offices or commissions in the state militia, shot at government supporters, reneged on an oath or been indicted. In Hampshire County alone, five hundred Shaysites had already been indicted on charges including "high treason, insurrection, riot, sedition or seditious acts"; another two hundred were indicted in Worcester County. In all, at least three hundred were arrested and faced court trials.

For two months, beginning in late March 1787, the state's supreme court justices traveled from county to county to hear the most serious charges. In Great Barrington, they sentenced six men to death; in Northampton, another six. In each of Worcester and Middlesex Counties, one man was sentenced to be hanged. Among the condemned were Job Shattuck, leader of the protests in Concord, and James White, who had been in the front ranks of the assault on the West Springfield arsenal. Many others fled across the state border to Vermont, whose leaders refused to return them to Massachusetts to certain condign punishment.

At the same time, the Bowdoin-dominated legislature voted to use taxpayer revenues to reimburse him and the others who had contributed to the fund to pay the mercenaries.

⁓

Even though Shays's Rebellion had been put down quickly, it thoroughly alarmed many American leaders, including Washington, who worried that the fragile Union was on the verge of collapse. In Virginia, Richard Henry Lee predicted that "the contagion will spread and may reach Virginia." It was the first of several frontier revolts in the next decade.[6]

In Paris, upon learning of Shays's Rebellion, Thomas Jefferson wrote to Abigail Adams in London, praising the Shaysites: "The spirit of resistance to government is so valuable on certain occasions that I wish it to always be kept alive. . . . I like a little rebellion now and then. It is like a storm in the atmosphere."[7] Learning that the Shaysites had surrendered, Jefferson wrote to Abigail's husband, John, advising amnesty: "God forbid that we should ever be twenty years without such a rebellion. The tree of liberty must be refreshed from time to time with the blood of patriots and tyrants."[8]

John Adams wasn't alarmed by the rebellion but his nineteen-year-old son, John Quincy, in his final year at Harvard, opposed any discussion of pardoning the Shaysites, confiding sardonically in his diary, "It is much to the credit of our government that a man who has stole [*sic*] £30 worth of plate should die for the offence while others commit treason and murder with impunity."[9]

~ ℓ ~

Retired and out of office for the first time in more than two decades, Hancock stayed quiet as reports of worsening economic conditions, unrest and then virtual civil war reached him atop Beacon Hill, where he was confined by his illness. Unable to travel for any long distance without intense pain, he felt cut off socially as well as politically. In addition, Hancock felt cut off from his family. To escape the heat and noise of Boston in the summer, Dolly took their son, her father, some close friends and three servants to the two summer houses the Hancocks maintained. There, refreshed by sea breezes, Dolly and her guests could take long strolls on the beach.

That summer, there were no dinner parties. Many of Hancock's business associates, including Bant and Palfrey and his closest friend, minister and confidant Samuel Cooper, had died. As Hancock could not entertain at home, he began once again to go out with friends. His favorite companion was a local hatter, Nathaniel Balch, whose wife was a frequent companion of Dolly's at Point Shirley. The tall, witty seller of beaver hats and the now slightly stooped Hancock were often seen drinking, dining and laughing together in taverns.

While Hancock remained personally close to his longtime lieutenant, Thomas Cushing, he now felt he needed a fresh political advisor. He found one in James Sullivan, an astute veteran legislator. His Irish immigrant parents had not sent him to Harvard; he was "lame" and epileptic. He had studied at home under his father's tutelage, while his older brother John went to Harvard and then tutored him in the law. At age twenty-three, Sullivan was able to open his own law practice in Georgetown, Maine, then part of Massachusetts. After being elected to the Provincial Congress, he became a judge of Admiralty, and in 1776 he received an appointment to the Superior Court of Judicature. In 1778 he bought a home in Groton, Massachusetts, and joined his brother John, then a Continental Army major general in command of American troops in the ill-fated Newport campaign. Hancock and Sullivan became close friends. Sullivan, an expert on Massachusetts politics who wielded a sharpened quill, was just the man Hancock would need to defend him in Boston's acerbic newspaper wars.

~⁓~

In January 1787, while two makeshift armies of former Massachusetts veterans faced each other in the Berkshires in bitter-cold weather, the Hancock family gathered on a Wednesday morning. Johnny, now eight, decided to go outside and engage in his favorite pastime, ice-skating. He took his blades and ran down the hill to a pond. Losing his footing, he fell, struck his head on the ice and fractured his skull. Three days later, he died.

His parents, who had lost their first child, once again lost their only child. They would have no more children. Hancock had hoped to revive the House of Hancock and pass its fortune along to his son, as his uncle Thomas had done for him. But the House of Hancock died that day, too. The funeral was plain, with the boy in a wooden coffin in Hancock's yellow coach. John and Dolly walked along behind with a small cortege of family and close friends, including Sullivan, who had also just lost a son. For years, John and Dolly had talked of making an extended trip to visit friends they had made in Fairfield, New York and Philadelphia during the Revolution. Now, waiting for winter to end, they prepared to leave behind the scene of their saddest day. To Henry Knox, Hancock wrote:

> The obtainment of health is now my pursuit. Journeying is much recommended to me and, as my situation is totally deranged by the untimely death of my dear and promising boy, I have no affectionate object to promise myself the enjoyment of what I leave.

Hancock said he was only "waiting [for] the roads to be good to set out with Mrs. Hancock . . . to New York and Philadelphia." He asked Knox "to engage lodgings in an airy place as will be suitable for Mrs. Hancock and myself and three servants. I wish for a decent place [with] two parlors; an handsome, well furnished chamber for us and decent rooms for my servants, for they lodge and eat at home as well as I do myself."[10]

~e~

In February 1787, before Hancock could leave for his trip, news of the rout of the Shaysites at Petersham reached Boston as sheriffs set out to round up the leaders of the insurrection. Thomas Cushing, who had stayed on as lieutenant governor under Bowdoin, led a delegation of Hancock's moderate supporters up Beacon Hill to implore him to return to office to avert civil war and restore calm. Despite his worsening gout, John Hancock decided he must quit his sickbed, cut short his retirement and return to politics to oust his nemesis.

While his health prevented him from actively campaigning, Hancock's surrogates spread the word. In the April elections, the electorate punished Bowdoin, the man who wanted to punish them, thrashing him at the polls in a record turnout. Despite the newly enacted Disqualification Act preventing some four thousand suspected insurgents—including half the electorate of Amherst in Hampshire County—from voting, Hancock won in a landslide, reelected to a sixth term as governor, receiving more than seventy-five percent of the vote.

In the boldest act of his long political career, once Hancock resumed control of both houses of the legislature, he pardoned all of the Shaysites other than the four leaders, expunging their convictions and restoring their voting rights. He also insisted that executions "should be avoided for the public good." In the end, only two men were executed: One who was convicted of looting and the other a horse thief were hanged because a sheriff failed to open a letter of reprieve in time to halt their demise.[11]

Instructing the legislature to forgo collecting state property taxes for the year 1787, Hancock approved laws that lowered court fees and exempted clothing, household goods and trade tools from seizure for debt. While curtailing government expenditures to lighten the tax burden, Hancock cut the governor's £1,000 salary by thirty percent and donated the balance of his pay to the state treasury.

Hancock had recovered sufficiently by the summer to take a victory lap in his yellow carriage through the rebellious Berkshire towns he intended to help in order to restore confidence in the state government. Crowds of grateful farmers cheered Hancock, and the tour reinvigorated him and doubtless further enhanced his popularity.

As part of cutting back government spending, Hancock pushed a bill that eliminated sinecures through the legislature. It especially targeted the post of captain of the castle, a ceremonial no-show job on Castle Island in Boston Harbor that until then paid a not-inconsiderable £450 ($67,500) salary to supplement the poorly paid post of lieutenant governor. After Thomas Cushing died the following year, General Benjamin Lincoln won a runoff for the number two state office. Hancock insisted that the sinecure was being abolished as an economic measure in straitened times. But the impecunious Lincoln, who had led the army of mercenaries that crushed Shays's Rebellion, depended on the income and saw losing it as a punishment.

~ℓ~

Hancock's pardons set a precedent for the rash of incipient taxpayer revolts that ensued in the decade after the United States gained its independence. As more Americans moved west, they turned their backs on the East Coast's commercial culture. Relying on bountiful harvests to produce surpluses that acted as currency in a cashless barter economy, they rebelled against control by distant politicians. Taxpayer revolts broke out from North Carolina to Pennsylvania, culminating in the Whiskey Rebellion.

The Whiskey Rebellion broke out in the Monongahela Valley of Pennsylvania in the summer of 1794. In his "Report on Credit" in 1792, Secretary of the Treasury Alexander Hamilton had before recommended a revenue-raising excise tax on home-distilled whiskey. Since Congress passed the tax in 1791, frontiersmen had resisted collection of the tax. When violence broke out against the backdrop of the French Revolution, Hamilton believed that the rule of law was seriously threatened. He recommended an immediate and massive display of armed force by the federal government to restore law and order.

When Hamilton's excise tax gatherers issued arrest warrants for home brewers, returnable three hundred miles and several days of arduous travel to Philadelphia, the servers of the warrants were repulsed. A crowd attacked a treasury official's house; one man was killed and the house burned to the ground. Washington decided that only force could stem further armed resistance. But Pennsylvania refused to call out its militia. In August, Washington sent federal commissioners west to offer amnesty in exchange for order. They sent back word of a strong armed minority that refused amnesty.

Issuing a proclamation to justify the use of troops, Washington called out twelve thousand militiamen from Pennsylvania, New Jersey, Maryland and Virginia to "exert the full force of the law" and crush the rebellion. Suffused once again with martial spirit in what was to prove his last outing as a soldier, the white-haired sixty-two-year-old Washington squeezed into his old uniform and traveled west with Colonel Hamilton at his side. Like Hancock, Hamilton loved nothing more than to be in his dashing officer's garb, prancing off to enforce laws of his own making. The militia rallied around their old commander, singing, "To arms once more, our hero cries / Sedition lives and order dies / To peace and grace then bid adieu / And dash to the mountains, Jersey Blue."

In Bedford, the army relieved the siege of a federal customs inspector who, cornered in his house, had engaged in a two-day gun battle. After robbing the mails, the whiskey rebels, seven thousand strong, gathered in a Bedford field. They threatened to burn Pittsburgh and march on the nation's then capital, Philadelphia. But when Washington and his army appeared, no resistance materialized. While the most dedicated rebels melted into the Northwest Territory, the militia rounded up some hundred fifty prisoners and herded them to Philadelphia. There, their two leaders were convicted of treason and condemned to death. But by 1795, President Washington, similar to Hancock eight years earlier, would pardon the men.

CHAPTER SEVENTEEN

"Radically Generous
and Benevolent"

As John Hancock swept to victory in the 1787 statewide elections, he was also elected as a delegate to the enfeebled Confederation Congress. For the fourth time, he was nominated to be the president. It was to prove to be the Confederation Congress's last session. Few states were consistently sending their delegates. It seemed to have become common knowledge that the confederation must be replaced by some new form of government that would be more able to deal with nationwide issues and avert the collapse of the Union. Individually and collectively, the states were unable to raise enough money to function properly. Foreign nations were hesitant to bargain with them or to lend them money while American debts were high and their currency virtually worthless; interstate commerce had become increasingly impossible.

Pennsylvania and Connecticut had actually gone to war over claims by settlers from Connecticut to northwestern Pennsylvania. New York City had barred farmers from New Jersey from landing their produce across the Hudson River. Pennsylvania, Delaware, Virginia and Maryland were at loggerheads over fishing rights to Chesapeake Bay. Georgia was unable to protect itself from Native American raiding parties from Florida armed and protected by Spain. Because many Americans were failing to repay prewar debts owed to British merchants and guaranteed by the Treaty of Paris, the British were refusing to withdraw their troops from forts on the northern frontiers.

Hancock was too weak to travel to Philadelphia to participate in congressional proceedings. He decided that he must both resign his seat as a delegate and decline to serve as president, even in absentia. While conducting the governorship from Beacon Hill, he resigned from Congress by mail.

When the Constitutional Convention convened in Philadelphia in May 1787, Massachusetts sent a divided delegation. Elbridge Gerry, a leading speculator in western lands and close ally of Samuel Adams, attended the intense summerlong debates, but then, after refusing to sign the draft Constitution, walked out, certain that Massachusetts would never approve the new, centralized form of government.

When the draft Constitution was nevertheless approved on September 17, it was sent to the Confederation Congress, still meeting in New York City; the Congress was then to forward it to the individual states for ratification or rejection by special statewide conventions. While Gerry and two other Massachusetts delegates to the Confederation Congress moved to censure the Constitutional Convention for exceeding its authority, they were outvoted by the overwhelming majority of delegates, who chose to send the document on to the states without further delays on September 20.

When the document reached Boston, Governor Hancock sent it on to the General Court—without comment. He refused to make public his decidedly mixed feelings. While he recognized the need for drastic reforms over trade and defense, he was reluctant to create a strong central government. The new Constitution would establish a central government possessing the power to regulate foreign and domestic trade, impose and collect taxes, borrow and coin money and organize military forces—powers no state government had been able to command. And without the inclusion of a bill of rights, it would do so without spelling out the individual rights of its citizens. Five states were already holding conventions; several others were balking; without a bill of rights spelling out the individual rights of citizens, the document seemed to be merely a frame of government that would not be accepted without amendments.

Hancock knew that Massachusetts would be divided into "Federalist" and "anti-Federalist" camps over ratification. The farmers, especially in the west, opposed remote government far from their local interests and believed a strong central power would deprive them of a voice in the government as in pre-Revolutionary times. Because of the state government's inept handling of its debts, eastern merchants, artisans and workers favored a federalized system that could spread the risks and rewards of a more coherent government, including issuing a stable currency, collecting customs duties, setting up and regulating banks and negotiating with foreign powers.

Boston was solidly Federalist; as a spokesman for merchants and artisans, Paul Revere wrote a resolution pledging their "warmest wish and prayer" for ratification and introduced it at the Green Dragon Tavern. Elbridge Gerry came back from Philadelphia vehemently and vociferously opposed to ratification, inveighing against it in the *Massachusetts Centinel*: "Beware! Beware! You are forging chains for yourselves and your children—your liberties are at stake!" Samuel Adams, Gerry's former mentor, organized opposition to ratification; ex-governor Bowdoin was a vocal advocate of ratification.

The selection of delegates to the ratifying convention portended a sharp division and assured lengthy debates. Included among those chosen from Boston were Hancock, Samuel Adams and Bowdoin. To pave the way, a few days before the convention's opening, Bowdoin invited the other delegates to a dinner. He intended to plump for ratification, but his strategy misfired. Two delegates, Hancock and John Winthrop, stayed home. The others enjoyed a good dinner before Samuel Adams announced that he had strong reservations about ratifying the Constitution. Ironically, Hancock's absence and silence suggested that he opposed Bowdoin's approval of ratification. For the first time in a dozen years, this assumption put Hancock on the same side of an issue as Samuel Adams.

The Massachusetts convention included the most delegates of any state. On January 9, some 364 delegates crowded into the State House in Boston to elect a president. Governor Hancock was ill and did not attend. Yet he was still elected, a testament to how much he was respected and trusted. His well-known condition made it a given that he would not attend every session. The delegates chose Thomas Cushing as vice president—expecting that he would fill in the president's chair more frequently than Hancock. So many delegates attended the proceedings that they had to be moved twice, first to Brattle Square Church and finally to Reverend Jeremy Belknap's Congregational church on Long Lane (later changed to Federal Street to commemorate the work there of the ratifying convention).

From the outset, it was obvious that the gulf dividing those

favoring and those opposed to ratification was wide, and their adherents were evenly split. The Federalists, who were largely merchants, lawyers, judges and officeholders, tended to be wealthy. The
anti-Federalists were so numerous that they might have won if they
had called for a vote the first day of the convention; uncertain that
they could muster enough votes, they backed away. The Federalists
preferred to wait and take more time to win over fence-sitters
through speeches and writings. On the fourteenth, with Hancock
still absent, the Federalists won a tactical victory when the convention voted to debate the Constitution "by paragraphs, until every
member shall have had opportunity fully to express his sentiments."[1]

While the debate raged in the convention, in newspaper essays
and in letters printed in the press, Hancock remained on Beacon
Hill, watching, waiting and studying reports he ordered sent to
him daily by both camps. He understood that Massachusetts, as
the initiator and first leader of the Revolution, was being watched
closely, its decision promising to influence other states. Thus far,
only five states had approved the Constitution. By now Hancock
had made his decision. He felt that the United States would not
survive unless the Constitution was ratified by the requisite two-
thirds of all states, and that only he had enough influence to win
over wavering delegates.

On Thursday afternoon, January 31, in the midst of a flare of
gout, Hancock ordered his coach. After Hancock rode with his
legs wrapped in red flannel, his servants carried him into the convention hall, where he took the chair. In what might have been his
most important achievement; in what his bitter rival Elbridge
Gerry conceded was a "dramatic presentation"; in a speech "wise
and plausible," Hancock declared "the anxiety of his mind."[2]

Hancock urged adoption of nine "Conciliatory Amendments"

that would evolve into the Bill of Rights. And probably most significantly to the longtime governor of a sovereign state, he proposed the Tenth Amendment: "that it be explicitly declared that all powers not expressly delegated to Congress are reserved to the several states, to be by them exercised."

As the last speaker, Hancock rose to address a silent hall and began:

> Gentlemen: Being now called upon to bring the subject under debate to a decision, by bringing forward the question, I beg your indulgence to close the business with a few words. I am happy that my health has been so far restored that I am rendered able to meet my fellow citizens as represented in this Convention. I should have considered it as one of the most distressing misfortunes of my life to be deprived of giving my aid and support to a system which, if amended (as I feel assured it will be) according to your proposals, cannot fail to give the people of the United States a greater degree of political freedom and eventually as much national dignity as falls to the lot of any nation on the earth.
>
> I have not, since I had the honor to be in this place, said much on the important subject before us. All the ideas appertaining to the system, as well those which are against as for it, have been debated upon with so much learning and ability that the subject is quite exhausted. But you will permit me, Gentlemen, to close the whole with one or two general observations. This I request, not expecting to throw any light upon the subject but because it may possibly prevent uneasiness and discordance from taking place amongst us and amongst our constituents.

That a general system of government is indispensably necessary to save our country from ruin is agreed upon all sides. That the one now to be decided upon has its defects, all agree. But when we consider the variety of interests and the different habits of the men it is intended for, it would be very singular to have an entire union of sentiment respecting it. Were the people of the United States to delegate the powers proposed to be given to men who were not dependent upon them frequently for elections—to men whose interests, either from rank or title, would differ from that of their fellow citizens—the task of delegating authority would be vastly more difficult; but as the matter now stands, the powers reserved by the people render them secure, and until they themselves become corrupt, they will always have upright and able rulers. I give my assent to the Constitution in full confidence that the amendments proposed will soon become a part of the system—these amendments being in no wise local, but calculated to give security and ease alike to all the states. I think that all will agree to them.

Suffer me to add that, let the question be decided as it may, there can be no triumph on the one side or chagrin on the other. Should there be a great division, every good man, every man who loves his country, will be so far from exhibiting extraordinary marks of joy that he will sincerely lament the want of unanimity and strenuously endeavor to cultivate a spirit of conciliation, both in Convention and at home.

The people of this commonwealth are a people of great light—of great intelligence in publick business. They know that we have none of us an interest separate from theirs; that it must be our happiness to conduce to theirs; and that we must all rise or fall together. They will never therefore forsake the first principle of society, that of being governed by the voice of the majority—and should it be that the proposed form of government should be rejected, they will zealously attempt another. Should it, by the vote now to be taken, be ratified, they will quietly acquiesce and where they see a want of perfection in it endeavor in a constitutional way to have it amended.

The question now before you is such as no nation on earth, without the limits of America, has ever had the privilege of deciding upon. As the Supreme Ruler of the Universe has seen fit to bestow upon us this glorious opportunity, let us decide upon it—appealing to him for the rectitude of our intentions, and in humble confidence that he will yet continue to bless and save our country.[3]

Hancock's sense of the gravity of the moment only enhanced his statesmanlike eloquence. As soon as he finished, Samuel Adams leapt to the podium and declared his support for Hancock's "conciliatory proposals." It was the first time the two men had agreed with each other on any issue in a dozen years; both were aware that neither could have prevailed without the other. One week later, Hancock called the vote. Massachusetts became the sixth state to ratify the Constitution, if only by a narrow margin, 187 votes to 168.

Across the state, Hancock was hailed as a hero, and he was even praised in a popular ballad:

Then Squire Hancock like a man,
Who dearly loved the nation

By a conciliatory plan,
Prevented much vexation.
Yankee Doodle, keep it up,
Yankee Doodle dandy,
Mind the music and the step,
And with the girls be handy.
He made a woundy Fed'ral speech,
With sense and elocution,
And then the 'Vention did beseech
T' adopt the Constitution.[4]

~e~

Until a two-thirds majority of the states ratified the draft Constitution, the framework of national government remained the Articles of Confederation. All measures involving the Confederation Congress required the unanimous vote of the states. Hancock quickly grasped the danger when Governor George Clinton of New York, the leading anti-Federalist, attempted to take advantage of the sharp division in some states, including his own. In the Confederation Congress, Clinton moved that a new national convention be summoned to replace the draft approved in Philadelphia. Hancock seized the moment to object on behalf of Massachusetts, blocking Clinton.

Massachusetts was the sixth state to ratify, after Delaware, Pennsylvania, New Jersey, Georgia and Connecticut, but three more states were needed to reach the necessary two-thirds majority for ratification. Maryland and South Carolina would soon follow suit. There was strong support for the Constitution in coastal New Hampshire, but its assembly voted to postpone its convention. The measure finally passed in June. Meanwhile, the sharpest resistance to the new form of government came in Virginia and in New York, where New York City overwhelmingly favored a strong federal government and everyone else in the predominantly agricultural state opposed it.

Shortly before noon on July 2, a Clinton attack on the Constitution was interrupted by "such a buzz through the House that little of his Excellency's speech was heard."[5]

Colonel William S. Livingston had ridden more than eighty-two miles of rough roads from New York City in ten hours, changing horses only twice, to bring the news from Madison in Congress that, over the powerful objection of Patrick Henry, Virginia had ratified. After it became apparent that, as Hancock had first proposed, a bill of rights must be appended to the Constitution, New York voted for ratification by a razor-thin three-vote margin, thirty to twenty-seven.

In Massachusetts's statewide elections in April 1789, Hancock swept to reelection by a three-to-one margin. He now saw his principal role as that of a conciliator. He persuaded the sixty-six-year-old Samuel Adams to run as lieutenant governor to block Lincoln from reelection. Adams was finally ready to concede that Hancock had done a remarkable job as governor, mediating disputes and bringing ancient rivals together for the good of Boston and the commonwealth. Adams ringingly endorsed Hancock for reelection to an eighth term:

> I am far from being an enemy to that gentleman, though he has been prevailed upon to mark me as such. I have so much friendship for him as to wish with all my heart that he is able to hold the reins of office with honor.[6]

That summer, Hancock's health improved so much that he was able to take a long-promised vacation trip with Dolly to Portsmouth, New Hampshire. As the country buzzed about the first presidential election—there never was a question that Washington would win—newspapers described the trip as Hancock campaigning for the vice presidency. Under the new Constitution, electors from each state would vote for the president, but the second-highest vote getter would become vice president. The *New Hampshire Gazette* prophesied that "Washington will undoubtedly be President and Governor Hancock Vice-President of the Union."[7]

While his political advisor James Sullivan urged Hancock to actively join the race, he seems never to have entertained the idea seriously, well aware that his chronic illness would make it impossible for him to travel or long preside at official functions. Still, he did not have his name stricken from the list of candidates.

In contrast, John Adams took Hancock so seriously that he wrote to Mercy Otis Warren that Hancock was "ambitious of being President or Vice President ... [and that] I stood in the way."[8] Benjamin Lincoln wrote to Washington, "Governor Hancock and ... Mr. John Adams are considered the candidates for that office.... The latter ... will be that man, for I cannot believe that the Governor would, under his present want of health, leave this government, even if he should be elected second in the new one."

In January 1789, Major William Jackson, Hancock's close friend and Washington's personal secretary, wrote to Washington that Hancock "has not been out of his chamber and is now confined to his bed with gout." He wrote again three weeks later, "Mr. Hancock remains very sick."[9]

When the votes were tallied, Washington had received all sixty-nine electoral votes for president. Among the remaining candidates, Adams received thirty-four votes. All of Massachusetts's electors voted for Adams. Hancock ranked fifth, receiving four votes. Despite his loss to Adams, Hancock was a friend of the future vice president. In June 1788, when Adams had come home from England, Governor Hancock arranged a splendid reception for him, even sending a note of welcome for Adams to the pilot at the Boston Light. As Adams's ship sailed into Boston Harbor, cannon on Castle Island boomed a salute and Boston's church bells chimed. Hancock's yellow coach waited dockside to carry the Adamses and their servants to Beacon Hill. There, the Hancocks greeted him, "wishing that you will tarry till you have fixed your place of abode." Dolly and her cooks laid out an especially lavish dinner for the Adamses.[10]

~e~

In the April 1789 statewide gubernatorial election, Hancock easily won along with his choice of lieutenant governor, Samuel Adams. While Hancock remained incapacitated, rarely leaving his mansion, Adams and Hancock's advisor James Sullivan effectively ran the state's administration from Beacon Hill, with Adams carrying out more and more of Hancock's official functions.

On April 30, Washington was inaugurated in New York City, cheered on by a crowd of ten thousand when he appeared on the balcony of Federal Hall. As he set about establishing the new nation's affairs, he was well aware that his every act would establish a precedent. He had to decide what he should be called, what he should wear and what amount of time he should allow to meet with the public. After choosing Cabinet officers, he personally screened and filled a thousand federal jobs, from judge to naval officer to postmaster. Service in the Revolution was an indispensable prerequisite.

In May, he wrote to Vice President Adams, "Many things which appear to be of little importance in themselves may have great and durable consequences from their having been established at the commencement of a new general government." If he accommodated the wishes for meetings with all the people who wanted to see him, he would be "unable to attend to any business *whatsoever.*" He sent Adams a list of nine questions, mostly dealing with his schedule of dinners, teas and receptions. Question eight queried:

> Whether during the recess of Congress, it would not be advantageous to the interests of the Union for the President to make the tour of the United States in order to become better acquainted with their principal characters and internal circumstances as well as to be more accessible to numbers of well-informed persons who might give him useful information and advice on political subjects?[11]

CHAPTER EIGHTEEN

"I Feel the Seeds of Mortality"

Washington planned his first presidential tour with all the precision of a military campaign, scheduling every stop and every hour of the next three weeks. He had become obsessed with time. He threatened to fire his personal secretary, Tobias Lear, for being a few minutes tardy; when Lear blamed his watch, Washington told him to get a new watch or get a new job.

At noon on October 15, Washington set off for New England accompanied by Lear and Major Jackson, a combat veteran and secretary of the Constitutional Convention. The two aides rode on horses on either side of Washington's carriage, which was pulled by four matched bay horses. Washington was attended by six servants, two of them enslaved. All the servants wore Washington's livery: blanket coats, jockey caps, buckskins and boots.

Washington had rehearsed a dramatic entrance into every town. Dressed in his navy blue general's epauletted uniform, he would climb down from his carriage and mount Prescott, a white charger trained to prance at the head of the presidential cavalcade while Washington waved his tricorne hat and half bowed left and right to the cheering crowd.

After passing through throngs in Philadelphia, New York City, New Haven and Hartford—where he substituted the locally made brown suit he had worn at his inauguration for his general's uniform—Washington crossed into Massachusetts. At Worcester, he spent a day fine-tuning his entrance into Boston. The Boston Select Board and officers of the Middlesex Militia had sent representatives to help him smooth out the details. The president would first be met by the militia in Cambridge; then he would cross over the Neck into Boston in a grand parade. Washington would confide to his diary that since "this ceremony was not to be avoided . . . I named the hour of ten to pass the militia . . . and the hour of 12 for my entrance into Boston."[1]

At Worcester, Washington also received a courier from Governor Hancock inviting him to stay at Hancock House. But Washington never accepted the invitations of politicians to stay in their private residences—a fact that Hancock should have remembered from 1776 when Washington had declined an invitation from President Hancock of the Continental Congress.

Thirteen years later, Washington again declined. He did, however, tactfully accept "your Excellency's polite invitation to take an informal dinner with you."[2] The next day, as Washington stopped over at Shrewsbury, he received another courier with a note from Governor Hancock. Hancock was not happy: "It would have given me pleasure had a residence at my house met with your approbation." Washington sent back word that this time he accepted.[3]

After reviewing a thousand militiamen and then crossing over from Cambridge, Washington, joined by Vice President Adams, followed the recently renamed Washington Street into Roxbury. The cavalcade was already behind schedule because the militia had assembled an hour late. Washington noted the delay in his diary, writing that "most of the militia having a distance to come were not in line until after eleven."[4] And he was due in Boston at noon.

During that hour, Washington, wearing his dress uniform, sat fuming on his elegant white charger, even more annoyed when he learned that Hancock would not be accompanying him into Boston. The governor had delegated Lieutenant Governor Samuel Adams to make his apologies to Washington: The governor was experiencing an acute flare-up of gout. Hancock had asked Adams to meet Washington's cavalcade and lead into Boston a parade consisting of Hancock's Corps of Cadets, a marching band and a long line of dignitaries.

It was becoming difficult for Washington not to interpret Hancock's repeated absences as deliberate snubs, as he likely didn't realize the governor was genuinely incapacitated. The president was making the tour in part to establish protocols for relations between the president and the states' chief executives and to determine just who should pay respect to whom and when and where they should do so. Washington wrote in his notebook that "(under a full persuasion that he would have waited on me so soon as I should have arrived) I excused myself upon his not doing it. . . . Dined at my lodgings, where the Vice President favored me with his company."[5]

Overnight, Samuel Adams conveyed to Hancock the extent of Washington's displeasure. When Washington returned to his lodgings after attending church, he found a note from a chastened Hancock: "The governor's best respects to the President. If at home and at leisure, the governor will do himself the honor to pay his respects in half an hour. This would have been done much sooner

had his health, in any degree, permitted. He now hazards everything, as it respects his health, for the desirable purpose."[6]

Washington answered with icy formality: "The President of the
United States presents his best respects to the Governor and has
the honor to inform him that he shall be at home till 2 o'clock. The
President of the United States need not express the pleasure it will
give him to see the Governor; but, at the same time, he most ear-
nestly begs that the Governor will not hazard his health on the
occasion."[7]

Within an hour, Hancock's carriage pulled up in front of Washington's lodgings. Hancock's servants—with Dolly's supervision—
had wrapped the governor's legs in layer after layer of red flannel to
minimize his pain during the jostling ride over rough streets. Two
burly servants carried Hancock, probably in a sedan chair, to Washington's rooms.

It had been thirteen years, a revolution and a war since the two
had last met—and Hancock was stunned by Washington. Others
had the same reaction. Senator William Maclay of Pennsylvania had
attended a speech Washington had recently made in New York
City. In his diary, he noted the toll the presidency was already exact-
ing. "He trembled and several times could scarce make out to read
[his speech]. He appeared to be emaciated, his uniform hanging on
him. His frame would seem to want filling up. . . . His complexion
was pale, nay, almost cadaverous."[8]

Hancock's appearance shocked Washington, too. Thirty-one
years later, Dolly Hancock told guests at a dinner given in her
honor by General Sumner Welles that Hancock had been in ex-
treme pain in both hands and legs that day. When Washington
saw that Hancock—his once elegant colleague in the Continental
Congress; the first man to sign the Declaration of Independence

and Washington's own commission as commander in chief of the Continental Army—had become an enfeebled old man who could no longer hold a pen, he wept. The next day, Washington joined the Hancocks for tea at their mansion on Beacon Hill.

On October 29—with a cavalry escort led by Captain Caleb Gibbs, the longtime leader of Washington's elite Life Guards—Washington decided to escape another throng by leaving Boston through the North End and across the new bridge Hancock had built across the Charles River.

~ℓ~

In the 1790 statewide elections, with Samuel Adams again as his lieutenant governor, Hancock easily won reelection and continued his agenda of moderating Massachusetts's Puritan rules. Only a few years earlier, no stage plays had been allowed. When one group of touring actors attempted to disguise a theatrical performance as a series of "moral lectures," an outraged Adams attended a performance and demanded that Hancock enforce a 1750 law. Boston's sheriff and his deputies shut down the theater by literally bringing down the house, dismantling the converted stable.

Hancock's legislative majority also relaxed the ban barring the return of the Loyalists. Now only actual combatants and former Crown officials would be excluded. The measure, undoubtedly supported by Governor Hancock, finally reunited Dolly Hancock and her sister Esther, whose husband, Jonathan Sewall, the former attorney general of colonial Massachusetts, had died in Halifax, where he was attorney general of New Brunswick. Esther had moved to join her sons in Nova Scotia. The little boy Johnny who had been terrified by the mob attack would become, like his father,

attorney general of a royal province. Now, Esther could visit her
sister in Boston.

Hancock continued to urge the legislature to appropriate more
money to improve education in a speech he made at a Harvard
commencement day delivered from a wheelchair. Late in 1792, he
finally arranged to pay the interest he still disputed owing Harvard
from his wartime years as the college's treasurer. He agreed to pay,
in 1793, the equivalent of simple interest but only for the time he
had physically retained the funds and was unable to invest them;
Harvard still was holding out for interest compounding since 1775.

Hancock now rarely left the mansion except to preside over
meetings of the General Court. He did not even leave to campaign
for governor, as he ran unopposed again in 1791, 1792 and 1793.
During brief periods of remission, Hancock took trips with Dolly.
In the spring of 1791, they traveled north to Portsmouth; in 1792,
south to Newport, then on to Fairfield, where they had married
seventeen years earlier and where they now reunited with their old
friends the Burrs. Hancock continued to invite legislative leaders
to his house atop Beacon Hill, but when Dolly and her staff served
their dinners, Hancock had to sit alone at a small table, his legs
wrapped in red flannel.

~·~

On September 18, 1793, Hancock presided over a meeting of the
General Court for the last time. He could no longer stand or read
his message asking the lawmakers to bar a suit brought by a Loyalist in Jamaica against Massachusetts for confiscating his lands.
Hancock's message had to be read by the secretary while Hancock
sat in a wheelchair. After the secretary finished reading, Hancock,

his hands shaking, his voice quavering, delivered his last speech extemporaneously:

> I beg the pardon of the Honorable Legislature, and I rely on your candor, Gentlemen, to forgive this method of address-ing you. I feel the seeds of mortality growing fast within me, but I think in this case I have done no more than my duty as the servant of the people. I never did and I never will deceive them, while I have life and strength to serve them.[9]

Hancock continued to serve as governor, now little more than a figurehead, his health broken.

On Tuesday morning, October 8, Hancock awoke too weak to speak or move, his breathing labored. Dolly sent for the doctor, but it was too late. One hour later, with Dolly and Nat Balch, his friend the hatter, at his bedside, John Hancock died. He was only fifty-six.

~e~

As word of his death spread across Boston, John Hancock lay in state in his beloved Hancock House for a week. According to the *Independent Chronicle*, the bells in all the churches and public buildings tolled for an hour, and the flags in town, on the castle and on the masts of ships in the harbor flew at half-mast as thou-sands of mourners from all over Massachusetts filed past his bier. Interim governor Samuel Adams declared the day of his burial a state holiday.

At two o'clock on October 14, in the largest funeral Americans had ever seen, a somber procession of twenty thousand from Bos-ton and nearby towns started a slow march from Beacon Hill across the Common, four abreast. Every militia unit from Boston and the surrounding towns stepped to the somber pounding of the drums. Swords drawn, they led all of the state's officials, including Samuel Adams and members of the executive council, who served as pallbearers. Hancock's Corps of Cadets followed with the four cannon that he had ordered seized at the outbreak of the Revolution and that had formed the nation's first artillery unit; the cannon were draped in black.

Behind Hancock's luxurious yellow coach, which bore his widow, Dolly, came twenty others. Vice President Adams followed with judges; members of the legislature; Harvard's president, Overseers and faculty; and Boston's selectmen. Cannon boomed as the hour-long procession wound slowly to Boylston Street, where it paused at the site of the Liberty Tree, then turned left and followed Washington Street to the State House and around it to the Granary Burying Ground, where Hancock was laid to rest beside his son, John George Washington Hancock, and his uncle Thomas. There, minuteman muskets fired thirteen salutes. Tributes poured in, many in long editorials. The *Independent Chronicle* simply proclaimed, in its largest font, "HANCOCK IS DEAD."[10]

Dolly Hancock lived another thirty-six years. Three years after Hancock died, she married his most trusted ship's captain and partner, James Scott, and moved with him to Portsmouth; when he died ten years later, she returned to Beacon Hill, avoiding some of the infighting Hancock had expected and dreaded over the disposition of his estate. To the surprise of many and the disappointment of some, Hancock left no will. By dying intestate, he left his estate, half what many had expected, to be divided three ways. Dolly received Hancock House; his mother and brother each received one-quarter of his estate. Hancock had given away half of the fortune left to him by his aunt and uncle to help win American independence, launch a new nation and attempt to improve the quality of life in his beloved Boston.

In 1812, John Adams, with his presidency and the political wars behind him, offered John Hancock—his childhood friend, schoolmate and longtime associate in early Revolutionary and national politics—a succinct encomium. John Hancock was

> radically generous and benevolent. I could melt into tears when I hear his name. . . . If benevolence, charity, generosity were ever personified in North America, they were in John Hancock. What shall I say of his education? His literary acquisitions . . . his military, civil and political services? His sufferings and his sacrifices?[11]

To William Tudor, Adams wrote in 1817, "I can say with truth that I admired him and more profoundly loved him."[12]

Hancock's generosity and hospitality were not forgotten by foreign soldiers and statesmen who had fought beside him and celebrated with him and Dolly over candlelight dinners atop Beacon Hill. In 1824, Lafayette, who had survived another revolution in France, reminded Americans of the glory and the agony of their Revolutionary birth. As President James Monroe's guest, he toured the nation. When his white-uniformed entourage reached Boston, Lafayette ordered it to pause as it passed by No. 4 Federal Street, where Dolly had moved after selling Hancock House. There stood seventy-seven-year-old Dolly Quincy Hancock Scott. Lafayette alighted from his carriage and bowed deeply to her; Dolly bowed back and said, in a barely audible voice, "Now I have lived long enough."[13]

John Hancock's openhandedness remained with French journalist Brissot de Warville after he had met many of America's Founding Fathers and before he went home to die in France's revolution. He had visited Beacon Hill in 1789 immediately after Hancock's brilliant speech securing the ratification of the Constitution:

> You know the great sacrifices he made in the Revolution and the boldness with which he declared himself at the beginning of the insurrection. The same spirit of patriotism animates him still. A great generosity, united to a vast ambition, forms his character; he has the virtues and the address of popularism; that is to say, that without effort he shows himself the equal and friend of all.[14]

Acknowledgments

In the half century since the Bicentennial in 1976 of the signing of the Declaration of Independence, researching early American history has become democratized. In large part, this is because of advances in technology that roughly parallel my own efforts to write the biographies of the Founding Fathers. This scientific evolution has made it possible for me now to chronicle the life of John Hancock despite the severe limitations on the accessibility of research materials imposed by the Covid-19 pandemic.

The Bicentennial celebration of America's independence unfolded against a backdrop of civil turmoil. The nation was riven by discord over the Vietnam War and reeling from the race riots and assassinations of the sixties. In contrast, the gathering and publication of multivolume collections of documents surviving from the nation's Founding Era were making them accessible to the public and laying the foundation for celebrating the nation's birth.

In 1969, the grand project was launched by creation of a Bicentennial Commission. Among its distinguished scholars was Catherine Drinker Bowen, author of the bestselling *Miracle at Philadelphia* and *John Adams and the American Revolution*. As a young features writer for the *Philadelphia Evening and Sunday Bulletin*, I was assigned to interview Ms. Bowen about her latest book, *Biography: The Craft and the Calling*.

Using state-of-the-art tools, a reporter's notebook and a pen, I was scribbling away when she graciously asked if I had ever considered writing a book. I told her I had been reading Benjamin Franklin's *Autobiography* and had been fascinated by his twice mentioning a son, opening the memoir, "Dear Son," then adding, "My son was of much use to me." I had recently been assigned to interview the governor of New Jersey and had come across a short book that profiled earlier governors, including the last under British colonial rule, William Franklin. "That is the last great untold story of the American Revolution!" Ms. Bowen exclaimed.

My editor at the *Bulletin*, B. Dale Davis, sent me off again with my notepad when he learned from Whitfield J. Bell, librarian of the American Philosophical Society, that a collector had just offered a large collection of the personal letters of the Founders, venturing that the *Bulletin* might find an interesting story among them. Davis gave me only one week to produce a piece for George Washington's birthday. But each morning for a month, I got up in the dark and drove across the city to Washington's Crossing. There I sat across the dining room table from Sol Feinstone, a real estate millionaire who had amassed 1,100 of the Founders' autographed documents. He handed me one letter at a time; I jotted notes until noon, then drove Feinstone into the city to the Philosophical Society—he didn't own a car!

Stretching the assignment to six weeks, I produced "George Washington's Love Letters," the lead Sunday feature. That article elicited kind words from Librarian Bell, who mentioned it to Ms. Bowen, a director of the Philosophical Society. The result: my first (modest) research grant, to write the first biography of William Franklin.

Invited to present a paper on Governor Franklin at the First International Conference on Loyalists in the American Revolution—he was to become the president of the Loyalists and went into exile in England before being disinherited by his more famous father—I met scholars from Britain, Canada and the United States. Several subsequently introduced me to archives that helped my project morph into a dual biography, *A Little Revenge: Benjamin Franklin and His Son.* James E. Mooney, then director of the Historical Society of Pennsylvania, was preparing a finder's guide to Loyalist papers; he also generously vetted my manuscript. Esmond Wright, director of the United States Institute at the University of London and a Benjamin Franklin biographer, challenged me to find anything new on the American Revolution and then arranged interviews and research privilege in England.

Elements of my father-son story next appeared in a series of monthly tabloids and a book, *The Founding City*, commissioned by the *Philadelphia Inquirer* as part of the Bicentennial. Freed from my investigative journalistic duties, I scoured the city's museums and historic sites and decided to return to school and retool as an historian specializing in biography. Over the years, I had borrowed heavily on the interlibrary loan privileges of Princeton University, which granted me visiting scholar status to complete my Benedict Arnold research and begin work on a biography of Thomas Jefferson. That research led me to archives from Virginia to California, where I found Jefferson's expense records—no one was reimbursing them—and followed the trail across Europe, through Italy and to the American Embassy in Paris, where hanging files were preserved for every American ambassador to France.

But the first meeting of my work with evolving technology and research techniques came at the University of Vermont, where I began to teach after graduate studies at Princeton University. Interest in the Loyalists had inevitably led me to Benedict Arnold, synonymous with "treason."

Thomas Jefferson once wrote, "I cannot live without books." I cannot live without librarians! There are no archives for America's most famous patriot turned traitor. My first challenge with Arnold was to track down his scattered papers. Joe and Bonnie Ryan, librarians at UVM, taught me about "not in" research: how to use a computer to narrow a search by excluding some depositories and collections in which the researcher does not expect to find anything unpublished. A trove of letters appeared from private and public collections.

The "not in" search ultimately led to the Loyalist Museum in St. John, New Brunswick, where I found the legal papers of Arnold's widow and executor, Peggy Shippen Arnold, left behind after the Arnolds' ultimate exile in London. At the same time, I learned about the massive collection of the *Naval Documents of the American Revolution*, available from the Government Printing Office, which unlocked Arnold's heroic naval exploits on Lake Champlain.

Until the technological revolution of the 1980s spawned the internet, historical researchers still had to rely on visits to archives, where curators not only guarded documents—no pens were allowed; pencils were still in fashion—but kept track of researchers' projects. Roberts Parks at the Morgan Library in New York City had heard that I was working on a biography of Jefferson: He alerted me that the Morgan had acquired letters Jefferson had written on the membrane of birchbark when he ran out of paper on a trip to Vermont with James Madison.

At this time, Project Gutenberg brought together the librarians of major universities with Google's search engines. Suddenly, hundreds of thousands of out-of-print books became available online, making it possible for researchers to work from their homes or offices without costly travel to archives and shielding priceless books from human handling and the possibility of damage or theft.

Combined with the assistance of interlibrary loan librarians, not only books but also journal articles became accessible through rapidly proliferating online databases. The librarian could request the cooperating library to make a hard copy and send it. For ten years, Brenda Racht, reference librarian at Champlain College—where I have taught American history for twenty-five years—tracked down materials from libraries as near as the University of Vermont and then down the street to England as I researched biographies of George Washington, Alexander Hamilton and Ethan Allen.

The evolution of new technologies brought on by a race to bring out faster, more efficient and more compact computers took place just in time to avert a calamity in research and publication at the outbreak of the coronavirus pandemic in 2020. Using these new tools, I have been able to retrieve materials and memories from earlier explorations into the lives and time of the Founders from my desktop computer. The democratization of research made it feasible for me to bring out *The Founders' Fortunes* during the pandemic and to undertake this book on the important contributions of John Hancock without the possibility of real-time visits to archives and libraries that were shut down for nearly three years.

At the same time, I owe thanks to many participants in this process. At Champlain College, longtime president Roger Perry supported some of my travel, making it possible to publicize my efforts. John W. Heisse Jr., longtime benefactor of the college, underwrote travel to France to study the life of Samuel de Champlain, namesake of the college and the lake he explored. His daughter, Karen, later helped me to do research in the Chesapeake Bay theater of the War of 1812 for my book *Unshackling America: How the War of 1812 Truly Ended the American Revolution*. Successive provosts at the college, including Laurie Quinn and Monique Taylor, have provided timely research grants.

As he has for many years, my friend, literary agent and wise counselor, Don Fehr, has helped me to bring this book to press. Brent Howard, my former editor at Dutton, first grasped the relevance of a study of the underappreciated contributions of John Hancock. Grace Layer, his successor, has cheerfully, skillfully and creatively completed the project, assisted by the meticulous fine-tuning of copy editor Frank Walgren. And as she has for forty years now, my lovely wife, Nancy Nahra, continues to inspire, encourage, and elucidate my life and my work, and our talented daughter, Lucy, a senior editor at Oxford University Press, wisely and patiently coaches me from the sidelines.

Abbreviations Key

AA—Abigail Adams
AP—Adams Papers
BN-L—*Boston News-Letter*
BPL—Boston Public Library
DQH—Dorothy Quincy Hancock
GW—George Washington
HLB—Hancock Letter Book, NEHGS
HUA—Harvard University Archives
JA—John Adams
JH—John Hancock
MAH—*Magazine of American History*
MHS—Massachusetts Historical Society
NEHGS—New England Historic Genealogical Society
NYPL—New York Public Library
PGW—Papers of George Washington
PMHB—*Pennsylvania Magazine of History and Biography*
PTJ—Papers of Thomas Jefferson
SA—Samuel Adams
TH—Thomas Hancock

Notes

PROLOGUE

1. Adams, "Portrait of an Empty Barrel," 161:431–32.
2. Beard, *Economic Interpretation of the Constitution*.
3. JA–William Tudor, June 1, 1817, in Allan, *John Hancock*.
4. Proctor, "New Soundings on an Old Barrel," 676.

CHAPTER ONE: "THE KNOWN WORLD"

1. William Waldron–Richard Waldron, December 25, 1723, Waldron Papers, 30, MHS.
2. Thomas Morton, *New English Canaan*, 123.
3. JA–Richard Cranch, PJA, MHS.
4. BN-L, March 4, 1725, BPL.
5. Ibid., May 6, 1736.
6. TH–Francis Wilks, June 24, 1737, Thomas Hancock Letter Book, Hancock Papers, NEHGS.
7. Ibid.
8. Ibid.
9. Ibid.
10. Ibid.

CHAPTER TWO: "NO PLEASURE WITHOUT PAIN"

1. Butterfield, ed., Diary and Papers of John Adams, 1:42–3.
2. *Sibley's Harvard Graduates*, 13:380.
3. Quincy, *History of Harvard University*, 2:97.
4. Faculty records, 1:322–23, 325; 2:211–12, HUA.

CHAPTER THREE: "MAKE A STIR FOR US"

1. Catherine Drinker Bowen, *John Adams and the American Revolution*, 214.
2. Ibid., 215.
3. TH–Christopher Kilby, May 21, 1760, MHS.
4. TH–JH, July 5, 1760, TH Letter Book, NEGHS.
5. TH–JH, March 16, 1761, MHS-P, 43:196.
6. JH–TH, January 14, 1761, MHS-P, 43:196.
7. JH–Mary Hancock, October 29, 1760, HLB.
8. JH–Ebenezer Hancock, December 27, 1760, HLB, MHS-P, 43:195.
9. BN-L, January 1, 1763.

CHAPTER FOUR: "WE ARE A GONE PEOPLE"

1. BN-L, January 3, 1765, BPL.
2. John Hancock–Barnard and Harrison, January 21, 1765, JH Letter Book, Hancock Papers, NEHGS.
3. John Adams–William Tudor, January 1, 1817, PJA, 10:259–60.
4. SA, "Instructions of the Town of Boston to Its Representatives in the General Court," May 15, 1764, BPL.
5. George Washington–Robert Cary & Co., September 20, 1765, PGW, Colonial Series, 7:402.
6. JH–Barnard & Harrison, June 23, 1764, MHS.
7. Ibid., April 5, 1764, MHS.
8. Ibid.
9. Ibid., September 11, 1765, in Baxter, *The House of Hancock*, 258.
10. Ibid., October 14, 1765, MHS.
11. Ibid., December 1765, MHS.
12. *Massachusetts Gazette Extraordinary*, March 22, 1766, BPL.
13. Ibid.
14. PJA, 2:259–61.

CHAPTER FIVE: "THE IDOL OF THE MOB"

1. Thomas Hutchinson, *History of the Province of Massachusetts*, 2:277.
2. Quincy, *History of Harvard University*, 2:194.
3. JH–William Reeve, September 3, 1767, HLB, NEHGS.
4. Quoted in Unger, *John Hancock*, 118.
5. Ibid.
6. Fowler, *Baron of Beacon Hill*, 100.
7. Customs commissioners to lords of treasury, May 12, 1768, in Knollenberg, *Growth of the American Republic*, 51.
8. Wells, *Life and Public Services*, 1:186.
9. *Boston Gazette*, August 4, 1768, BPL.
10. JA, papers, microfilm, reel 189.
11. John Wilkes–William Palfrey, July 14, 1769. Colonial Society of Massachusetts Publications 34:414.

CHAPTER SIX: "A SINGULAR DIGNITY AND GRACE"

1. Legal papers of John Adams,.3 vols., HUA.
2. Everett, *Eulogy of Thomas Dowse*, 8.
3. 1874 register, 182, NEGHS.
4. JH–George Hayley, August 24, 1768, JH Letter Book, Hancock Papers, NEGHS.
5. JH–George Hayley, November 14, 1772, in Allan, *John Hancock*, 125.
6. Fowler, *Baron of Beacon Hill*, 161.
7. JA, Butterfield, ed., Diary and Autobiography of JA, 2:332.
8. Wells, *Life and Public Services*, 1:186.
9. Ibid.
10. JA, Diary and Autobiography, 2:332.

CHAPTER SEVEN: "REMOVE IMMEDIATELY FROM BOSTON"

1. Lincoln, *Journals of Each Provincial Congress.*
2. JH–Massachusetts Committee of Safety, April 24, 1775, in Alden, *General Gage*, 107–9.
3. Sumner, Incidents in the Life of JH, MAH 19:505.
4. JH–Dorothy Quincy, March 25, 1775, in Alden, *General Gage*, 241.
5. Sumner, Incidents, MAH 19:505.
6. Randall, *Ethan Allen*, 20.
7. Fischer, *Paul Revere's Ride*, 178; Sumner, Incidents, MAH 19:505.
8. JA, diary, August 29, 1774; Butterfield, ed., Diary and Autobiography of JA; Smith and Gephart, *Letters of Delegates to Congress* 1:5.
9. JH–Joseph Warren, June 18, 1775, in Allan, *John Hancock*, 198.

CHAPTER EIGHT: "A SHADOW AS PALE AS ASHES"

1. JH–GW, July 10, 1775, in Sears, *John Hancock*, 191.
2. Force, ed., *American Archives*, 6:420.
3. JH–GW, July 10, 1775.
4. JA–AA, JA Papers.
5. JH–GW, May 21, 1776; Allan, *John Hancock*, 222.
6. GW–JH, March 19, 1776; Force, *American Archives*, 6:429.
7. JA in Boldt, ed., *Founding City*, 75.
8. Benjamin Rush–Charles Thomson, Boldt, *Founding City*, 191.
9. Child, *An Historic Mansion*, 14.
10. MAH 19:506.
11. Stoll, *Samuel Adams*, 174.
12. JA–AA, November 4, 1775, AP, MHS.
13. GW–JH, March 19, 1776, in Force, *American Archives*, 6:429.
14. JH–Thomas Cushing, June 12, 1776, HL, MHS.

CHAPTER NINE: "WHY ALL THIS HASTE?"

1. JA, diary, May 13, 1776.
2. Thomas Jefferson, *Autobiography*, 1818.

CHAPTER TEN: "CONSTANT APPLICATION TO PUBLIC BUSINESS"

1. JH–William Palfrey, October 29, 1777, BPL.
2. JH–Thomas Jefferson, October 25, 1777, in Smith and Gephart, *Letters of Delegates to Congress*, 2:534.
3. SA–James Warren, November 4, 1777, in Smith and Gephart, *Letters of Delegates to Congress*, 2:541.
4. Thomas Jefferson–Richard Henry Lee, July 8, 1776, PTJ, 1:456. For list of depositaries of Jefferson's papers, see page xxii of volume one of PTJ.
5. William Ellery–Governor Nicholas Cooke, January 4, 1777, in Staples, *Rhode Island in the Continental Congress*, 110.
6. *Massachusetts Magazine* 1 (1908): 52, BPL.
7. Isaac Cazneau–JH, April 4, 1776, in Watkins, "How the British Left the Hancock House," 194–95.
8. James Warren–SA, May 31, 1778, MHS.
9. Ibid.
10. Samuel Holten, journal, June 6, 1778, in Allan, *John Hancock*, 279.
11. JA, diary.

CHAPTER ELEVEN: "TOO PRECIOUS A KEEPSAKE"

1. JH–DQH, June 20, 1778, MHS.
2. William Ellery, June 28, 1778, "Diary of the Honorable William Ellery of Rhode Island," PMHB, 11:477–78.
3. Douglas Southall Freeman, quoted in Boatner, *Encyclopedia of the American Revolution*, 1071.
4. Ibid., 565.
5. Ibid., 585.
6. Montross, *Rag, Tag and Bobtail*, 293–94.
7. JH–DQH, August 19, 1778, BPL.
8. Christopher Ward, in Boatner, 592.
9. Sullivan et al., in Boatner, 793.
10. Lafayette, in Boatner.
11. JH–Jeremiah Powell, August 28, 1778, NYPL.
12. Lawrence, *Music for Patriots*, 79.

CHAPTER TWELVE: "THE FRENCHMEN ATE VORACIOUSLY"

1. GW–JH, August 24, 1778, in Boatner, 793.
2. Ellery, diary, June 28, 1778, PMHB, 11:477–78.
3. Quoted in Boatner, 1071.
4. JH–DQH, June 20, 1778, MHS.
5. Montross, *Rag, Tag and Bobtail*, 293–94.
6. Ibid.
7. Samuel Phillips Savage–SA, October 1778, *Proceedings of the Massachusetts Historical Society* 43:335, MHS.
8. SA–Samuel Phillips Savage, November 1, 1778, Thomas Cushing Papers, 4:87–88.
9. AA–JA, PJA Papers.
10. JH–Henry Quincy, August 30, 1779, in Fowler, *Baron of Beacon Hill*, 242–43.

11. JH–Jeremiah Powell, August 28, 1778, NYPL.
12. John Scollay–GW and Freeman, quoted in Boatner, 713.

CHAPTER THIRTEEN: "I HAVE LOST MANY THOUSANDS"

1. Allan, *John Hancock*, 303.
2. SA–Scollay, December 30, 1780, in Allan, *John Hancock*, 303.
3. Miller, *Sam Adams*, 365.
4. Brandes, *John Hancock's Life and Speeches*, 239.
5. William Heath–JH, September 22, 1781, MHS, seventh series, 5:262.
6. William Palfrey–JH, December 18, 1780, JH Letter Book, Hancock Papers, NEHGS.
7. William Hoskins–Joseph Palmer, January 17, 1783, JH Letter Book, Hancock Papers, NEHGS.
8. William Hoskins–James Warren, February 11, 1783, JH Letter Book, Hancock Papers, NEHGS.
9. JH–James Scott, n.d., JH Letter Book, Hancock Papers, NEHGS.

CHAPTER FOURTEEN: "A DELICATE BUSINESS"

1. Morison, *Three Centuries of Harvard*, 145.
2. Ibid.
3. Ibid.
4. Ibid.
5. Ibid.
6. Ibid.
7. JA, works, 2:325.
8. Sullivan, *Familiar Letters*, 12–13.
9. Catherine Wendell Davis–John Wendell, November 1782. "A Gentleman of Boston," AASP 29 (1919): 266–67.

CHAPTER FIFTEEN: "*PERHAPS* RESTORE OUR VIRTUE"

1. *Massachusetts Centinel*, January 1785.
2. JH–General Court, January 29, 1785, in Brandes, *John Hancock's Life and Speeches*, 289.
3. SA–JA, July 2, 1785, Thomas Cushing Papers, 4:316.
4. Randall, *Alexander Hamilton*, 319.

CHAPTER SIXTEEN: "A STORM IN THE ATMOSPHERE"

1. SA, papers, 3:246.
2. "Knox Report," in Richards, *Shays's Rebellion*, 11.
3. General Henry Lee–GW, PGW, digital edition, Library of Congress.
4. GW–General Henry Lee, PGW, digital edition, Library of Congress.
5. James Madison Jr.–James Madison Sr., November 1, 1786, PJM, 9 and 154.
6. Richard Henry Lee–James Madison, October 25, 1786, Founders Archive Online.
7. Thomas Jefferson–AA, February 22, 1787, PTJ, 11:174.
8. PJA, papers, MHS.

9. John Quincy Adams, eds. David Grayson Allen et al., Diary, November 1779–December 1788, 2 vols., 2:93.
10. JH–Henry Knox, March 14, 1787, MHS.
11. Hancock speech in Brandes, *John Hancock's Life and Speeches*, 184.

CHAPTER SEVENTEEN: "RADICALLY GENEROUS AND BENEVOLENT"

1. Peirce, *Debates and Proceedings in the Convention*, 55.
2. Allan, *John Hancock*.
3. Brandes, *John Hancock's Life and Speeches*, 327–29.
4. Allan, *John Hancock*, 335.
5. Randall, *Alexander Hamilton*, 359.
6. Schiff, *The Revolutionary*, 315.
7. *New Hampshire Gazette*, February 20, 1788, BPL.
8. JA–Mercy Otis Warren, quoted in Unger, *John Hancock*, 327.
9. William Jackson–GW, PGW, digital edition, Library of Congress.
10. JH–GW, PGW, digital edition, Library of Congress.
11. PJA papers, MHS.

CHAPTER EIGHTEEN: "I FEEL THE SEEDS OF MORTALITY"

1. Philbrick, *Travels with George*, 83.
2. GW–JH, PGW, digital edition, Library of Congress. Philbrick, *Travels with George*, 96.
3. Ibid., 83.
4. Ibid., 91.
5. Ibid., 96.
6. JH–GW, in Philbrick, *Travels with George*, 97.
7. Philbrick, *Travels with George*, 97.
8. William Maclay in Philbrick, *Travels with George*, 98.
9. Sumner, "Incidents," in Philbrick, *Travels with George*, 97.
10. *Independent Chronicle*, October 10, 1793.
11. JA–Richard Rush, July 30, 1812, in Allan, *John Hancock*, 364.
12. JA–William Tudor, June 1, 1817, Allan, *John Hancock*, 364.
13. Sumner, *Reminiscences*.
14. Brissot de Warville, *New Travels in the United States of America*, 373.

Bibliography

Abernethy, Thomas Perkins. *Western Lands and the American Revolution.*
Charlottesville: University of Virginia Press, 1937.
Adams, James Truslow. "Portrait of an Empty Barrel." *Harper's Monthly Magazine,*
September 1930.
Alden, John Richard. *General Gage in America.* New York: Greenwood Press, 1969.
Aldridge, Alfred Owen. *Benjamin Franklin: Philosopher and Man.* Philadelphia:
J. B. Lippincott Company, 1965.
Allan, Herbert Sanford. *John Hancock: Patriot in Purple.* New York: Beechhurst
Press, 1953.
Alvord, Clarence Walworth, and Clarence Edwin Carter. *The New Régime,*
1765–1767. Springfield: Illinois State Historical Library, 1916.
American Archives: Documents of the American Revolutionary Period. Edited by
Peter Force. Washington, DC, 1846.
Anderson, D. K., and G. T. Anderson. "The Death of Silas Deane." *New England*
Quarterly 62 (1984): 98–105.
Andreas, Peter. *Smuggler Nation: How Illicit Trade Made America.* New York:
Oxford University Press, 2013.
Appleby, Joyce O. *The Relentless Revolution: A History of Capitalism.* New York:
W. W. Norton, 2011.
Bailyn, Bernard. *The Ideological Origins of the American Revolution.* Cambridge,
MA: The Belknap Press of Harvard University Press, 1967.
———. *The Ordeal of Thomas Hutchinson.* Cambridge, MA: The Belknap Press of
Harvard University Press, 1974.
Baker, Mark Allen. *Spies of Revolutionary Connecticut.* Charleston, SC: History
Press, 2014.

Barrow, Thomas C. *Trade and Empire: The British Customs Service in Colonial America, 1660–1775*. Cambridge, MA: Harvard University Press, 1967.

Baxter, W. T. *The House of Hancock: Business in Boston, 1724–1775*. Cambridge, MA: Harvard University Press, 1945.

Beard, Charles A. *An Economic Interpretation of the Constitution of the United States*. New York: Macmillan, 1913.

Beeman, Richard. "The British Secret Service and the French-American Alliance." *American Historical Review* 29, no. 3 (1924): 474–95.

———. *Our Lives, Our Fortunes and Our Sacred Honor: The Forging of American Independence, 1774–1776*. New York: Basic Books, 2013.

———. *Plain, Honest Men: The Making of the American Constitution*. New York: Random House, 2009.

Bemis, Samuel Flagg. *The Diplomacy of the American Revolution*. Bloomington: Indiana University Press, 1957.

Berkin, Carol. *A Sovereign People: The Crises of the 1790s and the Birth of American Nationalism*. New York: Basic Books, 2017.

Bernstein, R. B. "Parliamentary Principles, American Realities: The Continental and Confederation Congresses, 1774–1789." In *Inventing Congress: Origins and Establishment of the First Federal Congress*, edited by Kenneth R. Bowling and Donald R. Kennon. Athens: Ohio University Press, 1999.

Bezanson, Anne, et al. *Prices and Inflation During the American Revolution, Pennsylvania, 1770–1790*. Philadelphia: University of Pennsylvania Press, 1951.

Billias, George Athan. *Elbridge Gerry: Founding Father and Republican Statesman*. New York: McGraw-Hill, 1976.

Boldt, David R., with Willard Sterne Randall, eds. *The Founding City*. Philadelphia: Chilton Books, 1976.

Bowen, Catherine Drinker. *John Adams and the American Revolution*. New York: Little, Brown, 1950.

———. *Miracle at Philadelphia: The Story of the Constitutional Convention, May to September 1787*. Boston: Little, Brown, 1966.

Bowen, H. V. *Revenue and Reform: The Indian Problem in British Politics, 1757–1773*. Cambridge, England: Cambridge University Press, 1991.

Bowman, Frank O., III. *High Crimes and Misdemeanors: A History of Impeachment for the Age of Trump*. Cambridge, England: Cambridge University Press, 2019.

Boyd, Julian P. "Silas Deane: Death by a Kindly Teacher of Treason?" *William and Mary Quarterly*, 3rd ser., 16, nos. 2–4 (1959): 165–87, 319–42, 515–50.

———, et al., eds. *Papers of Thomas Jefferson*. Princeton, NJ: Princeton University Press, 1950.

Brandes, Paul D. *John Hancock's Life and Speeches*. Lanham, MD: Scarecrow Press, 1996.

Breen, T. H. *Tobacco Culture: The Mentality of the Great Tidewater Planters on the Eve of the Revolution*. Princeton, NJ: Princeton University Press, 1985.

Brissot de Warville, Jacques-Pierre. *New Travels in the United States of America, Performed in 1788*. London: J. S. Jordan, 1792.

Brown, Robert E. *Middle-Class Democracy and the Revolution in Massachusetts, 1691–1780*. Ithaca, NY: Cornell University Press, 1955.

Buel, Richard, Jr. *In Irons: Britain's Naval Supremacy and the American Revolutionary Economy*. New Haven, CT: Yale University Press, 1998.

Bunker, Nick. *Young Benjamin Franklin: The Birth of Ingenuity*. New York: Alfred A. Knopf, 2018.

Burnett, Edward Cody. *The Continental Congress: A Definitive History of the Continental Congress from Its Inception in 1774 to March, 1789*. New York: Macmillan, 1941.

Burstein, Stanley M. "The Classics and the American Republic." *History Teacher* 30, no. 1 (November 1966): 29–44.

Butz, Stephen D. *Shays' Settlement in Vermont: A Story of Revolt and Archaeology*. Charleston, SC: History Press, 2017.

Calloway, Colin G. *The Indian World of George Washington*. New York: Oxford University Press, 2018.

Carlton, Mabel M. *John Hancock, Great American Patriot*. Boston: John Hancock Mutual Life Insurance Company, 1922.

Carp, E. Wayne. *"To Starve the Army at Pleasure": Continental Army Administration and American Political Culture, 1775–1783*. Chapel Hill: University of North Carolina Press, 1984.

Chapin, Joyce E., ed. *Benjamin Franklin's Autobiography*. New York: W. W. Norton, 2012.

Chastellux, Marquis de. *Travels in North America, 1780–82*. New York: Library of Congress, 1828.

Chernow, Barbara Ann. "Robert Morris: Land Speculator, 1790–1801." PhD diss., Columbia University, 1974.

Child, Frank S. *An Historic Mansion: Being an Account of the Thaddeus Burr Homestead, 1654–1915*. Fairfield, CT: n.p. 1915.

Coe, Alexis. *You Never Forget Your First: A Biography of George Washington*. New York: Viking, 2020.

Coleman, Peter J. *Debtors and Creditors in America: Insolvency, Imprisonment for Debt, and Bankruptcy, 1607–1900*. Madison: University of Wisconsin Press, 1974.

Collier, Christopher. *Roger Sherman's Connecticut: Yankee Politics and the America Revolution*. Middletown, CT: Wesleyan University Press, 1971.

Daughan, George C. *If by Sea: The Forging of the American Navy—From the Revolution to the War of 1812*. New York: Basic Books, 2008.

Davidson, James West, and Mark Hamilton Lytle. *After the Fact: The Art of Historical Detection*, 5th ed. New York: McGraw-Hill, 2004.

Dickerson, Oliver M., ed. *Boston Under Military Rule 1768–69*. Boston: Mount Vernon Press, 1936.

Doerflinger, Thomas M. *A Vigorous Spirit of Enterprise: Merchants and Economic Development in Revolutionary Philadelphia*. Chapel Hill: University of North Carolina Press, 1986.

Downing, Ned W. *The Revolutionary Beginning of the American Stock Market*. New York: Museum of American Finance, 2010.

Dull, Jonathan R. *A Diplomatic History of the American Revolution*. New Haven, CT: Yale University Press, 1985.

East, Robert A. *Business Enterprises in the American Revolutionary Era*. New York: Columbia University Press, 1938.

Ellis, Joseph J. *His Excellency: George Washington*. New York: Alfred A. Knopf, 2004.

———. *The Quartet*. New York: Alfred A. Knopf, 2015.

Ernst, Joseph Albert. *Money and Politics in America 1755–1775: A Study in the Currency Act of 1764 and the Political Economy of Revolution*. Chapel Hill: University of North Carolina Press, 1973.

Everett, Edward. *Eulogy of Thomas Dowse*. Boston: John Wilson and Son, 1858.

Feer, Robert A. "Shays's Rebellion and the Constitution: A Study in Causation." *New England Quarterly* 42, no. 3 (September 1969): 388–410.

Fenster, Julie M. *Jefferson's America: The President, the Purchase, and the Explorers Who Transformed America*. New York: Broadway Books, 2016.

Ferguson, E. James. *The Power of the Purse: A History of American Public Finance, 1776–1790*. Chapel Hill: University of North Carolina Press, 1961.

Ferling, John. *Independence: The Struggle to Set America Free*. New York: Bloomsbury Press, 2011.

———. *John Adams: A Life*. Knoxville: University of Tennessee Press, 1992.

Ferris, Robert G., and James H. Charleton. *The Signers of the Constitution*. Flagstaff, AZ: Interpretive Publications, 1986.

Fischer, David Hackett. *Paul Revere's Ride*. New York: Oxford University Press, 1994.

Fleming, Thomas. *Liberty! The American Revolution*. New York: Viking, 1997.

———. *The Perils of Peace: America's Struggle for Survival After Yorktown*. New York: HarperCollins, 2007.

Flower, Milton E. *John Dickinson: Conservative Revolutionary*. Charlottesville: University of Virginia Press, 1983.

Force, Peter, ed. *American Archives*, 1846.

Fowler, William M. *The Baron of Beacon Hill: A Biography of John Hancock*. Boston: Houghton Mifflin, 1980.

Franklin, Benjamin. *The Autobiography of Benjamin Franklin*, edited by Leonard W. Larrabee et al. New Haven, CT: Yale University Press, 1964.

Freeman, Douglas Southall. *George Washington: A Biography*. 7 vols. New York: Scribner's, 1948–1957.

Gilje, Paul A. *Rioting in America*. Bloomington: Indiana University Press, 1996.

Gipson, Lawrence Henry. *American Loyalist: Jared Ingersoll*. New Haven, CT: Yale University Press, 1971.

Gordon, John Steele. *Hamilton's Blessing: The Extraordinary Life and Times of Our National Debt*. New York: Walker, 2010.

Green, James N. "Benjamin Franklin as Publisher and Bookseller." In *Reappraising Benjamin Franklin: A Bicentennial Perspective*, edited by J. A. Leo Lemay. Newark: University of Delaware Press, 1993.

Gross, Robert A., ed. *In Debt to Shays: The Bicentennial of an Agrarian Rebellion*. Charlottesville: University of Virginia Press, 1993.

Gruber, Ira D. *The Howe Brothers and the American Revolution*. New York: Atheneum, 1972.

Hammond, Bray. *Banks and Politics in America: From the Revolution to the Civil War.* Princeton, NJ: Princeton University Press, 1957.

Hancock, David. *Citizens of the World: London Merchants and the Integration of the British Atlantic Community, 1735–1785.* Cambridge, England: Cambridge University Press, 1995.

Hart, Albert Bushnell, ed. *Commonwealth History of Massachusetts.* 5 vols. New York: Russell and Russell, 1966.

Hoffert, Robert W. *A Politics of Tensions: The Articles of Confederation and American Political Ideas.* Boulder: University Press of Colorado, 1992.

Horgan, Lucille E. *Forged in War: The Continental Congress and the Origin of Military Supply and Acquisition Policy.* Westport, CT: Greenwood Press, 2002.

Humphreys, David. *Life of General Washington*, edited by Rosemarie Zagarri. Athens: University of Georgia, 1991.

Hutchinson, Peter Orlando, ed. *The Diary and Letters of His Excellency Thomas Hutchinson, Esq.* 2 vols. Boston: Houghton Mifflin, 1886.

Hutchinson, Thomas. *The History of the Province of Massachusetts Bay, from 1749 to 1774*, edited by John Hutchinson. London: John Murray, 1828.

Indian Treaties Printed by Benjamin Franklin, 1736–1762. Philadelphia: The Historical Society of Pennsylvania, 1938.

Irwin, Douglas A., and Richard Sylla, eds. *Founding Choices: American Economic Policy in the 1790s.* Chicago: University of Chicago Press, 2011.

Isaacson, Walter. *Benjamin Franklin: An American Life.* New York: Simon & Schuster, 2003.

Jay, William. *The Life of John Jay.* 2 vols. New York: J. & J. Harper, 1833.

Jensen, Merrill. *The Articles of Confederation: An Interpretation of the Social-Constitutional History of the American Revolution, 1774–1781.* Madison: University of Wisconsin Press, 1959.

———. *The Founding of a Nation: A History of the American Revolution, 1763–1776.* New York: Oxford University Press, 1968.

———. "The Idea of a National Government During the American Revolution." *Political Science Quarterly* 58, no. 3 (September 1943): 356–79.

Jillson, Calvin, and Rick K. Wilson. *Congressional Dynamics: Structure, Coordination, and Choice in the First American Congress, 1774–1789.* Stanford, CA: Stanford University Press, 1994.

Johnson, Paul. *A History of the American People.* New York: HarperCollins, 1998.

Journals of the Continental Congress, 1774–1789. 34 vols. Washington, DC: Government Printing Office, 1904–1936.

Ketcham, Ralph. *James Madison.* Charlottesville: University of Virginia Press, 1990.

Kiernan, Denise, and Joseph D'Agnese. *Signing Their Lives Away: The Fame and Misfortune of the Men Who Signed the Declaration of Independence.* Philadelphia: Quirk Books, 2019.

Knollenberg, Bernhard. *Growth of the American Republic 1766–1775.* New York: Free Press, 1975.

———. *Origin of the American Revolution: 1759–1766.* New York: Free Press, 1961.

Konkle, Burton Alva. *Thomas Willing and the First American Financial System.* Philadelphia: University of Pennsylvania Press, 1937.

Labaree, Benjamin Woods. *The Boston Tea Party*. New York: Oxford University Press, 1964.

Larson, Edward J., and Michael P. Winship. *The Constitutional Convention: A Narrative History from the Notes of James Madison*. New York: Modern Library, 2005.

Lawrence, Vera Brodsky. *Music for Patriots, Politicians, and Presidents*. New York: Macmillan, 1975.

Lengel, Edward G. *First Entrepreneur: How George Washington Built His—and the Nation's—Prosperity*. New York: Da Capo Press, 2016.

Lincoln, William, ed. *The Journals of Each Provincial Congress of Massachusetts in 1774 and 1775, and of the Committee of Safety*. Boston: Dutton and Wentworth, 1838.

Liss, Peggy K. *Atlantic Empires: The Network of Trade and Revolution, 1713–1826*. Baltimore: Johns Hopkins University Press, 1983.

Magazine of American History. A. S. Barnes, 1877–1893.

Maier, Pauline. *American Scripture: Making the Declaration of Independence*. New York: Alfred A. Knopf, 1997.

———. *From Resistance to Revolution*. New York: W. W. Norton, 1972.

———. *The Old Revolutionaries: Political Lives in the Age of Samuel Adams*. New York: Alfred A. Knopf, 1980.

Main, Jackson Turner. *Political Parties Before the Constitution*. Chapel Hill: University of North Carolina Press, 1973.

Massachusetts Magazine, Devoted to Massachusetts History, Genealogy and Biography, Salem Press Co., 1908–18.

McAnear, Beverly. "Personal Accounts of the Albany Congress of 1754." *Mississippi Valley Historical Review* 39, no. 4 (March 1953): 727–46.

McCraw, Thomas K. *The Founders and Finance*. Cambridge, MA: The Belknap Press of Harvard University Press, 2012.

McCullough, David. *John Adams*. New York: Simon & Schuster, 2001.

McCusker, John J., and Russell R. Menard. *The Economy of British America, 1607–1789*. Chapel Hill: University of North Carolina Press, 1985.

McDonald, Forrest. *Novus Ordo Seclorum: The Intellectual Origins of the Constitution*. Lawrence: University Press of Kansas, 1985.

———. *We the People: The Economic Origins of the Constitution*. Chicago: University of Chicago Press, 1958.

McGrath, Tim. *Give Me a Fast Ship: The Continental Navy and America's Revolution at Sea*. New York: NAL Caliber, 2014.

Middlekauff, Robert. *The Glorious Cause: The American Revolution, 1763–1789*. New York: Oxford University Press, 2005.

Mitchell, B. R. *British Historical Statistics*. New York: Cambridge University Press, 1988.

Montross, Lynn. *Rag, Tag and Bobtail*. New York: Harper & Brothers, 1952.

Morgan, Edmund S., and Helen M. Morgan. *The Stamp Act Crisis: Prologue to Revolution*. Chapel Hill: University of North Carolina Press, 1953.

Morison, Samuel Eliot. *Three Centuries of Harvard, 1636–1936*. Cambridge, MA: The Belknap Press of Harvard University Press, 1936.

Morton, Brian M., and Donald C. Spinelli. *Beaumarchais and the American Revolution*. Lanham, MD: Lexington Books, 2003.

Morton, Thomas. *The New English Canaan of Thomas Morton*, edited by Charles Francis Adams. Boston: Prince Society, 1883.

Murphy, Orville T. *Charles Gravier, Comte de Vergennes: French Diplomacy in the Age of Revolution: 1719–1787*. Albany: State University of New York Press, 1982.

Nash, Gary B. *The Unknown American Revolution: The Unruly Birth of Democracy and the Struggle to Create America*. New York: Viking Penguin, 2005.

Noble, John. "A Few Notes on the Shays Rebellion." *Proceedings of the American Antiquarian Society* 15 (1903): 200–232.

Padover, Saul K. *The Living United States Constitution*. New York: Meridian, 1995.

Patten, Robert H. *Patriot Pirates: The Privateer War for Freedom and Fortune in the American Revolution*. New York: Pantheon Books, 2008.

Patterson, Stephen E. *Political Parties in Revolutionary Massachusetts*. Madison: University of Wisconsin Press, 1973.

Paul, Joel Richard. *Unlikely Allies: How a Merchant, a Playwright, and a Spy Saved the American Revolution*. New York: Riverhead Books, 2009.

Peirce, Bradford K., et al., eds. *Debates and Proceedings in the Convention of the Commonwealth of Massachusetts*. Boston: William White, 1856.

Philbrick, Nathaniel. *Travels with George: In Search of Washington and His Legacy*. New York: Viking, 2021.

Phillips, Philip Lee. "Washington as Surveyor and Map-maker." *Daughters of the American Revolution Magazine* 55, no. 3 (March 1921): 115–32.

Platt, J. D. R. "Jeremiah Wadsworth: Federalist Entrepreneur." PhD diss., Columbia University, 1955.

Proctor, Donald. "New Soundings on an Old Barrel." *Journal of American History* 64, no. 3 (December 1977): 652–77.

Puls, Mark. *Samuel Adams: Father of the American Revolution*. New York: Palgrave Macmillan, 2006.

Quincy, Josiah. *The History of Harvard University*. Boston, 1869.

Rakove, Jack N. *The Beginnings of National Politics: An Interpretive History of the Continental Congress*. New York: Alfred A. Knopf, 1979.

———. "The Collapse of the Articles of Confederation." In *The American Founding: Essays on the Formation of the Constitution*, edited by J. Jackson Barlow, Leonard W. Levy, and Ken Masugi. Westport, CT: Greenwood Press, 1988.

Randall, Willard Sterne. *Alexander Hamilton: A Life*. New York: HarperCollins, 2003.

———. *Benedict Arnold: Patriot and Traitor*. New York: William Morrow, 1990.

———. "Burgoyne's Big Fail." *MHQ: The Quarterly Journal of Military History* 32, no. 3 (2020): 42–51.

———. *Ethan Allen: His Life and Times*. New York: W. W. Norton, 2011.

———. *The Founders' Fortunes: How Money Shaped the Birth of America*. New York: Dutton, 2022.

———. *George Washington: A Life*. New York: Henry Holt, 1997.

———. *A Little Revenge: Benjamin Franklin and His Son.* Boston: Little, Brown, 1984.

———. *Thomas Jefferson: A Life.* New York: Henry Holt, 1993.

———. *Unshackling America: How the War of 1812 Truly Ended the American Revolution.* New York: St. Martin's Press, 2017.

Randall, Willard Sterne, and Nancy Nahra. *American Lives.* 2 vols. New York: Longman, 1997.

———. *Forgotten Americans: Footnote Figures Who Changed American History.* Reading, MA: Addison Wesley Longman, 1998.

Rappleye, Charles. *Robert Morris: Financier of the American Revolution.* New York: Simon & Schuster, 2010.

———. *Sons of Providence: The Brown Brothers, the Slave Trade, and the American Revolution.* New York: Simon & Schuster, 2006.

Reid, John Phillip. *In a Rebellious Spirit: The Argument of Facts, the Liberty Riot, and the Coming of the American Revolution.* University Park: Pennsylvania State University Press, 1979.

Richards, Leonard L. *Shays's Rebellion: The American Revolution's Final Battle.* Philadelphia: University of Pennsylvania Press, 2002.

Roberts, Cokie. *Founding Mothers: The Women Who Raised Our Nation.* New York: William Morrow, 2004.

Rossiter, Clinton. *1787: The Grand Convention.* New York: W. W. Norton, 1987.

Sankovitch, Nina. *American Rebels: How the Hancock, Adams, and Quincy Families Fanned the Flames of Revolution.* New York: St. Martin's Press, 2020.

Schiff, Stacy. *The Revolutionary: Samuel Adams.* New York: Little, Brown, 2022.

Sears, Lorenzo. *John Hancock: The Picturesque Patriot.* Boston: Little, Brown, 1912.

Sibley, John Langdon. *Biographical Sketches of Those Who Attended Harvard College.* Boston, 1873.

Signer, Michael. *Becoming Madison: The Extraordinary Origins of the Least Likely Founding Father.* New York: Public Affairs, 2015.

Smith, Paul H., and Ronald M. Gephart, eds. *Letters of Delegates to Congress, 1774–1789.* 26 vols. Washington, DC: Government Printing Office, 1976–2000.

Smith, Richard Norton. *Patriarch: George Washington and the New American Nation.* Boston: Houghton Mifflin, 1993.

Staples, William R. *Rhode Island in the Continental Congress, 1765–1790,* edited by Reuben Aldridge Guild. Providence, RI: Providence Press Company, 1870.

Stewart, David O. *The Summer of 1787.* New York: Simon & Schuster, 2007.

Stoll, Ira. *Samuel Adams: A Life.* New York: Free Press, 2009.

Stuart, I. W. *Life of Jonathan Trumbull, Sen.* Boston: Crocker and Brewster, 1859.

Sullivan, William. *Familiar Letters on Public Characters, and Public Events.* Boston: Russell, Odiorne, and Metcalf, 1834.

Sylla, Richard, and David J. Cowen. *Alexander Hamilton on Finance, Credit, and Debt.* New York: Columbia University Press, 2018.

Szatmary, David. *Shays' Rebellion: The Making of an Agrarian Insurrection.* Amherst: University of Massachusetts Press, 1980.

Taylor, Robert J. *Western Massachusetts in the Revolution.* Providence, RI: Brown University Press, 1954.

Unger, Harlow Giles. *John Hancock: Merchant King and American Patriot*. Edison, NJ: Castle Books, 2000.

Van Alstyne, Richard W. "Great Britain, the War for Independence, and the 'Gathering Storm' in Europe, 1775–1778." *Huntington Library Quarterly* 27, no. 4 (August 1964): 311–46.

Van Doren, Carl. *Benjamin Franklin*. New York: The Viking Press, 1938.

———. *Secret History of the American Revolution*. New York: The Viking Press, 1941.

Van Schreeven, William J., et al., eds. *Revolutionary Virginia: The Road to Independence*. 7 vols. Charlottesville: University Press of Virginia, 1973–1983.

Van Vlack, Milton C. *Silas Deane: Revolutionary War Diplomat and Politician*. Jefferson, NC: McFarland, 2013.

Ver Steeg, Clarence L. *Robert Morris: Revolutionary Financier*. Philadelphia: University of Pennsylvania Press, 1954.

Watkins, Walter K. "How the British Left the Hancock House." *Old-Time New England* 13 (1923): 194–96.

Wells, William V. *The Life and Public Services of Samuel Adams*. 3 vols. Boston: Little, Brown, 1865.

Wiencek, Henry. *An Imperfect God: George Washington, His Slaves, and the Creation of America*. New York: Farrar, Straus and Giroux, 2003.

Wood, Gordon S. *The Creation of the American Republic, 1776–1787*. New York: W. W. Norton, 1972.

Woodbury, Ellen C. D. Q. *Dorothy Quincy, Wife of John Hancock*. Washington, DC: Neale Publishing Company, 1905.

Wright, Esmond. *Franklin of Philadelphia*. Cambridge, MA: The Belknap Press of Harvard University Press, 1986.

Wright, Robert E. *One Nation Under Debt: Hamilton, Jefferson, and the History of What We Owe*. New York: McGraw-Hill, 2008.

Wright, Robert E., and David J. Cowen. *Financial Founding Fathers: The Men Who Made America Rich*. Chicago: University of Chicago Press, 2006.

York, Neil L. "Clandestine Aid and the American Revolutionary War Effort: A Reexamination." *Military Affairs* 43, no. 1 (February 1979): 26–30.

Zobel, Hiller B. *The Boston Massacre*. New York: W. W. Norton, 1970.

Index

About the Author

During his seventeen years as a journalist, **Willard Sterne Randall** was a feature writer for the *Philadelphia Bulletin*, a magazine writer for the *Philadelphia Inquirer* and an investigative journalist for *Philadelphia Magazine*. His reportage won the National Magazine Award for Public Service from the Columbia Graduate School of Journalism, the Standard Gravure Award, the Hillman Foundation Prize, the Gerald Loeb Award and the John Hancock Award for Excellence in Financial Writing. Since pursuing advanced studies in history at Princeton University—where he received the Davis Prize in British History—he has authored biographies of Benjamin and William Franklin, Benedict Arnold, George Washington, Thomas Jefferson, Alexander Hamilton and Ethan Allen. His Benedict Arnold biography received four national best book awards, was a *New York Times* Notable Book and was a finalist for the *Los Angeles Times* Book Prize. *Publishers Weekly* deemed his biography of Jefferson one of the ten best biographies of 1993. He received the American Revolution Round Table's Award of Merit, its highest honor, and the Thomas Fleming Award for Outstanding Military History Writing from *MHQ: The Quarterly Journal of Military History*. He has participated in the Historians' Survey of Presidential Leadership since its inception in 2001. He has taught American history at John Cabot University in Rome, at the University of Vermont and at Champlain College, where he is Distinguished Scholar in History and an emeritus professor. He lives in Burlington, Vermont, with his wife, Nancy Nahra, a literary scholar, writer and prizewinning poet.